Ecomusicology

MARK PEDELTY

ECOMUSICOLOGY

Rock, Folk, and the Environment

TEMPLE UNIVERSITY PRESS
Philadelphia

TEMPLE UNIVERSITY PRESS
Philadelphia, Pennsylvania 19122
www.temple.edu/tempress

Library of Congress Cataloging-in-Publication Data

Pedelty, Mark.
  Ecomusicology : rock, folk, and the environment / Mark Pedelty.
     p.   cm.
  Includes bibliographical references and index.
  ISBN 978-1-4399-0711-5 (cloth : alk. paper)
  ISBN 978-1-4399-0712-2 (pbk. : alk. paper)
  ISBN 978-1-4399-0713-9 (e-book)
  1. Rock music—History and criticism. 2. Folk music—History and
criticism. 3. Environment—Songs and music—History and criticism.
I. Title.

  ML3534.P38 2012
  781.64'159—dc23   2011048804

Printed in the United States of America

2 4 6 8 9 7 5 3 1

To my brother, sister, nieces, and nephews

Contents

Acknowledgments

First, thanks go to Mick Gusinde-Duffy at Temple University Press for his enthusiastic support and faith in the project and to Amanda Steele for her hard work. Thanks also go to Jane Barry and Lynne Frost for their highly professional editing, to Gary Kramer for his promotional efforts, and to the entire Temple University Press staff.

I owe a large debt of gratitude to the American Musicological Society's Ecocriticism Study Group (ESG) and to ESG Chair Aaron Allen in particular. Their pioneering work in ecomusicology made this book possible. I am also indebted to Tyler Kinnear, Andrew Mark, and Brooks Toliver for helpful suggestions and assistance.

I greatly appreciate the efforts of the anonymous scholars who reviewed this manuscript for Temple University Press. Their thoughtful, careful, and helpful reviews significantly improved the finished product.

Much appreciation goes to BMI, Nora Guthrie, Jorge Arevalo, and the entire staff of the Woody Guthrie Archives. They not only gave me access to Woody's notes, diaries, lyrics books, drawings, and more, but also granted me the BMI Woody Guthrie Foundation Fellowship to fund that once-in-a-lifetime experience. A posthumous thank-you goes to Woody Guthrie for inspiring all of us to think more about the relationship between music, people, and place.

This brings us to the incomparable Billy Bragg. I am grateful to Billy not only for tremendous music and tireless work on behalf of all that is good and green but also for contacting me in person to grant permission to use his lyrics. After I begged and paid music publishers for the rights to reprint the lyrics fragments peppered throughout this book, I found it refreshing—and emblematic of the man—that Billy sent me a kind note offering up his lyrics for free.

To the same end, I thank Pete Seeger for a handwritten note, penned just days before his ninetieth birthday. While preparing to perform for tens of thousands, Pete took the time to respond in full to my request. Such acts of kindness mean so much to academic researchers and music fans alike.

I am grateful to University of Minnesota colleagues who have informed this book through contacts ranging from hallway discussions to careful reads. The following are just a few of those who helped out: Bill Beeman, Annette Digre, Heather Dorsey, Teresa Gowan, Jay Hatch, Murray Jensen, Linda Keefe, Richard Leppert, Pat Nunnally, Laurie Ouellette, Desdamona Racheli, Gil Rodman, Ed Schiappa, Brian Southwell, Catherine Squires, Shayla Thiel-Stern, Melissa Thompson, Mary Vavrus, Tom Wolfe, and Marco Yzer. I thank Jon Foley, director of the Institute on the Environment (IonE) and Ann Waltner, director of the Institute for Advanced Study (IAS), as well as my fellow Fellows at both institutes. Their interdisciplinary input has helped me better understand the relationship between ecological systems, music, and soundscapes. I am also indebted to hundreds of University of Minnesota students who have informed the book through conversations, presentations, and creative example.

Metro Blooms and Executive Director Becky Rice inspired not only the film discussed in Chapter 4 but also much of the rest of the book. It is a true pleasure and privilege partnering with a community group that makes such a difference in people's lives. Their music resonates throughout the community, from roots to rain barrels.

Arianna Winkle, a band's best friend, created our logo, developed album art, and took pictures of individual band members. I am truly grateful to Ari—her contribution has meant a lot! I also owe a great debt of gratitude to Cindy Poch for her professional photography services. We'll be back.

Hearty thanks go to the Hypoxic Punks for letting me leech off their talent, knowledge, and hard work. That group includes current members Leon Hsu, Bryan Mosher, and Bob Poch; founding members Desdamona Racheli and Pete Noteboom; and Tim Bornholdt, Randy Jezierski, Jesse Mandell-McClinton, and Wally "Tubaman" Wallrath. They let an ethnographer and musician-in-training play along. They are even willing to perform my songs. Amazing—still not sure how I talked them into it. The same goes for the audience—I thank each member for showing up, listening, and indulging us. And I thank Steve and Juli Groath for listening, laughing, and playing along.

I would like to thank my mother, Jane Pedelty. In addition to being an accomplished organist and pianist—as well as an excellent model for community-oriented musicianship—her help with this project was invaluable.

Speaking of audience members, there is a good reason this book is dedicated to my siblings, nieces, and nephews. They are not only inspirational and creative spirits but also the most dedicated audience one could hope to find. I hope the experience has not caused them any permanent damage. I owe them more than I'll ever be able to repay.

Above all, I am indebted to Karen Miksch, my wife, for her endless support, inspiration, ideas, and much more.

If I have forgotten anyone, it is a sign of failing memory, not ingratitude. Rest assured, I will be walking to work some freezing morning when I will suddenly remember that I left a person of significance out of these acknowledgments. I hope that any unacknowledged contributors will not hesitate to point out my oversight.

Any errors or shortcomings that remain in this book are entirely my own. Thanks for reading it.

Introduction

U2 hates the planet. At least their 360° Tour made it seem that way. With "a steel structure rising 150 feet from the floor over a massive stage with rotating bridges" (U2 Station website), the band's stadium show was the height of industrial excess. This giant stage apparatus was erected before each show, disassembled afterward, and trucked on to the next city. David Byrne criticized U2's tour as "excessive" (*New Musical Express* 2009a):

> Those stadium shows may possibly be the most extravagant and expensive (production-wise) ever: $40 million to build the stage and, having done the math, we estimate 200 semi trucks crisscrossing Europe for the duration. It could be professional envy speaking here, but it sure looks like, well, overkill, and just a wee bit out of balance given all the starving people in Africa and all.

Residents of the neighborhood surrounding Dublin's Croke Park stadium protested U2's artistic overkill by blocking the stadium exits. U2's trucks were held up, missing a ferry scheduled to ship the massive operation on to Sweden. "Have U2 Created a Monster?" the *Belfast Telegraph* headline asked (Grant 2009).

U2's lead guitarist, The Edge, provided this defense: "I think anybody that's touring is going to have a carbon footprint" (*New Musical Express*, 2009b). "I think it's probably unfair to single out rock 'n' roll," he continued. "There's many other things that are in the same category but as it happens we have a programme to offset whatever carbon footprint we have." The U.K. firm CarbonFootprint Ltd. estimated that at least 20,000 trees would need to be planted in order to even begin to offset the tour's carbon emissions. Clearly the band was not too worried. The first page of their tour website bragged about the "massive" moving structure (u2 .com/tour/). In response to the criticism, however, U2 hired Michael Martin's MusicMatters group to lessen the environmental impact of their tour. Martin has been the driving force behind rock's green movement for over two decades. He retired from investment banking in 1990 to form a non-profit group called Concerts for the Environment. His first project was the wildly successful Earth Day concert on the Washington Mall, an event that brought out 500,000 fans and led to what has become an annual celebration around the world. Martin has done far more than anyone else to lessen the environmental impact of rock.

Martin showed me the "enviro-rider" that U2 and their tour sponsor, Live Nation, signed in order to shrink the tour's environmental footprint. New provisions included supplying reusable water bottles for the concert crew, putting recycling bins in backstage offices, collecting food scraps from the crew dining room for composting, creating a fan rideshare program, facilitating fans' purchase of optional carbon offsets, and recycling ink cartridges. Carbon offsets are calculated based on the energy used by the production and transportation teams. A second company provides the actual offset. Martin helped U2 reduce the vehicle fleet for the tour by 10 percent as well.

In addition to representing an impressive effort to mitigate the impact of a band that one environmental consultant referred to as a "multinational corporation," all these arrangements do as much to illustrate the enormity of the problem as they do to solve it. Pop spectacle is clearly at odds with environment. As in the case of U2, many musicians are just beginning to reconcile the obvious contradictions between their environmental intentions and the actual material effects of their tours, increasingly calling in specialists like Martin's Effect Partners and his subsidiary group, MusicMatters. Rock may not be ruining the planet, but it's certainly not helping. At least not yet.

One answer might be to do away with the big tours and move toward local and participatory music. However, environmental impact is not just a concern for globe-trotting "multinational corporations" like U2. Local musicians struggle with the same problem of making their music more sustainable. Consider a small rock band from Minneapolis: the Hypoxic Punks. The Punks performed for the North Star Chapter of the Sierra Club in Stillwater, Minnesota, as part of the Tour de St. Croix. Billed as the "14th Annual Land Use Conference on Wheels," the tour was designed to promote sustainable land use. It was a zero-waste event. All materials were reused, recycled, or composted. Like U2's 360° Tour, the Sierra Club event was not completely harmonious with nature. For starters, most of the participating bikers drove cars and trucks to the reunion point. The parking lot was full of minivans and SUVs. Only bike racks and eco-friendly bumper stickers differentiated it from any other school, mall, or business parking area. However, the organizers and participants can hardly be faulted for driving: there was no alternative for most participants. The contemporary car culture and infrastructure require that most of us drive, especially in rural areas, a reminder that what we do individually is only half as important as what we do collectively.

However, the Land Use Conference on Wheels was remarkable in that it helped participants imagine better ways of getting around and, more importantly, better ways to organize our land-use policies and transportation system. Despite participants' fossil fuel inputs, the Tour de St. Croix was a strong net gain environmentally.

The musical entertainment was more problematic. The Sierra Club invited a local group, the Hypoxic Punks, to perform. After the bikers completed their 26-mile trek through the beautiful St. Croix River Valley, they dismounted, unloaded their recyclables, drank some water, used the portable toilets, and huddled in the small patches of shade available. A few listened to the band, but most hopped right into their cars, anxious to get home. The Hypoxic Punks consisted of four professors and two students from the University of Minnesota. They performed upbeat tunes as the bikers finished their long tour of the scenic valley.

I was part of that band (Fig. 1). My participation was, and is, "ethnographic." In other words, I was an anthropologist pretending to be a musician in order to better understand the local popular music culture from a musician's perspective. More specifically, I wanted to explore the political ecology of rock from the inside.

What I learned is that rock and roll is energy-intensive, even for "acoustic" setups like ours. Compared with most bands, we were not particularly tech-heavy on that unusually hot September day, but we still needed a public address (PA) system to properly mix and project our instruments and voices, especially outdoors. Cables ran in all directions from the mixing board across the newly mown grass. We drove a van and two cars to get there as well, hardly equivalent to U2's massive fleet of trucks, jets, and ferries, but a fairly impressive amount of energy use for 45 minutes of live music. We plugged into a solar generator, which greatly lessened the band's impact and carbon footprint, but the obvious disjuncture between a human-powered, zero-waste event and the band's energy-intensive performance raised a few troubling questions.

FIGURE 1 The Hypoxic Punks perform for the Sierra Club. Bryan Mosher on bass and Mark Pedelty on guitar are pictured here. *(Photo by Kevin Pedelty.)*

First, did our musical performance add enough to any participant's environmental awareness, action, or enthusiasm to justify our environmental impact? The cost-benefit ratio is questionable. Our contribution to the low-energy event was either a wash or an example of greenwashing on a pathetically small scale. Either way, it is worth thinking about, and perhaps doing differently. Can rock evolve a less energy-intensive profile, or would that acoustic downsizing make it something other than rock? Is the environmental crisis ultimately a genre crisis for rock, hip-hop, and other energy-intensive musical styles?

The second question is one of aesthetics and message rather than material impact. Did the sight and sound of our plugged-in Americana rock advance the Sierra Club's environmental message? Was it the right sound for that setting? Perhaps not. Philip Tagg argues that rock is the consummate urban sound (2006). He notes that heavy metal vocalists and electric lead guitarists use "sharp timbres at high pitch" to cut through the urban din (2006, 44). Audiences applaud a rock band's victory over the urban soundscape, argues Tagg, partly because it represents our desire for individuality in anonymous and alienating city settings. Perhaps the message of a rock band performing in a bucolic setting like the St. Croix River Valley is more about contradiction than conservation. Much like the urban punk who "looks so sick in the sun," as the Clash sang in 1979, rock aesthetics tend to contradict environmental outlooks. Later on we will see that this does not have to be the case, but it was that day in the St. Croix River Valley. An ethnographer hopes for those "aha" moments during fieldwork, and perhaps nothing brings home the problem better than the subjective experience of *being* the problem. This book is about that problem: the conundrum of making music sustainably— as well as related questions. How might music actually promote and inspire the sort of collective action needed to make our towns, cities, and nations more sustainable? What are some of the material, aesthetic, aural, lyrical, and even visual considerations that we need to keep in mind when aiming toward more sustainable music? And, most importantly, what's really at stake?

Why talk about popular music and the environment? The answer is easy: because popular genres like rock, pop, hip-hop, and country are what most people listen to and love. They form the basis of a major global industry. If there is little to no relationship between popular music and the environment, then we may have already identified the problem. How could the music we love ignore the greatest crisis we face? The deceptively simple answer to the problem of unsustainable music is for all of us to start making more of it locally. However, whether one is a global star like U2's Bono or a local unknown, we deal with many of the same challenges, contradictions, conundrums, and opportunities. As shown by the Sierra Club example, the big environmental problems do not go away with diminishing scale. Granted, locally based musicians perform at radically different levels of material and social effect than globe-trotting rock stars like Byrne and Bono, but the basic problems remain the same. How can we make our music more sustainable? Or, to put it in more positive terms, how might our music proactively promote sustainability? Can music be put to work? For example, could musicians be doing more in relation to environmental movements? If so, how? Those are some of the questions behind the research and writing of this book.

Where Music Takes Place

The main purpose of this book is to understand the ecological potential, and pitfalls, of contemporary popular music, with an emphasis on the contrasting genres of rock and folk. While other methods will be brought to bear, my main entry into the problem is ethnographic. However, there are many other ways to study music and the environment. For example, scientists have studied sounds made by other species, including birds (Roper 2007), whales (Tougaard and Eriksen 2006), and even beetles (Cummings 2006). Similarly, musicians have engaged in performance-based research with nonhuman species, such as David Rothenberg's seminal explorations with birds and whales (2005, 2008).

Perhaps the most influential approach to date, soundscape studies, was pioneered by the Canadian scholar R. Murray Schafer (1994). His work and that of his students not only identified some of the most fundamental problems, but also led to the development of new listening environments. Designers influenced by the soundscape design studies movement have created structures and landscapes that combat noise pollution and inspire more sustainable orientations.

Conversely, musicologists interested in the ecocriticism tradition, initiated in literary studies, have tended to focus on musical texts rather than listening contexts, using ecocritical theory to build philosophical taxonomies for better understanding musical meanings. They borrow the literary critics' toolkit—semiotic, narrative, genre, and discourse analyses—supplementing those methods with music-specific theories and concepts. The musicological ecocritics' goal is to better understand musical discourses and histories. The *Grove Dictionary of American Music* (forthcoming) defines "ecomusicology" as "the study of music, culture, and nature in all the complexities of those terms. Ecomusicology considers musical and sonic issues, both textual and performative, related to ecology and the natural environment." The Summer 2011 issue of the *Journal of the American Musicological Society* (*JAMS*) most effectively introduces ecomusicology and promises to become a foundational publication for the emerging field. From Aaron Allen's overview in the Colloquy, "Ecomusicology: Ecocriticism and Musicology" (391–394), to Holly Watkins's essay brilliantly recasting "musical space as a virtualization of social and natural spaces" (407), the *JAMS* issue is must reading.

Unfortunately, these explorations have not reached far beyond academically sanctioned musical styles, including classical and jazz. One of the few exceptions is David Ingram's *The Jukebox in the Garden: Ecocriticism and American Popular Music since 1960* (2010). It is a truly excellent ecocritical survey of popular music history over the past half-century. *The Jukebox in the Garden* provided extremely useful historical context for this study.

This book draws a bit from each of the above fields: ecocriticism, classical musicology, and biological ecology, as well as ethnomusicology and environmental communication. When applied to environmental issues, these fields can be collectively described as "ecomusicology," a multidisciplinary moniker that is rapidly gaining acceptance. As previously mentioned, my main research method is ethnography, meaning that I have engaged in long-term ecomusicological fieldwork to better understand music as a form of environmental communication, ecological art, and advocacy. The book deals with all three aspects of popular music—(1) communication: music as a means of mediating environmental matters; (2) art: music as a creative, aesthetic, symbolic, and affective expression of environmental meanings; and (3) advocacy: music as an attempt to inform, inspire, and persuade audiences.

To explore those questions, the book moves from the global stage to local campfires. The first three chapters deal with the environmental struggles of famous musicians, starting at a global scale (Chapter 1) and then working down to national contexts (Chapter 2), before finally focusing on the ways in which music helps to create regional identities in relation to specific environmental projects, such as the damming and un-damming of iconic rivers and watersheds (Chapter 3). Those chapters focus on major concerts, such as Live Aid and Live Earth, and well-known musicians and bands: U2, Jack Johnson, Sheryl Crow, David Byrne, Soundgarden, Woody Guthrie, Mos Def, Peter Gabriel, Pete Seeger, Ani DiFranco, and others whose music continues to shape the American soundscape.

But what about the rest of us? Millions of us make and listen to music in our neighborhoods, homes, watersheds, and communities. Is there more we can do to align our musical lives and environmental interests? Is there some way for us to put music into the service of local sustainability? Or must we simply watch the show unfold elsewhere, in London, Los Angeles, and cyberspace? Answering those questions is the main goal of Chapter 4 and, ultimately, the book as a whole. As such, this book takes up Ursula Heise's challenge to find "imaginative strategies and devices that allow individuals and communities to form attachments" to "different kinds of space" (2008, 5). Like Heise, I find it necessary to go from "the local and regional level all the way to the national and global" (ibid.) in order to find satisfactory answers. Place is no longer purely local. Conversely, global culture is no longer distant, somewhere "out there" beyond our immediate grasp. Every day we bathe in sounds made and manufactured somewhere far away, making them part of our intimate surroundings via the magic of television and digital listening devices. While these four levels of analysis—global, national, regional, and local— are by no means distinct, covering each in turn allows us to better understand the ecology of musical production and consumption.

As an anthropologist, I mainly use ethnographic methods to understand music. Chapter 4 presents the results of eight years of musical fieldwork in Minnesota and Washington State, drawing on what I previously learned from working with musicians and audiences in Mexico City. Throughout that time I learned from expert informants while performing alongside them, doing what anthropologists refer to as "participant observation." I learned an instrument, composed music, formed a band, recorded CDs, and performed for local audiences. In other words, I made a fool of myself. In doing so, I learned a little bit more about what it is like to be a musician.

But don't worry, this book is not about me. We become anthropologists because other people are infinitely more interesting than we are. I completed hands-on fieldwork in order to gain backstage access and a stage-eye view of the problem. Just as there is value in the work of musicological analysts and critics, there are also benefits to ethnographic fieldwork. Ethnographers experience text in context. Most importantly, the ethnographer goes through a painful process of enculturation. Like children learning their own cultures, we are willing to make fools of ourselves in the field, to get things wrong in order to eventually get them right. That is how both children and ethnographers learn: through trial and error, deep engagement at the sites where cultural text meets social life. Unlike armchair criticism of finished products like musical compositions and recordings, ethnography is a messy and complicated business, mirroring the messy and complicated ways in which music (or sausage) is made. And so, through learning to compose, write, and perform music, I learned a lot about local performers and performance. I watched and interviewed musicians, learning from them by becoming one of them.

As indicated in the Sierra Club story above, this book will not glorify local music or suggest that it holds all of the answers to environmental engagement, community building, or social change. Today, globally distributed music is often experienced more intimately than music created and performed locally. Thanks to global culture industries, worldwide distribution networks, and digital listening technologies, we are more likely to feel close to music made by someone half a world away than music performed down the street. This intimate conversion of global production into local listening has resulted in audiences whose consciousness tends to be more global and national, musically speaking, than local or regional. The globalization of music has also made live concerts more magical than ever. During these special, highly ritualized occasions, we share physical space with digitally omnipresent figures like U2, Soundgarden, or Lady Gaga.

Live concerts bring "our" music back home, allowing each of us to feel connected to something larger than ourselves and the physical spaces we inhabit. That deep sense of emotional investment is part of what defines ritual. Instead of God, we get Lady Gaga. Popular music critics once imagined that mass production, repetition, and global distribution would demean the live musical experience. However, the truth is quite different. Social distance heightens audiences' emotional investment and attraction to spectacle. Whether speaking of Mayan ritual, the classical music of Western empires, or globally commodified rock, the physical locales we cohabit are often less important than imagined communities and cultural spaces far away.

In other words, our minds are often elsewhere, and our music comes from somewhere far beyond the horizon. Communication prosthetics like televisions, iPods, and video game consoles provide a magical sense of transcendence, enriching our lives in the globalization age. However, such displacement can become a problem when it comes to creating sustainable places closer to home.

As global musics multiply, local and regional musicians struggle to make their sounds resonate. In fact, even hyper-local musicians must react to global soundscapes. Globally distributed sounds and sensibilities tend to dominate the music of local performers. Local musicians perform globalized music to go where the audiences' consciousness resides: "out there" rather than right here. The most successful local musicians, by far, are cover bands.

This raises a set of questions for those seeking to make environmentally conscious music. What *is* local music? How does local music relate to local ecologies, if at all? In a globalized sound system, what should local musicians do?

As distant places become more familiar, local spaces can become less so. Geographically proximate and distant environments alike become part of an electronically mediated market and consciousness. The modern consciousness seeks escape from place, and modern technologies, from thermostats to earbuds, provide it. Rather than becoming oriented toward the physical environments immediately surrounding our bodies, ears, and mouths, our minds are quite literally elsewhere. We are here and not here, there and not there. We are everywhere and nowhere in terms of physical space. A series of simulacra color our sense of reality, no matter how grounded we imagine ourselves to be. That magical engagement includes soundscapes, creating challenges for those who seek to sustain local environments through music.

Because it is hard to know what local music is anymore, it is difficult to make. Rather than force the issue, I decided to concentrate less on making local music and more on making music locally. My starting premise was that anyone, even an anthropologist, could make a positive musical contribution to his or her surrounding community and environment. Everyone has the capacity to learn an instrument, to sing, and to join others in the making of music. From the outset, I assumed that "citizen-musicians" could make a difference. Few performers have U2's bully pulpit, but all of us have the ability to make sound matter together in our homes, parks, and bars.

To a certain extent the experiment succeeded. I learned to make music with others. If an anthropologist can do it, anyone can. However, I also learned to question the hopeful assumptions surrounding "participatory music" in the musicological literature. In truth, making music involves hard work. It is also expensive and time-consuming. That might be because I took things a little too far. Perhaps the ultimate lesson is that one does not need to play music in bands and clubs for it to matter, and that doing so can even become a profound distraction. However, even getting together with friends and neighbors to make music takes serious time, effort, and money. Taking the next step—making music serve the interests of sustainability—makes that task even more challenging.

Fortunately, one does not have to learn an instrument and perform to make music. A recurrent theme in this book is that audiences make music through listening, dancing, downloading, and playing recorded music in social contexts. When those social contexts include community building and environmental action—and not just entertainment and consumption—amazing things can happen. People don't need to hold instruments in their hands to make music matter.

Why Music?

In order to study music ecologically, it is necessary to consider connections between sound, people, and place. Ecomusicology requires us to go beyond composition, classroom, and concert hall to explore the resonance of entire ecosystems (Guy 2009). If we claim that pop's main message is conspicuous consumption, we have to show what that means in the lives of musical consumers. If we are interested in activists singing around the campfire (greatly expanding their carbon footprint), we have to go beyond musical affect to consider material effect as well. In other words, neither material nor cultural reductionism will suffice. Yet, including material systems is new and uncomfortable for many musicologists, who prefer to remain in the realm of aesthetics and meaning. Unfortunately, no ecological analysis is complete without consideration of the material world as well.

Material analysis is not only important for sound ecology, however; it is also a useful way to discover musical meanings. What makes for good music, in the aesthetic sense, has always been partly dependent on what makes music good, ethically. That implies some recognition of material effect. In one of the most insightful studies of genre, Simon Frith concludes, "It is through genres that we experience music and musical relations, that we bring together the aesthetic and the ethical" (1996, 95). If the ethical problem is environmental sustainability, then musical meaning is partly dependent on material contexts and effects.

Whether or not the ethical dimension is made explicit in critics' aesthetic assessments, it is always part of the argument. Past debates about musical ethics have mainly revolved around sexuality, identity, and power (Blecha 2004). Sustainability, including its material dimensions, must enter the debate for ecomusicology to become truly ecological.

But why would we choose to make music in a time of environmental crisis? Didn't Nero get in trouble for doing that? One answer is that we never choose to make music; it is a fundamental human behavior. Music is an outcome of evolution, a species-defining trait (Levitin 2006). We make music because we can, because we express our humanity through musical sound as well as our connection to each other and a shared sense of place. In other words, it is not so much a question of *why* we would make music for, in, or with an environment—we have been doing it all along. Instead, it is a question of how we might make music better, environmentally speaking. What makes music "good" shifts from generation to generation, culture to culture, and genre to genre. Sustainability is just entering the discussion.

Of course, all music has environmental implications and meanings. The last beat of Britney Spears's "Toxic" (2004) is not found in the final measure of the song, but rather in the metallic "thunk" a broken iPod makes when it hits empty soup cans in a local landfill. Aaron Allen addresses material connectivity particularly well in his groundbreaking study of violin production. Allen argues that "if we want to protect the environment, we need to make both cultural and ecological arguments;

and if we want to preserve cultural traditions, we need to recognize and address their environmental impacts as well" (2010, 13).

People, places, and technologies generate songs. In return, music helps define who we are and mediates our imagination of place. Drawing connections between music and environment is not an unnatural act. The unnatural act is assuming that music is somehow separable from the contexts in which it is made and consumed. From acoustics to aesthetics, the places where we live, work, and play influence what music means and how it functions. Environmental crises have reawakened us to such connections, reminding us of what Yaqui deer dancers, griot drummers, and studio engineers have known all along: music is more than organized sound. Music is movement, languages, and places. Music is even material. The origins and consequences of music come from, and extend far beyond, a musical piece or performance. Therefore, ecological synthesis is not just important for achieving more sustainable musics but also for understanding music more holistically and, therefore, better understanding what music is.

As William Gardiner explained in the nineteenth century, music is one of humanity's most direct connections to nature (Gardiner 1838). Based on over sixty years in the music business, New Orleans musician Harold Battiste argues, "Musicians who are close to nature make the best music" (2010). Whether or not that is true, music can help listeners become closer to nature. From Ferde Grofé's *Grand Canyon Suite* (1932) to Pete Seeger's "My Dirty Stream" ("The Hudson River Song," 1966), from Ani DiFranco's "Your Next Bold Move" (2001) to Peter Gabriel's "Down to Earth" (2008) from the *WALL-E* soundtrack, music contains a reaffirming energy and the capacity to reconnect us to the living world.

1

Pop Goes the Planet

Global Music and the Environmental Crisis

A long line of cars motored slowly down the road. It was a burning hot day in the high desert of Washington State, July 30, 2011. The metal pilgrims inched toward their holy shrine, the Gorge, a natural amphitheater on the Columbia River. Soundgarden's faithful fans would be ritually released that night, their troubled minds and aging bodies forgotten with the assistance of grunge metal's high priests. The fans' liberated spirits would soar above the Gorge, floating on dry ice vapors and a haze of cannabis smoke.

The cars were still crawling past young women in yellow safety vests as the first act took stage. Event staff directed each vehicle to the next parking attendant, shouting questions back and forth: *¿Dónde quiere estacionar ése?* Cars, SUVs, and large recreational vehicles rolled onto the burnt grass field as the Meat Puppets opened a four-band show in the Gorge below. The band led with "Plateau," a song many fans interpret as a condemnation of suburban sprawl and environmental degradation. Not tonight, however. Few had come to hear the Meat Puppets. The grunge devotees had gathered for Mastodon, Queens of the Stone Age, and Soundgarden. Clearly, most of them had never heard of the Meat Puppets, a 1980s punk band that inspired 1990s grunge. The crowd was too young to know pre-grunge punk, but too old to still be cool. Fading tattoos and receding hairlines betrayed their liminal age and status. The grunge bands they loved were either defunct or beginning reunion tour afterlives, as was Soundgarden.

That same afternoon, two hundred and fifty miles to the west, folk artists Sharon Abreu and Michael Hurwicz, otherwise known as the Irthlingz, performed two sets of songs about environmental conservation on Orcas Island. A small crowd—enthusiasts of various ages—had gathered to celebrate their collective struggle to preserve Turtleback Mountain. They raised $18.5 million to preserve Turtleback for future generations of hikers, bikers, flora, and fauna. Musicians and artists like the Irthlingz played an essential role, as did Orcas resident Gary Larson, of "Far Side" fame, who dedicated a cartoon to the effort and provided substantial funding for Turtleback Mountain preservation.

As members of the San Juan Preservation Trust enjoyed a feast of barbequed salmon, salad, watermelon, freshly baked bread, and cookies supplied by the Orcas Village Store, the Irthlingz performed "Wild, Wild River," "The Food Chain Song," and other original songs. They also borrowed a few tunes from close friends, including Tony Ultimate's "Calling the Salmon Home" and "Solar Energy Shout" by the Banana Slug String Band.

Meanwhile, back at the Gorge, the Meat Puppets were mostly ignored. A few audience members stopped drinking, smoking, and shouting long enough to exclaim, "Hey, those guys are covering Nirvana!" They got it backward: Nirvana covered the Meat Puppet's "Plateau," not the other way around. But the sentiment was stupid and contagious, to paraphrase Cobain. Tweets repeating the mistake made the rounds as the Meat Puppets rounded out their set with the folk classic "The John B. Sails," conspicuously repeating, "I want to go home" and showing apparent punk derision for their disinterested audience. The fans of nineties grunge gathered at the Gorge appeared to be, for the most part, as oblivious to the Meat Puppet's musical slight as to their own musical roots.

Rock eats its ancestors. Other than a few music scholars, critics, and bookish fans, each generation assumes that their beloved music and musicians represent a radical break from those that came before. Later, each assumes that the next generation's musical "crap" will lead to rock's inevitable decline. Of all rock traditions, this cycle of exaggerated change is most constant. The ecology of rock is built on a foundation of forgetting.

As the Columbia River rolled by, tamed by one of the world's largest hydrological control systems, reveling rockers at the Gorge probably did not reflect on the musical history of that amazing place either. As we will see in Chapter 3, it was in the Columbia River basin that Woody Guthrie composed songs like "Roll On, Columbia," now Washington's official state song. If fans were oblivious to the fact that the Meat Puppets had inspired grunge in the late eighties, they probably did not give too much thought to Guthrie's musical life there in the forties.

Reliving the glory days of grunge, the audience erupted as their headliners hit the stage. Soundgarden brought chart-topping hits back to life as the sun set over the Gorge's high west canyon wall. "One of the prettiest fucking places I've ever seen!" said one sinewy fan to his much less enthusiastic picnic partner, a young woman along for the ride. Who knows what music moved her, but it clearly wasn't Soundgarden. She and a woman two blankets over shared a bemused look whenever the group of guys surrounding them erupted into shouts of ecstasy, each perfectly timed and orchestrated by Chris Cornell. The women looked like atheists hanging out a Baptist convention. Whoever developed the Gorge as a concert venue must have foreseen that it would be the sort of place where accidental fans and involuntary concert-goers like these could at least enjoy a picnic, even if they were not especially into the show itself.

The town of George, Washington (population 528), is known for two things: it is the only town that uses the first president's full name and it is home to the Gorge. The Gorge is a natural landform carved by the Columbia River, bordered on each side by high plateaus and scrubland. Just before sunset an eagle cruised the canyon's rim, looking for the wayward rabbit or careless snake down below. The urban sound of rock meets nature at the Gorge. The venue brings in tens of thousands of fans each summer to camp, throw tailgate picnics, and party through the night. The cheapest ticket to the Soundgarden concert cost $85, plus taxes and fees, but that did not deter these fans. Nor did camping fees of $40 to $110 stop them from pitching their tents just outside the venue. Even in a down economy, rock is considered an American staple, like food, shelter, and beer.

Among Soundgarden's songs is the environmental anthem "Hands All Over" (*Louder Than Love*, 1989). Composer Chris Cornell has repeatedly described "Hands All Over" as an environmental song and has taken part in several benefit concerts, including Live Earth. In a 2007 interview he described influences ranging from hiking in the Pacific Northwest to the Iraq war, all of which moved him to speak out and sing about environmental issues (Artisan News Service 2007). "We are a couple of generations away from being in serious trouble, and if I have the opportunity to be part of an event that raises awareness for these issues I'm definitely going to do it . . . it is what I do, so it's so easy . . . the one thing I know how to do that people are going to bother to check out." Fan Ringoo of Montclair, California, dubbed "Hands All Over" the "Coolest earth conscious song ever!!" adding, "maybe it's the only cool one there is." Cornell is clearly aware of his audience. He carefully crafted one very good song about environmental destruction to bring home the point. If he had gone so far as to make sustainability a central theme of his music, he would risk turning off the audience. Soundgarden did not perform "Hands All Over" that night at the Gorge.

No one would mistake the July 30 concert at the Gorge for the Irth-lingz' environmentally themed performance at Turtleback Mountain. Other than an advertisement by insurance giant Esurance—"Keeping the Gorge Green Since 2007" (see esurance.com/gorge)—there was nothing to indicate that the Soundgarden concert was about anything more than consuming conspicuous amounts of rock music, bottled soft drinks, alcohol, and drugs. Granted, there is a longstanding bacchanalian strain in American environmentalism, and we could probably use more of it, but this was not part of that tradition either.

It would be hard to design a more wasteful concert event. For starters, Soundgarden and Live Nation moved their audience to the concert, rather than the reverse. Music fan Maradee writes:

> I realize that the Gorge is the most beautiful venue in the Pacific Northwest but it's also really, really, really inconvenient. It's 4.5 hours from Portland. Almost 3 hours from Seattle. 2.5 hours from Spokane. Because of the distance you pretty much have to camp at their shitty campground because there really isn't any camping anywhere else nearby. And if they are playing the Gorge, that also means there's a really good chance they're going to skip Seattle altogether, which really sucks. (soundgardenworld.com/forum/7101)

Reverse economy of scale: if you can get the consumers to drive hours from all directions, tour transportation costs go way down and profits increase. But at what environmental cost? Of course, it is a matter of damned if you do, damned if you don't. U2 raised the critics' ire for transporting a massive stage apparatus around the world. Whether you take a massive apparatus around the world or bring the audience from far away, the energy needs of live rock remain a problem.

So what is the take-away from this concert comparison? Is it that placed-based, activist-oriented, folk music is better for the environment than high-energy stadium rock? From an ecological perspective, probably, but that is not the point. Big rock is not going away. It is enjoyed by more people, more passionately, and in more places than local, place-based music. Cornell's balancing act, with his strategic insertion of one song about the environment into an otherwise apolitical corpus, might do more on a wholesale scale than local music does on the retail level. As he seeks to "push the button of awareness" (Artisan News Service 2007) for his relatively apolitical fan base, Cornell's nod to environmental issues might do as much as or more than the Irthlingz' deeper musical commitment to ameliorating environmental problems. Both types of musical activism are needed. Both have limits. Both are useful. Although musical movements like rock and hip-hop will one day become folk—no longer very popular but preserved as a historical tradition—for now they are the most popular genres, the living music of our time and place. Therefore, in terms of sheer numbers, energy, and presence, rock, hip-hop, and other top-selling styles matter most from a purely material, ecological perspective. We will return to local artists in Chapter 4, but first we need to understand the types of musicians and music most people listen to most of the time, starting with global rock.

Don't Know Much about Ecology

Does popular music help us deal with environmental crisis, or are we merely amusing ourselves to death, as Neil Postman suggests (2006)? Human ecology has grown to global scale (i.e., human impacts and material exchanges are planetary rather than localized), leading to environmental crisis on the same planetary scale. There is relatively strong scientific consensus around the claim that we are facing an environmental crisis, or crises, but much less agreement as to why. Take capitalism. Some believe that capitalism is a major cause of the world's most extreme environmental problems. Historically, crude accumulation on the capitalist model motivated colonial exploitation, creating a basic pattern of haves and have-nots that remains to this day (Wallerstein 2004). Global corporations seek to find profit everywhere and by every means, including the transformation of biodiverse environments into ecosystems that provide short-term profits, turning forests, wetlands, and prairies into farms, mines, and strip malls. Consumers perform a central role in capitalist ecology, purchasing, consuming, and displaying as many goods and services as possible, regardless of the consequences for future generations. Those of us lucky enough to live in the overdeveloped world— people David Korten refers to as "Stratos Dwellers" (2001, 107–120)— prosper at the expense of others' natural resources and labor (N. Klein 2010). Others believe that capitalism is the solution and that we will innovate our way out of the problem, with large corporations leading the way. They argue that capitalist modernization, development, and free markets have led to greater political freedom and prosperity worldwide. For such theorists, the best model for fixing the current predicament is more capitalism (de Soto 2000). The market will cure all.

What do theories of political economy and the global environment have to do with popular music? Everything. U2's internal contradictions reflect the cognitive dissonance of contemporary capitalism: a rhetoric of sustainability matched by unsustainable acts of consumption. Like the rest of us, they want to have their cake and eat it too. David Byrne picked an easy target in U2, whose massive 360° Tour clearly clashes with the band's public advocacy for more sustainable ways of life. Presumably U2 are calling for sustainability to start somewhere outside the stadium grounds. Rather than posit himself as the solution, Byrne is playing the role of court jester, fitting a musical persona he cultivated so well through songs like "(Nothing But) Flowers" (2006). Dada at heart, Byrne loves to point out the absurdity in everything from malls to mass movements. Maybe that is art's most important role, to provoke and poke holes, to show us that the emperor in all of us has no clothes.

However, Byrne's provocative jab calls attention not only to aesthetic inadequacies—the emperor's nakedness—but material contradictions as well. U2 failed Byrne's cost-benefit analysis (100 trucks + x gallons of gas = unsustainable performance) *and* aesthetic judgment. The band's touring edifice presents a visual contradiction for anyone who pays attention to the band's activist rhetoric. The disjuncture sparked a visceral response among environmentalist music fans. Several email responses to a *Chicago Tribune* story about the tour called for U2 to "scale down" (Kot 2009).

While ecological assessment may seem like a rather coarse way of dealing with music, the truth of art has always been partly contingent on its wider social resonance. How we make music in relation to context—environment—has always influenced interpretation. Music is sometimes perceived as less artful when message and means contradict each other, as evidenced by Byrne's critique and critical fan responses. Therefore, when art evokes a sustainable aesthetic, visual and material contradictions are inevitably brought into the listeners' interpretive assessments. Given the success of their tours, most U2 fans clearly could not care less— or maybe they buy into the idea of massive offsets. As environmental concerns continue to grow, however, it is inevitable that such questions will increasingly impact art: 2009's beautiful stage structure may become 2019's abomination, something that music fans look back on in disgust. U2's tour may become the symbol of a past age of extreme musical excess. Either that, or people are reading this in 2019 and laughing at me.

Of course, discord, irony, polysemy, and contradiction are also important. There is nothing more boring than puritanical art, and environmental music has too often fallen into that trap. As neuroscientist Daniel Levitin explains, sound becomes music when composers and performers fulfill the listeners' desire, anticipation, and expectation for predictable sound patterns as demanded by a given genre (2006, 111–113). However, if music only does that, if it simply panders to audience expectations, it fails. That is the problem with Muzak, easy listening, and bubblegum pop: they simply fulfill expected musical formulas. Therefore, they leave most audiences unimpressed, if not annoyed. To be considered truly musical, organized sound also needs to contain selective and purposeful violations of culturally defined patterns, violations that both surprise and please an audience (ibid.). The same dynamic distinguishes melodrama from more artfully developed narratives.

As listeners we require artists to fulfill our expectations, but we react favorably to a few artfully conceived surprises. Art that goes too far in either direction turns audiences off. The search for a seamless and holistic synthesis between nature and music is laudable, but also impossible. Music demands innovation to remain vital.

In other words, if U2 had purposely juxtaposed industrial excess with sustainable intent, they might have artfully provoked the audience. Unfortunately, irony is only artful when intentional. As evidenced by their initial evasion and defensive remarks, U2 are not attempting to provoke a conversation about musical contradiction; they *are* the contradiction.

Live Earth: The Planet

U2 became the focus of criticism because they are the standard-bearers for stadium rock. Their case raises a question: is it possible to take music "firmly located within the commitment to mobility and consumerism" (Grossberg 1993, 202) and also make it compatible with environmental goals? Is rock done for? Will a more environmentally conscious culture shove rock from its golden age into its golden years? Having long since evolved from avant-garde to popular art, will rock now complete the cycle by fading into folk (Pedelty 2004)? Already the genre preservationists are erecting museums and creating academies of rock, unintentionally killing the wild thing they once loved. A growing number of bands are referring to themselves as "post-rock," another sign of rock's waning vitality. Or perhaps rock could be reborn, remaining just as vital in this century as it was in the last one, continuing to serve the needs of rebelling youth and beer marketers alike.

For now, however, rock and pop account for over half of the world's music sales (Media Literacy Clearinghouse 2010). Closely related subgenres make up much of the remainder. Although there are thousands of musical styles around the world, only a few have widespread global recognition. Rock and pop circulate across borders, diasporas, and cultures.

As was true of world religions and food, music has generally been spread by empire. The most popular forms of popular music are produced and mediated in dominant metropoles. Today as in the past, culture industries are headquartered in wealthy nations. Regardless of how that reality came about, the dominance of the United States, Western Europe, and the Anglophone world has turned rock and pop music into global phenomena. Once out of the box, however, they have slowly become everybody's music. Modern pop comprises Cleveland rock and Indonesian dangdut, almost in equal measure.

Ecomusicology must grapple with the most widespread and popular of global musics. Rock and pop provide a meaningful place in the world for billions of people. Musicologists might prefer classical genres, and the academy might still reward that preference, but that is not what most of the world downloads and desires. Rock and pop provide the soundtrack for the world system. Ecomusicology needs to come to grips with that reality.

Before moving on to Live Earth, it is time to define what I mean by "space" and "place," words that I have used repeatedly. I follow Lawrence Buell's definitions (2005). "Space" for Buell "connotes geometrical or topographical abstraction" (2005, 63). "Place" is space made meaningful. In other words, places are created when ideas and identities are attached to spaces. Roughly speaking, space is a signifier, the raw material of meaning, and place is a sign, a complete unit of meaning. Although spaces exist independently of human occupation and understanding, we cannot know them as "real" spaces, as watersheds, mountains, or aquifers. We know them as the Mississippi River Watershed, Turtleback Mountain, or, in the case of aquifers, as scientific models. Physical space becomes place through cultural mediation, including music. As Hamlet remarks, "There is nothing either good or bad, but thinking makes it so." Evaluations of music as good or bad are context-dependent and multiperspectival. A department chain manager who uses Muzak to chase street musicians away from the store's entrance considers that a socially positive act. Street musicians view that same action as the privatization of public space (Hempton and Grossman 2009, 57). The manager and musician hold very different interpretations of what makes music "good."

In other words, neither music nor conceptions of place are neutral. Some deeply held conceptions of place have disastrous human consequences. Ursula Heise uses the example of the Nazis' place-based rhetoric (2008, 48). Music can have negative consequences as well. Bruce Johnson and Martin Cloonan present convincing evidence that of "all the elements in the modern soundscape, music is among the most invasive"

(2009, 163). One person's musical pleasure might be a neighbor's sonic annoyance. The question is not just whether we manage to make music in relation to place, but also how and toward what end. Ecomusicology is inevitably a question of ethics.

Furthermore, places do not exist independent of our actions but are instead constructed through meaning-making processes and articulation within larger histories, language, texts, myths, and ideologies. That is why my version of the American West might be different from yours, and our collective understanding of the American West might be, in turn, quite different from that of someone who has never seen a Clint Eastwood movie. We might both hear same eight haunting notes every time we glimpse an image of the American desert, but someone who has never seen *The Good, the Bad, and the Ugly* would hear a different desert altogether.

To complete the point, none of our conceptions of the American West are fully real or completely false. Even though I have spent a fair amount of time in the desert Southwest, my "American desert" was filmed far away, in Andalucía, Spain. Each conception of place has a specific history and a range of intertextual associations in the present, not all of which spring from actual, material experience in the referenced space. And each conception of place has different environmental consequences.

Rebee Garofalo's studies of musical mega-events remind us of that fact (1992). The politics of "place" go well beyond local phenomena to include images, sounds, and ideas culled from throughout the world. There is a globalized consciousness at play in contemporary popular music every bit as consequential politically, and ecologically, as songs, singers, and performances dedicated to local music. In fact, ecocritic Greg Garrard argues that our dominant "idea of place as locale has provided us with no sense of the place of the whole Earth in contemporary culture" (2004, 178). Garrard's point is well taken. Earth is becoming a central "place" in our musical consciousness. That is evidenced by the growing number of references made to the planet as a whole in music, including the highly problematic, yet promising, Live Earth.

Taking place on July 7, 2007, "Live Earth was," according to its executive producer, Kevin Wall, "a carbon-neutral event on a global scale, reaching an estimated 2 billion people with a message about climate crisis" (quoted in Waddell 2008, 34). The 2 billion estimate might be a bit high. There were 19 million television viewers in the United States and 100 million unique hits online, although it is not clear if the latter number accounted for all world watchers or just those in the United States. According to the *Hollywood Reporter*, Live Earth ratings were on the "cool side," at just 2.7 million viewers, less than the 3 million NBC averaged on a typical summer Saturday night in 2007 (Gough and Woodson, 2007). The event garnered fewer television viewers than 2005's Live 8, perhaps one of the reasons the "successful" Live Earth was never repeated.

Still, in comparison with previous global mega-benefits, Live Earth marked an important shift in terms of how mega-events are mediated. More people viewed Live Earth online than on television. Not only have economics and ecology come into conflict with the mega-event tradition, but the dispersed nature of digital media may be bringing an end to "the whole world is watching" phenomenon, as marked by the ascendance and decline of television as the world's most important mass medium. Rather than all watching the same thing at the same time, we are more likely to share bits and pieces of a broadcast at various times well after the event has taken place. In the digital media culture, even the largest, most captivating, and singular events get blown up into little bits and bytes to be consumed a million different ways at a million different times. That dispersal changes the nature of both an event and a recording of an event, turning them into one and the same, with neither being more essential than the other. Quite simply, Live Earth felt less important than Live Aid and the big concerts that gave rise to both.

Live Earth presented 150 musical acts over a 24-hour period, making it the largest global media event ever staged. Although similar to the Olympics or the World Cup in terms of estimated carbon emissions, Live Earth sent only 19 percent of its material waste to landfills, and the purchase of carbon offsets allowed the producers to claim neutral greenhouse gas emissions. The goal was to demonstrate that massive outputs could be offset by equally intense environmental mitigation. Before assessing Live Earth from an ecological standpoint, however, a bit of history is in order.

A Brief History of the Global Mega-Benefit

Earlier mega-benefits had nothing to do with the environment. The global concert movement started in 1971 with the Concert for Bangladesh. Held in New York City, organized by George Harrison and Ravi Shankar, the concert featured Bob Dylan, Ringo Starr, Eric Clapton, and Billy Preston. It would take over a decade for someone to stage another benefit concert on the same international scale.

The groundbreaking 1985 Live Aid concerts in London and Philadelphia raised roughly $300 million for Ethiopian famine relief. The landmark event transformed its creator, the Boomtown Rats' talented songwriter and singer, Bob Geldof, into a household name and, eventually, Knight Commander of the Order of the British Empire. It was an ironic honor for the man who penned "Another Piece of Red" (1981), a song mocking the British empire. From new wave to world stage, Geldof took pop music to new heights, proving that rock and roll could do more than get musicians laid. After the "me generation" of the seventies, Geldof's concert series was viewed as saving rock from itself. In that way, it represented the ultimate success of the punk and new wave generation.

A year before Live Aid, Geldof and Midge Ure had written "Do They Know It's Christmas?" (1984) to raise money for Ethiopian famine relief. Recorded by Band Aid, it remained the United Kingdom's best-selling song for over two decades. Geldof has since referred to it as the worst song ever written but still gives it credit as the inspiration for Live Aid. While performing at Live Aid, Bob Dylan suggested that some of the proceeds be spent to pay off American farmers' debts. In 1985, Willie Nelson and John Mellencamp joined Dylan to create Farm Aid. Each year, Farm Aid concerts raise money for struggling U.S. farm families and advocate for family-farm-friendly policies. By focusing on the sustainable food movement, Farm Aid became the most environmentally relevant mega-concert project.

Tibetan Freedom concerts resuscitated the waning mega-benefit movement in 1996 and remained vital until 2001. Led by the Beastie Boys, those concerts were designed to raise awareness of the Chinese occupation of Tibet or, from another perspective, to highlight human rights issues in China's Tibetan region. It is reasonable to assume that the Tibetan Freedom concerts increased American awareness of those issues, although American media and audiences still demonstrate relatively little knowledge of the topic (Moyo 2010). As with other mega-events, it is unclear whether the Tibetan Freedom concerts made much of a difference outside the stadium. Other than international antiapartheid concerts, there is little evidence that any mega-events led to long-term structural change. Please note: I am not claiming that musical concerts undid apartheid, but rather that, unlike most mega-benefits, they were articulated within a much larger, longstanding, and ultimately successful movement.

Bob Geldof went at it again in 2005. His Live 8 events put pressure on the leading industrialized nations of the Group of Eight (G8) to increase aid to African countries, negotiate fairer trade rules, and provide debt relief. Unlike other rock stars, Geldof cannot be accused of one-off politics. He has continued to advocate for people living in extreme poverty.

The Live 8 concerts were a great success in terms of attendance, but by no means did policy follow suit. Perhaps Live 8's demands presented too strong and specific a challenge to prosperous nations. Or the opposite might be true. Perhaps Live 8 failed to radically challenge the assumptions upon which global deprivation and wealth are predicated. Live 8 rhetoric is somewhere in the middle, calling attention to the disastrous debt cycle, but not going so far as to challenge the ideology, policies, and military actions that fuel it. More resistant politics are left to radical rockers like Rage Against the Machine, Propagandhi, and Anti-Flag. Geldof and the bands in Live 8 trade critical specificity for global breadth; or, looked at from another angle, rock acts like Rage sacrifice global reach in order to advocate for more radical policy changes.

Live Earth: The Concert

Coming two years after Live 8, and produced by the same team, Live Earth was in part an attempt to demonstrate that mega-events remained relevant, effective, and sustainable. The goal was to transform music fans into activists. Each audience member was asked to take a seven-point pledge (Azios 2007):

> I pledge . . .
>   To demand that my country join an international treaty within the next two years that cuts global-warming pollution by 90 percent in developed countries and by more than half worldwide in time for the next generation to inherit a healthy earth;
>   To take personal action to help solve the climate crises by reducing my own CO_2 pollution as much as I can and offsetting the rest to become "carbon neutral";
>   To fight for a moratorium on the construction of any new generating facility that burns coal without the capacity to safely trap and store the CO_2;
>   To work for a dramatic increase in the energy efficiency of my home, workplace, school, place of worship, and means of transportation;
>   To fight for laws and policies that expand the use of renewable energy sources and reduce dependence on oil and coal;
>   To plant new trees and to join with others in preserving and protecting forests; and,
>   To buy from businesses and support leaders who share my commitment to solving the climate crises and building a sustainable, just, and prosperous world for the 21st century.

"There are changes happening . . . but in general when you read these scientific reports that keep coming out you realize that these problems didn't just go away because we did a concert, or a movie won an Academy Award, or Al Gore won the Nobel Peace Prize," explained Executive Producer Kevin Wall. "This crisis is only going to go away because real actions are taken" (quoted in Waddell 2008).

Trying to leverage the power of Live Earth, Wall joined Al Gore in the unsuccessful attempt to get a "Kyoto 2" treaty ratified by the nations that produce the most greenhouse gases, including the United States. That attempt failed. Like the rest of us, the concert organizers watched in frustration as the United States, China, and other foot-dragging countries increased, rather than curtailed, their use of coal and other greenhouse-gas-emitting fuels. Even a concert of Live Earth's dimensions is dwarfed in scale relative to the oil and coal industries' PR resources. In addition to advocating policy changes and new treaties, the producers of Live Earth published green event guidelines for use by the music industry and a consumer-oriented guide to help individuals cope with climate change: *The Live Earth Global Warming Survival Handbook* (de Rothschild 2007). In *The Ecologist* Mark Anslow praised the Live Earth handbook as a potentially effective text for friends "who drive 4X4S and look at your copy of the *Ecologist* as if it were Mein Kampf" (2007, 63). Some criticize such publications and events for fostering the notion that individual acts are sufficient by themselves, offering a neoliberal, consumer-oriented solution to a problem caused by neoliberal economics, ideology, and institutions. Anslow agrees that much of the book may be "too simplistic," and in the case of aviation, "typically understated" (ibid.). Nevertheless, as he points out, it is better than nothing.

In 2008, *Billboard's* Ray Waddell noted that rock bands were moving away from "press releases touting massive production and a fleet of semis." As we have seen in the case of U2, not everyone got that message. In fact, nothing illustrates the energy-intensive aspect of rock better than musicians' claims to have radically reduced their footprints through offsets. For example, Sheryl Crow claims that her total carbon reductions for a 2010 tour were equivalent to 81 homes going without electricity for a year (Crow 2010). The implication is that, thanks to Crow, massive amounts of energy were conserved. In truth, a great deal of energy was expended, twice—first for the tour and then for producing offsets that, theoretically, will soak up enough carbon to make the original energy expenditures climate-neutral. As was pointed out in the Introduction, the ecological accounting is not yet based on firm science;

offsets are a matter of serious debate among environmental scientists and economists.

Crow not only seeks carbon neutrality, however, she also uses her music to advocate for action. For example, she joined forces with the Natural Resources Defense Council to protest against mountaintop removal mining in Appalachia (Webster 2010). Therefore, my point is not to lambaste Crow and other conscientious musicians but rather to point out that they act out our collective conundrums in public. To the degree that such global stars bring attention to environmental dilemmas, they do a great service. To the degree that they use these actions to cover over the complexities of ecological challenges and promote all-too-easy answers like carbon offsets, they do a disservice. Live Earth did the latter on a global stage.

The 2007 Live Earth concert deserves a postscript. The producers planned on repeating Live Earth the following year in India, but terrorist attacks in Mumbai led them to cancel the event. However, in 2010 the Dow Live Earth Run for Water took place in cities throughout the world, sponsored by the same chemical company accused of poisoning groundwater worldwide. Dow was attempting to improve its international image by sponsoring clean-water events and developing low-cost water-filtration systems. Understandably, the International Campaign for Justice in Bhopal and Amnesty International boycotted the event. Dow is the parent corporation of Union Carbide, the company that killed between five thousand and fifteen thousand people in Bhopal, India, in one of the worst environmental catastrophes on record. Angered by what they viewed as greenwashing, activists signed up to run the race under the names of fictitious environmental organizations as a guerilla protest to embarrass Dow. Thanks to Dow's sponsorship, by 2010 much of the environmentalist community viewed Live Earth as a greenwashing project and nothing more. However, some environmental organizations took part in the fun runs and received funding in turn (liveearth.org/run).

As noted in Anslow's review of the Live Earth handbook, an important message of Live Earth was that consumerism and environmentalism could be made compatible if practiced correctly. Not surprisingly, industrial publications for the advertising, public relations, marketing, and the accounting professions uniformly praised the event (Accountancy 2007). "Ad Community Rallies around Al Gore's Live Earth Campaign," proclaimed one (Rivard 2007). Indeed, Live Earth pleased industry.

The reviews were much more mixed among environmentalists, audience members, and music critics. As usual, contradiction was the main theme. In blogs and letters to the editor, some fans complained about stars with lavish lifestyles asking audiences to reduce their consumption while the same celebrities own multiple homes, fly private jets around the world, and advertise wasteful consumer products (Graillat 2007). Gore and his ally Sir Richard Branson have been criticized for peddling forms of conservation that they don't practice themselves. Richard Peet, Paul Robbins, and Michael Watts use Branson and Gore as critical foils to lead off their book *Global Political Ecology*, which contains a photo of airline CEO Branson tossing a globe into the air while Gore smiles at his side (2010).

While playing up the principal performers' contradictions, however, surprisingly few critics questioned Live Earth's carbon-offset premise. Perhaps the concept was too new at that point. Since then, scientists, environmental accountants, and activists have raised questions about the validity of specific offset schemes and algorithms (Rogers 2010). Others have questioned the basic premise: the claim that one expenditure of energy can successfully offset another (e.g., planting a grove of trees). Offsets might even the score in terms of total greenhouse gasses released and absorbed, but in terms of the entire ecological system, such massive actions are likely to have other deleterious consequences. Often such schemes ignore the multiple inputs required by offsets, such as the energy required to grow and transport plants, foster tree growth in disturbed soils, and so on. A report on NBC's rival ABC, "Critics: Live Earth Not So Green," estimated that the sponsors would need to plant 100,000 trees to offset Live Earth's massive carbon emissions (ABC News 2007). Clearly, it would be better to reduce the energy used by the concert and model environmental stewardship more directly.

The *Harvard Law Review* said it best, arguing that the concept of carbon offsets "allows people to 'do their part' without changing what they do" (2010, 2066). In that light, events like Live Earth ritually legitimate high-consumption lifestyles by obfuscating their real consequences. Rather than leading toward sustainable societies, these relatively empty gestures serve to garner cultural capital for those who can afford to make them, a form of noblesse oblige rather than authentic environmental action.

When assessing environmental action, of course, it is important to ask, "Compared to what?" In terms of environmental impact, Live Earth was benign in comparison with most previous mega-events. If the music industry is going to continue to hold live global spectacles, Live Earth presents a better model than the norm. Performer John Mayer had this clever response when asked about his "eco-sins": "I don't know . . . but tell the editors back at Glass Half Empty that I said hey" (quoted in Freydkin, Gardner, and Grumman 2007).

The man behind Live 8 and Live Aid, Sir Bob Geldof, questioned the point of Live Earth. "Why is [Gore] actually organizing them?" he asked. "To make us aware of the greenhouse effect? Everybody's known about that problem for years" (ABC News 2007). Responding to such criticisms, Gore explained that Live Earth was just the beginning of a three- to five-year campaign destined to bring important change. Given that July 7, 2012, marks the event's five-year anniversary, it is not apparent what campaign Gore was referring to. However, that might be the best lesson of Live Earth. If well-intentioned rituals like Live Earth are ultimately unsustainable and unsuccessful, what does that say about our individual and collective lifestyles? We are all failing at this together.

Music and Movements

Rolling Stone's Brian Hiatt skewered the featured acts of Live Earth as life-less, emotionally uncommitted, and unable to ignite a stadium crowd. He wrote that the music felt "as hot as a climate-displaced polar bear" (2007, 82), reminding us that no matter how well intentioned or struc-tured, a ritual must be enacted well to achieve its intended effects. Of course, some critics were more favorable, but Hiatt's scathing assessment raises questions about the ecological role of musical performance.

Musical ritual tends to emphasize emotional impact. Music can achieve a collective catharsis, connecting on a more emotional level than dry didacticism (e.g., a scientific lecture) or narrative (e.g., environmental documentaries). It is more ephemeral, yet also more deeply felt than more explicitly educational acts. Music plays an important role in pro-ducing ritual's magical catharsis. From dictatorships to marketing direc-tors, that lesson has not been lost on the powerful. Spectacular musical rites have reproduced institutional power the world over.

In addition to understanding that universal principle, specific cultural knowledge is essential for ritual performance to succeed. For example, the Bosavi composers of Papua New Guinea craft *gisalo* songs "with the delib-erate intention of moving others to tears" (Feld 1982, 36–37), especially at funeral ceremonies (86–87). Similarly, it is "normal for the Tuvans to cry when they hear music" (Levin 2006, 3)—but one should never cry at a Tuvan funeral; in fact, "people would take you away" if you did (ibid.). Bosavi and Tuvan musicians are well aware of their own cultural pre-scriptions and proscriptions and incorporate that knowledge into per-formance. The Tuvans' proscription against crying at funerals would seem quite foreign to the average Mexican music fan. However, the idea that music moves listeners to tears is very familiar. While conducting field research in Mexico, I witnessed stoic men bawling their eyes out over ranchera songs and associated rituals. Ritual provides structure to collective catharsis, and music impels it. The mariachi musician is a ritual expert on par with Bosavi and Tuvan musicians.

And so are rock musicians. What distinguished Live Earth from an Al Gore speech was music. Environmental information was placed into a rich ritual context with all of the cultural proscriptions, prescriptions, and liturgy that implies. From Live Earth on down to the club concerts described in Chapter 4, popular music rituals are designed to make us feel a sense of collective catharsis. Occasionally, that might entail instructing us as to how we might achieve new possibilities, momentarily transporting us to theoretical worlds and altered states: heaven, nirvana, a successful "hook up," sustainability, peace, the American Dream, etc. Musical rituals promise us that such transcendent worlds await. The ritual simulacra is designed to give us a glimpse into those magical worlds and experiences, if we follow the ritual protocol in good faith. However, it takes years to build such ritual apparatuses, and a good deal of effort to pull off ritual performances successfully. The priest class earns its pay.

Although that may not be their manifest rationalization, well-conceived rituals are designed to show us what a better world might actually look, feel, taste, and sound like. Their latent and more important purpose is to encourage us to feel a special connection to each other, to make us feel something, together. Special sound, sight (e.g., ritual architecture), movement, taste, and touch are intended to transport us from the profane to the sacred, providing a glimpse of collectively conceived utopias. Of course, the subtext is that you will earn these things if you faithfully obey basic precepts as laid down by the state, institution, or individual sponsor. As Joe Hill of the Industrial Workers of the World sang, "You'll get pie in the sky, when you die (that's a lie)!" (KUED 2012). He contested one set of rituals with another. Indeed, politics is performed via competing rituals, each with an opposing collective destiny, and utopia, in mind.

Ritual precepts are in play at secular events like Live Earth as well. Musicians and audiences acting in concert (to borrow the title of Mattern 1998) gain a liminal glimpse of the impossible dream, an indication that something better might be possible. "Music," explains Simon Frith, "offers us not argument, but experience" (1996, 157). When articulated to political movements, musical rituals encourage meaningful action. At least, they do if performed well.

Ritual is an ecological system in and of itself, requiring close articulation of movement, sound, sight, smell, and taste within a unique architectural space, as well as disciplined attention to liturgy, drama, and narrative based on cultural custom. Successful ritual performance brings great rewards. However, violating the integrity of a ritual code brings scorn and ridicule, as failed regimes have learned time and again. Hologram projections of Al Gore were just one of the elements in Live Earth that appear not to have worked for critics or audiences. The effort was too transparently promotional, and too weakly articulated with more profound cultural norms. Despite the best intentions, Live Earth appears to have been a mostly dysfunctional ritual.

Put more positively, Live Earth was an expression of hope that greater global unity might be possible in the face of growing collective risk. The event provided evidence "that increasing patterns of global connectivity" tied to "broadening risk scenarios" were finally beginning to be reflected in music (Heise 2008, 210). However, Live Earth's theme of sustainability may have been ritually contradicted by its ostentatious rock context, message and means effectively canceling each other out. Whether Live Nation, U2, Al Gore, and others want to admit it or not, the global music industry is faced with a major conundrum: medium is contradicting message.

Live Earth's producers recognized that music needed to be brought into the matter. "We won't understand climate change by focusing only on its physicality," notes Mike Hulme. "We need to understand the ways in which we talk about climate change, the variety of myths we construct about climate change and through which we reveal to ourselves what climate change means to us" (2009, 355). Live Earth was an attempt, no matter how awkward, to create better ways to tell the story of climate change. Our conception of climate has gone from local to global in a matter of decades (Hulme 2009, 18). A confluence of cultural, scientific, environmental, and economic changes have expanded human consciousness, making us more adept at thinking about global abstractions like climate, yet at the same time rendering us less able to understand our immediate surroundings. When traveling in rural Mexico and Central America, I am constantly struck by the depth of knowledge local farmers demonstrate in regard to their environs. Even small children can identify and use features in the natural landscape to enrich their lives, from knowing when a tree fruit will ripen to associating seasonal changes with community events. Current crises require both local consciousness and global awareness, and the ability to link the two—no easy task.

Live Earth was a purposeful ritual in that regard, designed to mediate the world audience's orientation to the planet. Was it successful? Based on the evidence, probably not. However, it was ambitious to say the least, and given that it was the first of its kind, Live Earth's utopian imagination may yet prove prophetic. We may be able to salvage both consumerism and environmentalism. Or it may be a matter of choosing one or the other, a dialectical battle rather than the hand-in-glove system envisioned by Gore and Branson.

Live Earth also demonstrates the need to combine music and movements more successfully, a recurrent theme throughout this book. To the extent that Live Earth had an impact, it was thanks to the audience's subsequent activism. To the extent that it failed, it was largely because the event lacked serious movement connections and was based on faulty premises. Rather than having an energetic cadre of environmentalists helping to promote the event, Live Earth put its energy into wooing and winning over the private sector. Environmentalists are understandably wary of embracing industry-driven events like Live Earth. As was made clear in the controversy surrounding U2's 360° Tour, tensions between industrial rock and grassroots environmentalism survived Live Earth.

Beyond Live Earth

Although Live Earth largely failed, individual rock acts are increasingly taking up the call. In the December 16, 2010, issue of *Rolling Stone*, Joe Coscarelli listed "The 15 Most Eco-Friendly Rockers." Musicians made the list by contributing time, money, or their celebrity image to an environmental cause or organization. Green Day, for example, made the cut by collaborating with the Natural Resources Defense Council. Rock stars could also get on the list by trying to make their shows carbon- and waste-neutral. Educating audiences was an additional criterion, as illustrated by Barenaked Ladies, who play a video about climate change before each concert.

The first band profiled on *Rolling Stone*'s list is Guster, whose nonprofit organization, Reverb, has worked with musicians "from Avril Lavigne to Arcade Fire" to "lighten their footprint." Many on the list have been involved in Reverb events. For example, Drake headlined Reverb's Campus Consciousness Tour. Reverb has borrowed Michael Martin's innovations, but operates differently. While Martin's MusicMatters prefers to remain backstage, the Reverb group has been highly self-promotional, placing their name alongside that of client bands.

The Dave Matthews Band provides a good illustration of how far rock has come in the past decade. In 2004, 800 pounds of the band's excrement was dumped into the Chicago River. As it came rushing out of the tour bus, a passerby got soaked with the sewage. Needless to say, the publicity was less than positive. This much publicized event led Dave Matthews to donate $100,000 to environmental projects around Chicago. After years of environmental efforts, greatly assisted by Martin and

MusicMatters, the band made number 3 on the "Eco-Friendly" list. Of course, the concern is that organizations like MusicMatters and Reverb specialize in both environmental mitigation and public relations, a mixture of functions that makes it hard to know where one begins and the other ends. It would be useful to have external environmental accounting involved as well.

Concert education, collaboration, and mitigation appear to be *Rolling Stone*'s primary criteria; musical content does not appear to matter much. Of the 15 stars who made the list, only one song was mentioned as evidence of environmental commitment, and it was a cover tune. What distinguishes rock as "eco-friendly" appears to have more to do with concert context than musical content.

Not only were songs about the environment missing, but so were efforts to scale down operations by producing smaller concerts or encouraging more sustainable, perhaps even participatory, events. "Eco-friendly" rock is still about celebrity and spectacle, massive apparatuses and media designed to project individual personas onto giant stages for large live audiences to enjoy. In our discussion, Martin equated his work with U2 with his consulting at Proctor and Gamble (interview, July 28, 2011). He argues that getting Tide to produce a cold-water laundry detergent did more for the environment than all of the small, niche-marketed, environmentally conscious cleaning companies combined. Big rock acts are going to continue putting on big shows as long as people will pay them to do so. Getting them to do so in a more environmentally responsible manner is laudable and, judging from Martin's innovative efforts, it is very hard work as well.

However, alternatives should not be forgotten. If brand activism completely supplants public action, we will be in deep trouble. Without noncommercial activism it is unlikely that industry would feel any pressure to change. More importantly, green consumerism can all too easily drift into greenwashing. The same dynamic holds true for rock, where alternatives to traditional stadium concerts need to be more seriously explored. In the late seventies, industrial rock was challenged by punk, new wave, ska, and do-it-yourself alternatives. Groups like the Untouchables poked fun at the alienated nature of commodified rock, supergroups, and stadium shows. Big rock is being challenged once again by a new generation, this time with a concern for ecology. Punk tried to save the soul of rock from corporate takeover. Small, eco-oriented festivals and participatory groups are presenting a similar challenge to mainstream rock today.

Predictably, mainstream press coverage of rock environmentalism tends to be promotional, rather than balanced or critical. That is particularly true of *Billboard, Rolling Stone,* and other industry trade magazines. Furthermore, the most polluting rock bands are ignored rather than criticized. Dissenting sources are almost never quoted, nor are nonindustrial alternatives brought to light. There is virtually no consideration of scaling down pop spectacle to make it more sustainable, nor serious consideration of mainstream rock's relationship to the marketing of consumer products and high-consumption, unsustainable lifestyles. Just as positive psychology asks us to gloss over real social problems for the sake of unrelenting optimism, industrially oriented green rhetoric tends to deflect readers from thinking about wider issues and dealing with them more effectively.

However, *Rolling Stone's* December 2010 piece ends on a thought-provoking note. The final musician profiled, Radiohead's Thom Yorke, hints at larger problems. Yorke has on several occasions threatened to quit touring over environmental concerns and even refused an invitation to discuss environmental issues with the prime minister, citing Tony Blair's weak environmental policies. The article quotes an interview Yorke gave to an Australian newspaper: "The job I'm in is a job that wastes energy left, right, and centre," he complained. "It's madness." Yorke is publicly struggling with a problem identified concisely by Timothy Morton: "When you think about where your waste goes, your world starts to shrink" (2007, 1). It is hard to "shrink" a rock tour, but Yorke's innovations in direct-to-consumer distribution indicate that he may be able to come up with more sustainable ways to perform as well. Yorke recognizes how hard it is to perform rock in an ecologically sound way. For starters, musical performance does not function according to an economy of scale. There are few added efficiencies with increased scale of production in live performance. Whereas there are potential environmental benefits in growing lots of crops where they grow best and then shipping them to consumers, for example, hauling sound equipment, musicians, and fans around the world does not harness scale to advantage. While high transportation costs for moving food and other material goods are often justified by the economy of scale argument, music can be transported digitally, without the environmentally costly spectacle and a "Long Line of Cars" (Cake 2001) bringing audiences to each venue. More troubling yet, online music delivery has yet to produce material savings and, therefore, environmental gains for the industry as a whole (Hogg and Jackson 2009, 133). From an ecological perspective, it is hard to justify stadium rock tours.

However, rock concerts have mass educational benefits if audiences take advantage of the resources that bands like Guster provide. Furthermore, such tours may be building meaningful communities around environmental issues. At the very least, eco-conscious tours are better than those that fail to take environmental costs into consideration.

Meanwhile, the recession and weak recovery are doing their part to reduce touring, and 2010 was a particularly bad year for the music business. "It's official," wrote the *Washington Post*'s Chris Richards. "The concert business had a lousy 2010." The industry, as currently constituted, needs high-energy concert tours to protect their already slim profit margins, and sponsors line up to support such tours. However, it is not clear to what extent fans are still demanding the big tours. Audiences aren't found; they're made. It takes a lot of marketing energy to create audiences. However, fans need to have disposable income and job security in order to buy expensive tour tickets. Recently, money for promotions has melted away along with ticket sales. A new concert model may be forced on the industry, scaled down to match the new economy. The ecology of rock may be experiencing a negative feedback loop, a regulatory mechanism necessary for any system to be sustained in the long term.

However, fans still want to share physical space with their favorite bands, to hear the music they love reproduced live. Musicians often measure their artistic worth through live performance. Meanwhile, given the low-profit business model of digital distribution networks, music companies need live concerts more than ever. Music producers' profit margins depend on the ad subsidies and merchandise sales concerts make possible. As much as we like to think of rock as cultural rebellion, it is not that different from any other business. As Richard Leppert has demonstrated, music tends to be a cultural force predicated upon "affirming political and economic policies" (1993, 116). Even Live Earth and cause-marketing concerts do little to challenge business as usual or adapt the traditional rock tour to a peak-oil planet. They simply make energy-intensive entertainment more palatable.

But would it be rock without the busses and trucks, the blinding light show, and massive stacks pumping out high-volume hits? Or maybe rock has lost itself? Perhaps it has strayed too far from the days when Buddy Holly, Big Bopper, and Ritchie Valens rocked the Surf Ballroom and other more intimate venues. Maybe some clues to rock's sustainable future are to be found in its brilliant past.

Looking forward, bands like Cloud Cult (Chapter 3) are incorporating environmental concepts directly into their musical artistry. They let their music travel the globe without following it with a phalanx of trucks, busses, planes, and ferries filled with equipment. In a few generations our great-grandchildren may find it odd that we felt compelled to move great quantities of material and people around the earth to produce sounds that could be made anywhere and everywhere.

Yet cultural inertia is a powerful thing, especially when propelled by profit. The music industry continues to struggle with environmental contradictions, as demonstrated by U2, Soundgarden, Live Earth, and all of us who turn out to see the big show. It is "as easy as breathing for us all to participate" (DiFranco 2001). Simply by attending a concert we affirm its value. Therefore, one thing we can do as an audience is to favor performers who have taken significant strides to make their performances sustainable. Another is to ask our favorite artists and concert producers to take sustainability more seriously during tour planning. Perhaps the best model for that is Jack Johnson.

Jack Johnson, All at Once

The slogan of Johnson's All at Once project—"An individual action, multiplied by millions, creates global change" (allatonce.org)—was created in collaboration with Michael Martin. In our interview, Martin argued that Johnson brings "hope and positiveness" to environmental musicianship. Perhaps the most striking thing about Johnson's All at Once is that it directly engages fans in environmental activities. In exchange for taking part in environmental work with one of 220 partnered nonprofits, participants receive "rewards" in the form of free music, including song downloads not available anywhere else. The goal is to get people involved at a deeper level. The project's website links people to global campaigns and local efforts, while providing educational resources to help fans become active volunteers. Partner nonprofits submitted one-minute videos to the website explaining their work; then Johnson donated a dollar for each video watched. That brought over a million people to JackJohnsonMusic.com and resulted in the most downloaded album in history. Jack Johnson concerts go well beyond industry standards. In addition to providing recycling bins for plastic bottles, for example, Johnson's concerts have "hydration stations," another of Michael Martin's many innovations. They also feature Martin's Eco-Village concept, educational centers where fans can learn more about ongoing environmental efforts and volunteer to help out.

The All at Once project and Jack Johnson's concerts are a major advance in terms of environmental performance. Johnson takes sustainability seriously, and his work has gone from impact mitigation to proactive restoration. Martin and Johnson are transforming rock performance from passive consumption into active engagement.

Martin's influence is considerable, and goes beyond Jack Johnson. Using his education and talents in cause marketing, Martin instituted what he calls an "effect marketing" model for rock. His goal is to "effect social change to grow an artist's brand" (interview, July 28, 2011). Minneapolis-based Martin invented the "enviro-rider" contract that Live Nation and rock acts sign in order to improve their ecological impact. He was the first to institute carbon offsets (through his subsidiary Native Energy), Eco-Villages, renewable-energy-powered festivals, and a fan passport system that rewards fan-activists for taking action. His clients have included over 150 major rock acts, from Sting and R.E.M. to the Black Eyed Peas and Dave Matthews. Martin's work brings home the point that ecomusicology is about much more than artists and audiences. "People want to think that Dave Matthews and Ben and Jerry's were sitting in a kitchen and came up with the idea for the Lick Global Warming campaign," explains Martin, "but the reality is that it took me 18 months of working that deal to get all of the players on board" (interview, July 28, 2011). And yet, he added, "People should view this as the artist doing it."

As fans we want music's logistical and material apparatus to remain backstage. However, ecomusicology requires examining the entire system of musical production, performance, and consumption. Martin was incredibly helpful in explaining all that goes into producing rock shows and, therefore, how difficult it is to reduce their environmental impact.

Globalization and the Changing Nature of Place

All at Once may portend a brighter future for the ecomusicology of rock. At present, however, it is one of only a few global rock projects that effectively link fans to environmental action in their own communities. This is a different form of globalization than that touted by neoliberal economists. All at Once is more authentically democratic and empowering than the corporate and consumer-oriented utopia imagined in the neoliberal mindset.

Regardless of which vision of globalization comes to the fore, it would appear that the consciousness of the typical resident of planet Earth is increasingly globalized, more cosmopolitan and less parochial. However, it is not clear whether we are becoming more globally conscious or just less locally aware. For example, does digital downloading increase listeners' global consciousness or merely reduce their connection to local music? No one knows the answer to that question. Nor does anyone know who first said, "Writing about music is like dancing about architecture," but it's true (Scott 2009). Verbal descriptions do not convey the full emotional depth or sociological complexity of music. It is difficult to express musical truths in writing or provide definitive answers to musicological questions, such as how music influences our consciousness.

Music engages and integrates a remarkable number of the brain's regions, which may be why it produces such pleasurable effects (Benzon 2001). Perhaps for the same reason, music helps us to form relationships to people and places (Osborne 2009, 546). For example, the city where I live is bisected by the Mississippi River, a waterway that evokes a musical history, place, and collective identity. Music is part of the cultural glue that bonds the local community to the local place. We identify ourselves and each other with the river. What happens to our sense of connection to such places when our consciousness moves increasingly "out there" into the world, as opposed to "right here" by the river? What is gained and what is lost? How does musical consciousness change?

Historically, music has connected communities to the places where they live. Lawrence Grossberg puts it best when he describes music as a "territorializing machine" (1993, 206). Geographer James Curtis and Richard Rose use the example of Woody Guthrie's Dust Bowl songs to demonstrate how people, places, and events are connected through music (1994). Chris Davies shows how Gumatji musicians in the Yirrkala region of Australia use rock music to advocate for greater autonomy, sustainable land use, historical redress, and social justice (1993).

But what does musical community mean when projected onto a global scale? Davies becomes pessimistic at that point. He worries that the rock he encountered in rural Australia is lost in translation to geographically and culturally distant audiences. Music is "museumized, touristicated, and rendered simulacra" as it enters the global marketplace (1993, 262). Ultimately, even Curtis's Dust Bowl example illustrates the same point. After all, Dust Bowl songs became the music of diaspora, written by the itinerant Guthrie, favored by folklorists and music producers in New York. Rather than cohering people and place, Guthrie's music created new places in the modern social imaginary, nostalgically re-imagined representations of the Dust Bowl that became metaphors and foils for distant audiences. The musical connection between people and place is never simple.

If the relationship between music and place is that complex at the local level, how can we begin to understand music as part of a global ecosystem? Will popular music help create a more sustainable world community and sense of place, or will it form the soundtrack for more destructive forms of globalization? The answer might be "both." During the colonial era, music was both dominating and resistant, depending on who wielded it and why. There was imperial march music as well as underground rites of resistance. However, their power was never equal. Judging from the sounds surrounding us today, popular music is more likely to form a soundtrack for excessive consumption than to inspire more sustainable orientations.

One way to examine music in the world system is to think about the cultural, economic, and technological means through which we are "interpellated" musically into the global community. Interpellation is the act of being "hailed" by a text or institution (Althusser 2001). For example, if we are spoken to by news media as consumers, we cannot help but take on that identity, at least in relation to news. News reports about airline strikes could be written under the assumption that we, the readers, are stockholders, citizens, workers, or inconvenienced travelers. The fact that reporters and news institutions routinely choose to speak to us as consumers, inconvenienced travelers, betrays a certain sense of what the corporate news media are institutionally, and who we are expected to be in relation to them. In a consumer-oriented, capitalist system, news is not really a commodity (we don't pay for news, ads do), but rather a medium through which news consumers' eyeballs are sold to advertisers. News consumers *are* the commodity. Not surprisingly, our primary identity in such a system is that of obedient consumer. We consume; therefore we are.

Is the same true of music? When the global music industries hail us via iTunes and Ticketmaster, how do we respond? What messages are sent, and how do we receive them? Answering that question in earnest could entail an entirely different project, but some informal observations are in order as we end this chapter.

The relationship between local and global becomes difficult to disentangle in a world that is increasingly de-territorialized (Deleuze and Guattari 1977). Often we are nowhere and everywhere at the same time. When first writing this sentence I was sitting in a chair at the Snohomish, Washington, Starbucks while watching a *YouTube* music video made in Venezuela and drinking cocoa grown in Ghana. Exactly where are we during musical moments like that? Do they represent postmodern dis-location or some new way of being in the world?

Such dislocation and/or global reach is both the problem and promise of digital communication networks. The same technologies that take our senses thousands of miles away can also remove our consciousness from the streams, trees, or toxins in our own backyards. Yet the same global communication technologies allow scientists, environmentalists, and citizens to deal with planetary-scale ecological crises such as climate change, population growth, and water pollution.

Yet, it is hard to imagine sustaining local places when so few of us are still deeply engaged in them. Leslie Marmon Silko explains that the "ancient Pueblo could not conceive of themselves without a specific landscape" (1996, 269). With our minds in cyberspace, it is hard to develop such a close connection to local landscapes. Via digital avatars, we are increasingly defined more by cyber-associations than by place-based identities (or, as represented in the film, Avatar, are digital prosthetics a new way of gaining physical, mental, and cultural access to local environments?). Environmental educators work hard to counter the de-territorializing trend, designing curricula that place children and adults in their local surroundings, places where they can gain first-hand knowledge of local ecosystems and an embodied sense of what it is like to live in a watershed and eat from a local food web.

On the other hand, there are plenty of technological optimists when it comes to digital music and consciousness. Aaron Cohen equates online music making and sharing to the "counter culture" of the 1960s and argues that online collaboration has the same revolutionary potential as Pete Seeger's participatory music (2006, 8). He believes that young people are turning away from mass media and turning toward social networking, dispersing power that had been centralized in the hands of a few media corporations. Cohen contrasts that way of being with traditional stadium rock, citing Live 8 not as a watershed global benefit, but as a "victory" for traditional media companies hoping to move their oligopolistic control of the music market onto online environments. Using manifesto-style rhetoric, Cohen warns traditional media companies to "buckle up" in preparation for the growing "participant generation" (2006, 8). In the 1960s C. Wright Mills warned that most people were "losing control of the very means of cultural production" as culture became "an adjunct of marketing, or the bureaucratic ethos, or of both" (quoted in Vannini 2004, 47). Cohen sees people taking cultural control back from those same culture industries. He argues that social networking makes it more difficult for the music industry to mediate consumers' relationship to music and believes that the consumer-citizen-listener is wresting control from the music industry. Is Cohen's technological optimism warranted, or is social networking just another, even more intimate way for corporate culture to take root in individual lives? Watching young people eagerly market themselves online, it would appear that the corporate ethos has pervaded and commodified even the most intimate forms of social communication.

Heise argues that the de-territorializing tendencies of modern life "might sometimes need to be resisted by some form of 'reterritorialization'" (2008, 210). If music is a "territorializing machine," as Grossberg calls it (1993, 206), then it can play a positive role in that resistance: "it is music which founds space" by "constructing the rhythms of our stopping and going" and by building walls "around a bit of space" so that we "are protected now to engage in whatever activities are necessary" (ibid.). Grossberg provides a useful metaphor for musical activists seeking to create more sustainable soundscapes. Music may be just as important as law (e.g., legal ownership of physical space) when it comes to creating spaces for meaningful action. At the very least, music imbues shared places—public squares, parks, or protest encampments—with greater meaning. In semiotic language, music "encodes" space with cultural meaning.

As for the initial question, global consciousness, the only conclusion to be drawn at this point is that digital media have the potential to draw us away from the places where we live and out into the world. Therefore, they also have the potential to help us think and act in concert with distant others, even at a planetary scale. Thanks to digital integration, we are increasingly subject to global institutions, but also able to take part in growing global conversations. That is as true for music as it is for any other form of communication.

Music is a form of communication. The question of digital technology, communications hardware, brings us to the more dynamic dimensions of musical communication: musical style, structure, genre, and instrumentation. It is worth noting that most explicitly environmentalist musicians emphasize acoustic instrumentation, a point taken up again in Chapter 4. Wood, metal, and other natural elements are understood to more faithfully represent the sounds of nature. The goal is acoustic balance rather than electronic dissonance. It is assumed by new age and folk musicians in particular that winds and strings achieve a natural balance better than wires and Stratocasters. Yet, as Peter Gabriel has demonstrated, the most advanced sampling synthesizers can be extremely useful as well. Besides, even acoustic folk artists share their music with the world via advanced digital communication technologies. As variable as music can be in terms of cultural inflection, style, structure, genre, and lyrical content, it all tends to travel the same routes of production, distribution, and consumption. All global music is, ultimately, electronic.

Therefore, it is partly a question of whether the composer wants to imagine natural worlds in the past, present, or future wilderness or draw our attention to the places where most of us live and breathe in the present. Given that we all live in electronically mediated cultures, electronic music is quite authentic, ecologically speaking. Brian Eno recognized that with his creation of "Ambient Music" (2001, 139). Eno's music strikes a chord of cultural authenticity for many. Ambient music is relevant to modern time and space. It is designed to "induce calm and a space to think" (ibid., 142).

Furthermore, through sampling, synthesizers can often more effectively evoke natural sound than acoustic technologies. Electronic music can be performed in the spirit of Schafer's soundscape design principles (1994)—and it more easily avoids what Morton calls "retroactive fantasy" (2007, 11). Electronic music takes us into the present rather than imagining some environmental Eden to which we must return, or fail. Ultimately, whether a more sustainable sensibility is forged through electronic prosthetics or dried goat skins stretched over djembes might matter less than how they are employed musically. Some new age instrumentalists travel the world to collect and market the exotic sounds of nature, burning copious amounts of jet fuel and wood in the process. Is that ecologically sound? Some punks make the best of their urban environments, capturing surrounding sounds and channeling them into critical performance. Which is more "authentically" environmental? Although the comparison is hypothetical, examples of that paradox abound. World-traveling environmentalists and environmental scientists often find themselves preaching to earthbound others. Professional musicians, traveling for a living, find themselves in a particularly poor position to lecture others.

However, that argument could be taken too far. Some media may be better than others at facilitating meaningful connections to ecosystems. Bernie Krause worries that "Western" voices, instruments, and "computers" make us incapable of "reaching back far enough in time to be able to make the important distinctions between what we have composed and orchestrated and what really exists in the wilderness" (2001, 216). Similarly, Ellen Waterman argues that "an appreciation of the soundscape begins with recovering our ability to listen" (2007, 114). I would argue that this more acute way of listening comes not from rejecting technological sound but rather through recognizing its omnipresence, utility, and limits. Perhaps we need to hear the engine's rattle as well as the brook's babble. The creation of more natural soundscapes might require the recognition of both the world as it is (Waterman's point) and the world as we want it to be (Krause's goal).

For some audiences, electronic music is transcendental (Ingram 2010, 135). From psychedelic rock to contemporary rave, electronic music facilitates escape. Acid House ravers, for example, feel a sense of immersion and suspension. How different is this from other types of transcendental music? In Papua New Guinea, Bosavi ceremonies are designed to be "like being at a waterfall or off in the bush," putting the listener in "a hypnotic, dreamlike state that brings the forest up close, immersing the listeners in a liminal suspension" (Feld 1982, 180). These Bosavi rites are not performed *in* the forest; they musically transport the ritual participant *to* the forest. This is not unlike the descriptions of Goa trance and other rave rituals.

In other words, whether one is in a longhouse ceremony or an urban dance club, music can stimulate a sense of connection to nature. The goal for some listeners is not to imitate the sounds of nature but rather to create music that effectively evokes it. Music is a human phenomenon; it is what we do to live in the world, not what the world does for us. For some that means listening to a clarinet concerto performed in the woods; for others it requires a reverberating sound system and 200 bodies listening, moving, sweating, and swaying together. Judgments on the nature of music across genre borders are more about cultural distinction than meaningful ecological assessments.

It is important to remember that every musical instrument is a form of human technology. West African talking drums made from animal skins, Mesoamerican teponaztlis formed from fallen trees, Tuvan xapchyks made from sheep bones and bull scrota (Levin 2006, 3), and Roland synthesizers are all technological developments rather than natural endowments. Is there a point at which the musical prosthesis goes from being an authentically natural expression to something unnatural? If so, why wasn't that point reached when the first instrument was created? Dichotomies fail upon closer inspection.

David Ingram says it best in *The Jukebox in the Garden* (2010, 70):

Listening to music, then, is an activity determined by biological, cognitive and social factors in a more complex way than that suggested by New Age and deep ecological philosophies. Moreover, such theories of music tend to assume a transcendental, universal human subject, often constructed in the third person plural ('we'). However, despite the fact that the basic physiology of human hearing is a cross-cultural universal, listening itself, as a cognitive activity, is socially relative.

Much like the traditional Pueblo storyteller, the ecomusicologist's goal might be to seek "a communal truth rather than an absolute" when it comes to ethically assessing the ecology of sound (Silko 1996, 269). Electronic music and mediation are a central part of modern life. They are part of daily life as *Homo digitalis*. If I fall prey to the first person plural in this book, it is often in reference to specific group identities and very basic, shared realities, such as the omnipresence of electronic mediation in modern life or nomothetic patterns of musical behavior across time. However, Ingram's point is very important: there is no universal human subject and there are as many ways of being, musically speaking, as there are people. On the other hand, supra-individual, social patterns also exist, which is the main point of doing social research.

In addition to being a major distractor, digital communication has been credited with making the world more self-aware and interconnected. Jaron Lanier argues that computers are "efficient ugliness machines" (2001, 91) that have tended to make horrible music, yet digital communities can also "blow, dance, and sing whole worlds into existence" (93), which can "distract us away from mass suicide" (94). Global networking has incredible environmental potential. Although it has not happened yet, digital compression of time and space could theoretically allow people to save more paper, travel less, and manage resources more efficiently, while developing richer, more immersive and satisfying communities. Once again, the digital simulacrum has potential to repress or liberate.

Perhaps no digital interface is more important than the iPod and similar personal listening devices. We have already briefly touched on the consequences of digital media for global consciousness and local space. More specifically, what does the spread of personal listening devices portend in ecological terms? Most authors have thus far focused on the negative. Several critics have claimed that listening to personal music players damages hearing and thus negatively impacts people's ability to listen to their surrounding environments. Research by John McCormick and Jonathan Matusitz determined that as much as 10 percent of the U.S. population may be suffering hearing loss due to prolonged exposure to personal listening devices (2010). However, an intriguing study of iPod use by individuals in four contexts found that listeners tend not to expose themselves to volume levels above Occupational Safety and Health Administration (OSHA) thresholds for safety (Epstein, Marozeau, and Cleveland 2010). Although iPods can certainly achieve volume levels well above safe limits, Michael Epstein and colleagues' research with 64 iPod users indicates that the critics' concerns may be overstated.

Johnson and Cloonan provide convincing evidence of hearing loss caused by personal and public music sources (2009), as do Vogel and colleagues (2009). Johnson and Cloonan argue that music-induced discord is a major problem in all urban environments, accounting for

80 percent of neighbor noise complaints in the United Kingdom (2009, 164) and causing half a million people a year to change residence (162). While a blaring stereo is quite the opposite of private iPod listening, Johnson and Cloonan argue that both technologies can work as social solvents, breaking down bonds between neighbors and communities. Likewise, Gordon Hempton's *One Square Inch of Silence* (2009) presents a moving account of sound-induced hearing loss, his own, while illustrating ways in which iPods isolate listeners from nature and each other.

Yet, like it or not, more and more people listen to music via portable digital listening devices. According to a Nielsen analysis of a media study conducted by the Council for Research Excellence, 90 percent of Americans listen to some form of audio media every day (Loechner 2009). As of 2009, 12 percent used portable mp3 players (Loechner 2009), and sales statistics show that the number is growing rapidly. According to the Pew Research Foundation, 47 percent of Americans owned a portable mp3 player in 2010 (Media Literacy Clearinghouse 2010). Increasingly, cell phones double as musical listening devices.

The ability to download and consume music practically anywhere appeals to many listeners. It has made the iPod, iPhone, and other portable listening devices important musical prosthetics, especially for younger audiences. Does this new form of listening cut people off from others and their immediate environments as Johnson, Cloonan, and Hempton claim? Is digital music consumption simply one more way that our identities, communities, and consciousness are de-territorialized? If so, does digital listening re-territorialize listeners' consciousness in a way that spans physical geographic borders? And toward what ecological ends? Does our ability to download Tibetan throat singing make us more concerned about Tibet or simply less aware of what is happening to a local wetland? If we are less local, how can we be sure we are, in exchange, really becoming more global?

The phenomenon is too new for us to know the answers. Fieldwork presented in Chapter 4 may provide some insight into the difficulties of making local music or, to put it another way, of making music locally. Conversations with club owners and local musicians reveal that people are less and less interested in local live music. That might be the flip side of people's increasing interest in music delivered digitally from other parts of the world. However, it has been a long time since music made down the road seriously competed with recorded music recorded far away. Even before the iPod we had the means to hear music made in Memphis, New York, or London. In other words, the iPod is more about evolution than revolution, incorporation rather than a radical break with past trends. Yet the digital personal listening device is the most intimately integrated musical prosthesis yet, making phonographs and CD players, with their moving parts and physical media, seem ancient. The iPod is less of an external tool than prior listening technologies, and using it is much less of a conscious act. It is more "naturally" integrated into our bodies, lives, and neural circuitry than the clunky listening technologies of the past. What can be more physically intimate than the iPod earbud or Bluetooth headset? We'll probably soon find out. In fact, students reading this in 2016 are probably already laughing at the out-of-date technology described here. Smartphones are already replacing the iPod by incorporating its functions. The smartphone will become a microchip earpiece, and so on.

The iPod is just one more way in which we have become incorporated within increasingly dense and active musical networks on a global scale. These networks are both decentralized (social networks) and centrally managed (Facebook, Google, Pandora, etc.) on a scale that past record producers could never have imagined. However, the same technologies that take us away from the local time and place also allow us to more easily experience music made in other locales. As Frith argues, it is important "to support not just one's own local music, but also 'local' music in general, 'different' music wherever it comes from" (1993, 23). It is easier to do that now than ever. So, once again, what does digital music mean for planetary ecology? Is it making a difference, environmentally speaking? For better or worse? It is, quite simply, too early to tell, but digital production, distribution, and consumption raise some very interesting new questions for ecomusicology.

Moving from hardware to software, however, one thing is clear: relatively few world-famous musicians are performing songs about environmental issues. This chapter ends with a consideration of why that is so.

Where Are All the Environmental Songs?

What if the world was being destroyed, but nobody sang about it? What if someone sang, but no one cared? Are we fiddling while the Earth burns? Popular music researchers are only now turning toward environmental questions in a serious way. As evidence of this growing interest, the theme for the 2010 annual conference of the Society for Ethnomusicology (SEM) was "Sound Ecologies," although a relatively small number of SEM papers referenced ecological research.

Only one paper covered the topic at the 2010 meeting of the International Association for the Study of Popular Music, U.S. Branch (IASPM-US), which took place in the heart of New Orleans, just five years after Hurricane Katrina. IASPM's scholarly neglect of environmental concerns remains puzzling. Weeks later the massive British Petroleum oil spill served as yet another reminder that environmental issues are not going away, no matter how difficult they are to deal with in musicology.

Serious research concerning environmental issues in popular music is rarer yet. The foremost example is David Ingram's insightful account of Pete Seeger and Malvina Reynold's *God Bless the Grass* (1966). Ingram (2008) describes Seeger's efforts as a watershed for folk music, but something of a lost opportunity as well, because so few others followed suit. So far, the story of environmental music research parallels that of its subject, including promising starts, inexplicable stops, and a sense of exigency that is repeatedly overcome by uncertainty. It is no wonder music researchers avoid the topic.

Musicians themselves, especially popular musicians, also have a tendency to avoid environmental themes. The examples described above— Irthlingz, Ani DiFranco, Jack Johnson—are exceptional cases. A few of the songwriters I interviewed and performed with helped me to understand why musicians are reluctant to sing about environmental issues. Several suggested that writing environmentally themed songs would feel forced and hypocritical, so they avoid writing them altogether. Folk singer Carolyn Cruso explained that she "tours in a car" and uses a fair amount of energy to make music, one of the reasons she avoids writing songs explicitly about environmental issues. Cruso is a light-traveling folk singer who works on an organic farm. If she is that concerned about environmental hypocrisy, it is hard to imagine the rest of us feeling comfortable performing eco-oriented songs. It might explain why even *Rolling Stone*'s "15 Most Eco-Friendly Rockers" shy away from them (2010). Feelings of hypocrisy can cause creative paralysis.

However, as Deena Weinstein reminds us, not only environmental advocacy, but overtly political popular music in general, is exceedingly rare (2006). As a result, relatively few musicologists have dedicated their research to the study of pop politics. A few have studied case histories of politically charged songs (Margolick 2000), community building through music (Mattern 1998), identity politics (Gracyk 2001), dialectics of power and resistance (Cloonan and Garofalo 2003; Sharp 1992), and musical movements (Garofalo 1992; Garofalo et al. 2005; Pratt 1994). If there is a consensus, it is that popular music can help build more cohesive and effective political communities. That conclusion has important environmental consequences. Nevertheless, given the dearth of environmental songs in global rock, it is hard to find that sort of community building taking place globally, apart from the hopeful examples cited earlier, such as All at Once.

With a world audience to win and thousands of divergent interest to appease, taking a stand on any issue entails risk for the would-be global superstar. Popular artists known for their political lyricism or activism tend to speak out only after achieving star status. For the musician who wants to make a living through music, melding pop and politics is a risk best taken after you have already made it (Pedelty and Racheli 2009). Rajmil Fischman explains that "resources commanded by the music industry and their access to mass communication imbue the artist with a disproportionate degree of power . . . and the messages of those who have not reached star status may be ignored" (1999, 53). Of course, there are exceptions, including bands like Rage Against the Machine and uncompromising musicians like Pete Seeger, artists who declare their politics from the outset. Doing so might make these musicians more complete artists than their apolitical peers, but in a market-driven system it is also riskier than sticking to songs about sex and romance. Apolitical art is safest in any society.

For most politicized artists, therefore, political artistry follows commercial success. Yet most popular artists never take that step, whether out of fear, lack of interest, or contentment with their status and the status quo. Music producers and audiences alike view environmental issues as political. Therefore, when looking at environmental musicians we are already studying a small and special subset of popular musicians, like Jack Johnson, who have decided to step out of line. Examining their stories tells us a great deal about what it takes to make music with environmental intent, and what is required for environmental pop to expand.

Perhaps one reason for the relative dearth of songs about environmental matters is uncertainty on the part of composers and performers as to whether environmental music really matters. In a crowded field of songs about romance and sex, what does environmentally oriented music mean? In a more functionalist sense, what does it actually *do*? If we were to examine the history of songs like Joni Mitchell's "Big Yellow Taxi" (1970), John Denver's "Calypso" (1975), the Beach Boy's "Don't Go Near the Water" (1971), Midnight Oil's "Blue Sky Mining" (1990), Michael Jackson's "Earth Song" (1995), or the Capitol Steps' "God Bless My SUV" (2006), would we find that they effectively communicate environmental messages to audiences? Do audiences use the resulting knowledge and inspiration to make meaningful changes in their individual or collective lives? Or are their environmental messages mostly ignored, while the songs are enjoyed in much the same way as any other pop tune, a sweet moment of pleasure loosely associated with life events? What do audiences actually do with these songs, if anything? For the most part, we don't know, especially on the global level. Making music remains largely an act of faith. Perhaps as the aperture shrinks to focus on a single country in Chapter 2, more specific answers will be found.

2

The Musical Nation

Popular Music and the American Soundscape

This chapter is about the ecological implications of American popular music. The journey will take us from Joe Hill to Ke$ha, from purple mountain majesties to the National Mall. The chapter will also feature the voices and perspectives of American activists. However, we will start with the songs that connect America, a nation of people, to America, the land.

"America the Beautiful," "God Bless America," and "This Land Is Your Land" present three distinctly different representations of America. They represent America not only as a nation, but also as nature. Written on Pikes Peak as the lyricist looked down at the "fruited plains" below, "America the Beautiful" evokes pastoral pride. It glorifies nature and is inspired by America as both a physical place and a fantastic dream.

"God Bless America" is different: it conscripts the landscape in an effort to instill nationalistic pride. "God Bless America" imagines America as a divine bulwark against European fascism. It is the most nationalistic of our national songs, prideful, boastful, and filled with the echoes of Manifest Destiny.

"This Land Is Your Land" was Woody Guthrie's conscious attempt to take the American soundscape back from Irving Berlin. Each of these three songs presents a very different vision for the American nation, state, and land.

"America the Beautiful" begins with the following verse:

> O beautiful for spacious skies
> For amber waves of grain,
> For purple mountain majesties

> Above the fruited plain!
> America! America!
> God shed His grace on thee
> And crown thy good with brotherhood
> From sea to shining sea!

"America the Beautiful" was written by Katherine Lee Bates in 1883. Looking out over one of America's most dramatic landscapes, she penned a poem that incorporates not only the nation's natural virtues—its "purple mountain majesties"—but also the "fruited plain" and "waves of grain" that Americans had created with that natural endowment. In this classic pastoral vision, Americans fit harmoniously into God's country. Bates's sun-soaked sense of "brotherhood" is blessed by Heaven and nature in equal measure. "America the Beautiful" is about balance.

Of course, the song changes with time and context. In 2007 American conservatives recruited "America the Beautiful" to make a point about gay marriage by reminding listeners of traditional American values. For example, they sang it repeatedly at the Iowa State Fair at a time when gay marriage was under consideration (it was made legal two years later). And yet, as Gerald Weissman points out, the poem's author lived in a committed and long-term "Boston marriage" with Katherine Coman, a woman from Michigan (2007, 3400). In other words, the author of "America the Beautiful" was gay. Once again, social and historical contexts are key to creating musical meaning; text does not speak for itself.

"God Bless America" had very different origins. Irving Berlin originally wrote the song in 1918 but revised it in 1938 as the United States was starting to emerge from the Great Depression. The rise of fascism in Europe had many Americans worried, including Berlin. He used his best pitch, religion, to rally the nation. A decidedly conservative song from the start, "God Bless America" was written in the form of a prayer. Walking a tightrope as he attempted to rally American patriotism to combat Hitler's rise in Germany without producing a right-wing anthem, Berlin replaced the phrase "to the right" with "through the night" (see Berlin 2012 for complete lyrics).

Nevertheless, many on the secular left saw "God Bless America" as an affront. Among them was folk singer Woody Guthrie. The 1930s witnessed the institution of a social safety net for the poorest Americans, laws regulating child labor, a shorter working day, greater access to education, and many other advances. By the end of the decade those progressive gains were meeting a serious backlash from conservatives. "God Bless America" was viewed as part of that backlash.

"God Bless America" is a more jingoistic, anthropocentric, and self-satisfied song than "America the Beautiful." Berlin's song puts more emphasis on a heavenly presence and divine blessing. We, the people, are exceptional. "America the Beautiful" humbly asks for God's "grace," whereas "God Bless America" has a palpable sense of Manifest Destiny and a triumphant tone from title to final refrain. It is American exceptionalism made manifest in song. Conservatives have attempted on several occasions to make it the national anthem.

"God Bless America" is the most effective kind of propaganda, the kind that intersects with dominant ideologies. Hegemony is more than a conscious belief: its subjects feel it all the way to the bone and make it part of their cosmology. "God Bless America" is the state hailing its citizens, and they answer back in joyful refrain. By the 1940s the hailing state was tired of being challenged. During the Great Depression corporate hegemony and wealth were brought into question; now, America was on a war footing. Freedom would again be articulated with the health of large corporations and that most godlike of abstractions: "the economy."

In 1940 Guthrie heard "God Bless America" on the radio one time too many and set out to write a musical response. "This Land Is Your Land" would transform him into an American folk hero and archetype, at least for the Left. The song encourages a deep, rapturous, and cathartic connection to the nation as physical space, much in the tradition of "America the Beautiful." It is a place-making song. However, it is more about political geography than either "America the Beautiful" or "God Bless America." "This Land" associates individualism with Americanism and makes the land an interlocutor between people and freedom. One hears the echoes of Thoreau's personal reflections in lines like, "As I was walking that ribbon of highway, I saw above me that endless skyway." The land was not made for some nebulously collectivized "us" or "America" to feel pride in. Instead, it was made for "you and me" to experience in unfettered fashion. The individuals in Guthrie's song are not defined by their nationhood but rather by the land itself and a collective right to walk and work it.

The last three verses are the ones that most clearly distinguish Guthrie's national anthem from Bates's poem and Berlin's hymn:

> In the square of the city, in the shadow of a steeple;
> By the relief office, I'd seen my people.
> As they stood there hungry, I stood there asking,
> Is this land made for you and me?

There was a big high wall there that tried to stop me;
Sign was painted, it said private property;
But on the back side it didn't say nothing;
That side was made for you and me.

Nobody living can ever stop me,
As I go walking that freedom highway;
Nobody living can ever make me turn back
This land was made for you and me.

Guthrie's national anthem argued for public land ownership and against privatization.

Mark Allen Jackson presents a compelling history of how "This Land Is Your Land" evolved from a protest song into one that "sings more like a national anthem than its intended purpose" (2002, 250). In the 1950s school administrators, textbook publishers, and church choir directors edited Guthrie's work down to three celebratory stanzas, keeping the rousing refrain. What began as a political challenge to "God Bless America" instead became its compulsory cousin. Another hallmark of hegemonic ideology is its ability to appropriate and incorporate dissent. What started as a challenge to conservative propaganda became its unwilling complement.

Guthrie made it easy to edit his songs for ideological purposes. He tended to start each song with several relatively apolitical verses, setting the scene and hooking listeners before hitting them with increasingly critical statements. That is true of his Columbia River chronicles (Chapter 3), his unpublished atom bomb songs, and a great number of other compositions. Whether he did this to piggyback critical messages on otherwise uncontroversial texts or to give performers several options, this pattern of composition made it easy for performers and others to edit out elements they did not like. That ideological filtering process transformed "This Land" from a song about inequality, private property, and religious hypocrisy into a simple, albeit elegant, celebration of national pride.

Each semester I ask students to characterize "This Land Is Your Land." Most place it in the same category as "America the Beautiful," referring to it as a "patriotic school song." When I ask them to imagine what Woody Guthrie must have been like, the most common response is "patriot." I then present a more complete version of the song, usually by showing a video recording of Bruce Springsteen, Arlo Guthrie, Little Richard, and others singing it as part of the filmed tribute *A Vision Shared* (Guthrie and Leadbelly 1988). In a lecture course with 140–220 students, only a handful claim to have heard those verses before, even though most can sing the rest of the song by heart.

Some students feel betrayed at having been taught a censored song, while others argue that it is appropriate to edit out the overtly political verses. A few suggest that the dropped verses are less poetic and compelling. Mirroring America, the students demonstrate that "This Land" is more than just a single song. "This Land," the place and song, is really made up of many lands and peoples. Yet the song and its conflicted history demonstrate that we share "a common stock of symbols," to use Mary Douglas's parsimonious definition of "culture" (1966, 122). Songs like "This Land" help us to perform and contest our differences through a common language.

In a sense the students' first impression of Guthrie is quite accurate. He certainly was a patriot, of sorts. The song, regardless of interpretation, is patriotic. Unfortunately, the label "patriot" hardly captures the full persona of a man who wrote for the *Daily Worker, Music Vanguard,* and other socialist periodicals while professing democratic socialist perspectives through his prolific lyrics, diaries, and letters. Guthrie was comfortable enough in his American skin to express patriotic sentiments in the form of a humanistic challenge. For example, his 1948 song "Deportee (The Plane Wreck at Los Gatos)" was ahead of its time in lamenting the abuse of Mexican immigrant farm labor. "Deportee" is another sign that Guthrie considered collectively owning, working, and sharing the land to be more important than patriotic allegiance to the state.

Guthrie was a left intellectual, but this rather scholarly, self-taught bookworm knew what to give the New York liberals who sponsored his early career. Musicologists, record producers, and liberal audiences in the city center were hoping to find in Guthrie an untutored and "natural" folk symbol. He gave them that, but only in exchange for the chance to do more through his music.

Guthrie's songs work on two distinct levels: documentary narrative on the surface, with a strong undercurrent of radical critique underneath. The documentary element, often presented in the form of cornpone verse, masks his more artistic and politically critical double meanings. Some are not willing to look at the cultural critique he embedded in his art. Others see Guthrie, the political critic, winking through a mask of folk narrative. His life and writings were a constant game of negotiation with urban liberals who could only see him as a two-dimensional man from the hinterland. Urban liberals engaged his persona as opposed to his person. Guthrie's musical afterlife has been more of the same; he continues to be marketed as an authentic and "natural" folk singer. There is no such thing.

Reading successive versions of Guthrie's songs, it is obvious how much work went into each word and phrase. As an artist, he would sculpt a song, starting with prosaic phrases like "God blessed America for me." He would then work them over and over, changing phrases in subtle ways until he could achieve more poetic statements like "This land was made for you and me." In the end most of Guthrie's songs are equal parts art, anthem, and critical subversion, neatly wrapped into one polysemic package. Those qualities gave the folk icon's songs an ability to remain relevant for over seventy years, as demonstrated at Barack Obama's inaugural concert on the Washington Mall.

Woody, Pete, Bruce, and Barack: The Hope for Audacity

On Sunday, January 18, 2009, Pete Seeger led Barack Obama and an audience of 400,000 in a spirited performance of "This Land Is Your Land," backed by Tao Rodriguez-Seeger, Bruce Springsteen, and a 125-member choir. From the steps of the Lincoln Memorial to the farthest reaches of the mall, celebrants at President Obama's Inaugural "We Are One" concert sang along. It was quite possibly the greatest number of people ever to sing "This Land" at one time.

As he has for decades, Seeger performed a version of "This Land" that most Americans never learned in school. The octogenarian folk legend performed all three of Guthrie's forgotten stanzas, the ones that best express Guthrie's thoughts about privatization, privation, and religious hypocrisy in America. Far from being God blessed and privately owned, the American landscape in Guthrie's song is under threat from the people who exploit and disenfranchise American farmers and laborers. During the "We Are One" concert, Seeger's performance invoked both histories of the song: "This Land" as a rallying cry for activists and "This Land" as a patriotic anthem.

Like the event itself, Seeger's performance represented a unifying sense of hope and national identity, a recognition of America's collective purpose. However, disagreement was lying just below the surface, as it does in all political rituals. While united by hope, the 400,000 in attendance and millions watching at home represented different visions of the nation, past, present, and future. Even at moments of ritual *communitas* like the inaugural, sublimated contests over meaning boil to the surface (V. W. Turner 1969).

Just months later, the voices of Obama's conservative opposition, including the Tea Party, would be matched by those of a very disillusioned

Left. Like the song itself, Seeger's performance represented a conflicted relationship between the activist Left, mainstream American liberals, and the conservative Right. Those ideological divisions have played an important role throughout the history of Guthrie's iconic anthem, whose heightened ambivalence and polysemy (with the last verses removed) has allowed the song to lead a double life, serving oppositional interests for decades.

"This Land" is a site of deeply shared difference, as beloved by conservatives (Minard 1992) as by socialists. It has served as an advertising jingle for Ford, a theme song for George McGovern's presidential campaign, and just about everything in between. "This Land" is the poster child for musical polysemy, a floating signifier as likely to snag on the right bank as on the left.

Guthrie felt that the American landscape belonged to all Americans, not just those with the capital to own it. We can assume that he felt the same way about music, which makes subsequent legal battles over his music disturbing. Those with copyright control over Guthrie's "folk" music have fought hard to retain that control, thus limiting people's ability to perform, record, and write about Guthrie's music, three and a half decades after the musician's death. Ironically, even "This Land" is privately owned—a point that was successfully disputed by the online parody site *JibJab*, which used the song without permission or charge (Electronic Frontier Foundation 2011).

Unfortunately, the question of legal ownership was not fully resolved by the courts. For example, Ludlow Music asked me to pay $50 to print the three stanzas above, and additional fees for other Guthrie lyrics. Ironic, given that one of those verses includes Guthrie's most strident critique of private property.

A battle over copyright somewhat similar to *JibJab v. Ludlow* took place following the inauguration. The cable network Home Box Office (HBO) argued that individuals who digitally recorded the "We Are One" concert and placed those images on *YouTube* were infringing upon HBO's exclusive contractual right to record and rebroadcast the concert. You read that correctly: the American inauguration was privatized.

"HBO is going over Youtube with a fine tooth comb and having all clips of the event pulled under copyright claims," wrote blogger Josh Marshall (2009). "Want to see the special moment where an 89 year old Pete Seeger sang This Land Is Your Land on the footsteps of the Lincoln Memorial?" he continued. "Tough luck." (According to the Motion Picture Association of America's copyright attorney, Ben Sheffner, HBO had ceased enforcing its inaugural copyright claims by January 23, 2009.)

Seeger's performance was in part an inspiring bit of salvage work for
an old friend. When I wrote to ask Seeger why he included those verses
in his "We Are One" performance, he responded:

> In February, 1940, Woody wrote six verses and one became a
> chorus. Later he wrote the verse, "Nobody living can ever stop me,
> as I go walking my freedom highway, etc." The school songbooks
> left this verse out, also two of the 'political' verses of the original
> six ('Was a great high wall there' and 'By the relief office I saw my
> people'). When Arlo was about age [missing word] Woody was
> allowed out of the hospital to visit his family, and he said, 'Arlo
> they're singing my song now but they left out the three most
> important verses' and he made Arlo write 'em down. So these
> verses I included on January 18 in D.C. (Letter, Seeger to author,
> 2009)

Jackson argues that singing the forgotten verses allows "This Land Is Your
Land" to become "a song with a history rather than a set of lyrics to
mumble through at some public occasion" (2002, 272).

It is not clear whether most of the audience on the mall thought
deeply about the words Seeger sang. After decades of institutional training, they may have simply heard the same celebratory song from their
school days. In both versions, the refrain remains the same. A cursory
analysis of news stories and blogs indicates that Seeger's reinsertion may
have gone largely unnoticed. A Lexis-Nexis search found 41 news articles
in "Major World Newspapers" using the terms "Seeger" and "This Land,"
of which 36 (88 percent) dealt with the "We Are One" concert. Yet only
5 (14 percent) of those mentioned Seeger's presentation of the oft-
missing verses. The same search terms and parameters in the Lexis-Nexis
"Blog" category retrieved 47 blogs, of which 31 (80 percent) dealt with
the inaugural concert. Ten of those (32 percent) mentioned the lost
verses. The missing verses tended to be mentioned by bloggers on left-
leaning websites and ignored by the others.

As Nick Spitzer of National Public Radio explained when discussing
the song's history: "It was these populist lyrics that had appealed to the
political Left in America" (2000). The same appears to be true of the "We
Are One" concert: the Left picked up on the critical significance of Seeger's
performance. Those with knowledge of the song and a history of participation in protest movements seem to have experienced a truly profound
catharsis hearing the song sung in its entirety. It was moving to see one

of their own—a musical icon who has persevered through decades of blacklisting, censorship, ridicule, and marginalization—take center stage and bring Guthrie's message back to life.

During the inaugural concert, such ideological divisions and distinctions were suspended, a taboo topic in their own right. Months later it was evident that fissures between the activist Left and centrist liberalism remained no less salient than those between American liberals and conservatives. Barack Obama would be led even further to the right after the Democratic party's electoral losses of November 2010, largely leaving his progressive base behind.

Given the way in which progressives are ignored in U.S. politics and mass media, it is little wonder that so large a part of critical discourse here takes place through music and popular culture. Whereas parliamentary democracies allow third and fourth perspectives into the policy discussion, in the United States the Left depends on bankable liberal candidates to give some voice to their concerns, as well as critical representation in popular culture (e.g., *The Daily Show*). Perhaps more than anything, the Seeger-Springsteen performance symbolized an uneasy and interdependent relationship between mainstream liberalism and more critical left voices among artists and activists.

For example, the Left tends to be more critical of the development policies of "conservative" politicians and corporations, whereas liberals have been much more conciliatory. Thus, efforts to curb greenhouse emissions have been strongly associated with the Left, weakly articulated by liberals like Barack Obama (and subordinated to economic exigencies), and strongly opposed by the Right. The increasingly libertarian base of the Republican party views all governmental attempts to regulate land use, pollution, or carbon release as unnaturally fettering the market and individual freedoms.

Symbolic of his conciliatory politics, Obama retained a lynchpin of George W. Bush's Middle East war policy, Robert Gates, as secretary of defense; named Arne Duncan, a proponent of No Child Left Behind, as education secretary; made Eric Holder, a man who supported the Patriot Act, the U.S. attorney general; and tapped Tim Geithner, an architect of Bush's bank bailout, as treasury secretary. In other words, from the starting gate Obama demonstrated allegiance to the basic neoliberal economic philosophy and policies that have held sway since the Reagan administration. From quickly reinstituting immigration raids to legal advocacy of Bush's rendition program, there has been much to disappoint the organized Left and little to encourage it beyond rhetorical support for

environmental sustainability. In the months following Obama's inauguration, environmentalists would be just as disappointed as those who
hoped for reduced military intervention and other changes. For example,
the new president sacrificed his campaign commitment to climate change
mitigation in order to spend dwindling political capital on a highly com-
promised health bill. Among the most disappointed are those nations
that expected regime change in America to lead to new international
treaties on climate change. Despite audacious hopes for change, the song
mostly remained the same.

Following Seeger's lead, environmental activists often perform "This
Land," using the song's popularity to advantage. Almost every American
already knows the first few verses and refrain, making it an easy interlocutor for environmental rallies. Although its social justice message is often
overlooked by audiences, the song's message is almost immediately recognized as advocacy for public land and environmental preservation when
sung in environmentally themed performance contexts. During British
Petroleum's oil spill in the Gulf of Mexico, for example, "This Land"
became a rallying cry for environmental activists demanding remu-
nerative justice and stricter regulation of public waters and tidelands
(McCollam 2010). Such performances belong to a long tradition of musical protest in America.

The Joe Hill Tradition

Contemporary environmental protest music needs to be understood as
part of a long tradition of musical advocacy, one that links folk to rock.
The first name associated with that tradition is that of Joe Hill (1879–
1915). Hill, a labor organizer and lyricist, spoke in the musical vernacular
of his time: sacred hymn. In the early 1900s people of all classes grew up
with songs crafted in the nineteenth-century Christian hymn movement.
Hymns were sung in church by parishioners, on street corners by mis-
sionaries, and in soup kitchens where itinerant workers took refuge.
When it came to reaching miners, lumbermen, and dockworkers, the
hymn was king. "A pamphlet, no matter how good, is never read more
than once," wrote Hill, "but a song is learned by heart and repeated over
and over" (quoted in Smith 1969, 19). Even when Hill wrote music to go
along with his revolutionary words, the lyrical tone and cadence sounded
as if they were taken straight from a hymnal. Consider "Workers of the
World Awaken" (1914): Hill wrote the words and composed the melody,
but you can tell simply by reading the words how closely the song
matches the tone and cadence of sacred hymn (KUED 2012):

Workers of the world, awaken!
Break your chains, demand your rights.
All the wealth you make is taken
By exploiting parasites.
Shall you kneel in deep submission
From your cradles to your graves?
Is the height of your ambition
To be good and willing slaves?

Arise, ye prisoners of starvation!
Fight for your own emancipation;
Arise, ye slaves of every nation
In One Union grand.
Our little ones for bread are crying,
And millions are from hunger dying;
The end the means is justifying,
'Tis the final stand.

Other musicians followed Hill's example. For example, John Brill transformed "What a Friend We Have in Jesus" into the classic labor anthem
"Dump the Bosses off Our Backs" (1916). Like many revolutionary
hymns, "Dump the Bosses" is easily adapted to rock (hear one version at
hypoxicpunks.org). Nineteenth-century hymns, twentieth-century folk
songs, and rock music have much in common, including a shared history
and strophic, verse-chorus forms lyrically evoking the American folk
vernacular.

Some critics complain when musicians profane the arts with politics
(Ingraham 2003). They can place much of the blame on Joe Hill. Hill
turned folk music into an incendiary art. At a time when singing about
labor unions and women's rights (e.g., "Rebel Girl") could land a musician in jail, Hill artfully combined the sound of sacred hymns with critical verse. He was, in a literal sense, profaning power, an age-old element
in the arts. Then as now, segregating politics from music would be as art-
less as letting ideology overwhelm it.

Hill's theatrical daring left a lasting musical mark, as did his execution
in front of a Utah firing squad in 1915. In 1925, as Hill's ghost was gaining mythical status among union activists, poet Alfred Hayes penned "I
Dreamed I Saw Joe Hill Last Night." Several years later Earl Robinson put
Hayes's poem to music. "I Dreamed I Saw Joe Hill Last Night" has served
as political code ever since, a way for committed musicians to show allegiance to a musical tradition that goes back to the Industrial Workers of
the World (IWW), better known as the Wobblies.

Paul Robeson was one of the first to popularize Robinson's song, making it part of his permanent repertoire, an act of musical daring at least as great as Joe Hill's seditious songwriting (1990). Woody Guthrie, hearing Robeson perform the song, was so moved that he wrote a rambling letter to the singer, praising the performance and noting how it had inspired him (Reuss 1968, 66–70).

Guthrie then carried on the tradition, as did his young friend and protégé Pete Seeger. The song has been handed down through the generations, a tradition carried into the present by Joan Baez, Utah Phillips, Ani DiFranco, Billy Bragg, Bruce Springsteen, the Dubliners, and countless others. Musicians ranging from Phil Ochs to Rage Against the Machine have expressed their allegiance to the tradition by writing new songs about Joe Hill.

Clearly, politicized rock owes much to Hill. Historically and thematically, the Joe Hill tradition forms one of many links between folk and rock. While mainstream rock is equally useful to liberal and conservative causes (Grossberg 1993), explicitly political rock tends to be oriented toward the Left, following the Joe Hill tradition. It is this tradition that most strongly articulated left politics in twentieth-century American music.

Granted, one can talk about the political meanings of almost any pop song, from Michael Jackson to Madonna. The song does not have to explicitly reference social problems or policies to have a political dimension. Cultural Studies scholars tend to study popular music from that perspective, what we might call *the politics of music*, drawing contextual associations between seemingly apolitical texts and larger social practices, structures, and ideologies. However, the Joe Hill tradition is more specific, denotative, and declarative. It is overtly *political music*, requiring a different form of analysis from that used in Cultural Studies to extrapolate political meaning from mainstream pop. In American folk and rock, such overtly political music has tended to signify a left tradition, so much so that even conservative commentators like Laura Ingraham identify it as such (2003). One of the most important ways to study overtly political music—in this case, environmental protest music—is to learn how it functions in environmental movements.

How Activists Use Music

In *The Jukebox in the Garden,* Ingram notes: "The extent to which popular music has actually inspired environmental action is an empirical question beyond the scope of this book" (2010, 168). This section is designed to provide a few answers to that difficult question, based on content analysis of fan blogs and, more directly, a survey of activists.

According to a content analysis Linda Keefe and I conducted on fan blogs in 2009, fans of musicians with political reputations are more likely to write about politics than are fans of mainstream musicians (Pedelty and Keefe 2010). In other words, fan discourse at least partly mirrors that of their favorite musicians. Of course, that does not imply cause; we have no idea if political people are drawn to political musicians or if music politicizes previously apolitical fans. My guess is the former. Music rarely has a strong autonomous effect; rather, it fits into the wider ecology of activism, as we will see in a bit.

More directly to the point, I surveyed American activists about their musical interests and motivations (Pedelty 2009). The most surprising result was the extent to which political music serves as an alternative headline service, especially for young listeners: 72 percent of the activists claimed to have drawn important information from songs. The following examples provide a snapshot: a 22-year-old first heard about "Strontium 90 affecting children's teeth" from a song; a 24-year-old was exposed to problems within the meat industry by the music of Propagandhi; a 29-year-old first learned about the animal rights movement through listening to bands like Earth Crisis; a 32-year-old became involved in Earth First! after hearing about the organization in campfire songs; a 33-year-old took an interest in Australian land policies and aboriginal rights after hearing "Bed's [sic] Are Burning" (1987) by Midnight Oil. A 35-year-old thanked Midnight Oil, R.E.M., and U2, for raising his or her (no gender data were solicited) awareness of "acid rain" and "food production" issues; a 36-year-old activist cited Midnight Oil's "Blue Sky Mine" (1990) for alerting him or her to asbestos mining issues in Australia; and a 38-year-old learned about "global warming" from "Al Gore's 'Live Earth.'" Clearly, musical knowledge can translate into action.

Like the blog study, the survey involved human rights, labor, peace, and environmental activists. Nevertheless, as evidenced above, the responses shed light on some of the ways in which music specifically relates to environmental awareness and action. It was common for respondents to be knowledgeable and active in at least two areas, showing how environmental activism is closely articulated with other causes in the United States, mainly under the left or "progressive" rubric.

Among the other responses, a 23-year-old stated that Joni Mitchell's "Big Yellow Taxi" (1970) pops into her mind each time she sees a ruined landscape. The song has inspired her to "work towards having a more sustainable campus." A 29-year-old described how music built a strong sense of community at his or her local farmers' market. A 46-year-old said that "an Earth Day event or Harmony Festival always inspires me to keep working to protect the environment." A 61-year-old noted Pete Seeger's work "along the Hudson River" as an inspiration. A 71-year-old lauded John Denver for building a sense of shared purpose at a "Sierra Club convention."

Survey respondents cited several examples of musicians who inspired them to take action: Fugazi's "Merchandise" (1990) motivated a 30-year-old to throw off "the shackles of consumerism." "Midnight Train" (1988) by the Men They Couldn't Hang moved a 38-year-old to work against the development of nuclear power. Seeing Bruce Springsteen in New Orleans after Hurricane Katrina strengthened a 49-year-old's resolve to assist in rebuilding the city. A 50-year-old mentioned Neil Young and credited "After the Garden" (2006) and "Prairie Wind" (2005) with making him or her "more politically and globally aware . . . to make changes in my way of life environmentally." A 57-year-old explained that Joni Mitchell's "Big Yellow Taxi" (1970) provided inspiration during a struggle to keep development in Fremont, California, from destroying 1,000 acres of local farmland. Another 57-year-old was moved to action by "the 1982 nuclear freeze concert in Central Park." A 59-year-old was inspired toward environmental action by the "last few lines" of the Doors' song "The End" (1967). "A Native American" musician "from Oklahoma" caused a 64-year-old "to feel more deeply" about global warming. A 86-year-old referred to "This Land Is Your Land" as "inspirational."

A 53-year-old credited a specific musical performance and local performer: "A folk singer named Danny motivated me about a year ago to work harder for forest protection, after a night of listening to him play songs he had written"—and yet the respondent could not recall his full name. Clearly it is difficult for people to remember the names of local musicians. Of the 676 examples offered, only 48 referenced local music making, and most of those were fairly generic descriptions of participatory events ranging from impromptu drumming at a rally to organized choral groups. Only a handful cited local performers by name, whereas the survey is peppered with the names of famous musicians.

Marketing students are told that an audience must hear something seven times before remembering it. That seems to be true of music as well. In a world where a relatively small group of music producers, distributors, musicians, and songs dominate the global market and soundscape, it is not surprising that we can recall their names so easily. Almost everyone has heard of Lady Gaga, even if many cannot name a single song she has written. Relatively few can recall the name of a local performer, however. We might assume that activists would be more interested in local alternatives, but "think globally, act locally" seems to apply to music as well as to political consciousness. Activists think about global music, even when their activism is mainly local. Perhaps this is an example of what some are referring to as "glocal" consciousness (Colmeiro 2009).

Interestingly, most of the surveyed activists referenced recorded music. Far fewer described live performance. A 27-year-old activist made this bold claim: "It is the duty of any citizen in the know to throw some Rage Against the Machine, Bad Religion, Slayer—whatever—on the good ol' iPod and take to Washington." A 21-year-old usually brings a recording of "inspiring songs" to protests. "Having even recorded music," argued a 64-year-old activist, "definitely improves the environment and helps to bring us together, as long as it's not too loud and intrusive to the proceedings or conversation." These comments suggest that loud music with a fast beat is good for personal motivation and group celebrations. Conversely, events predicated on group communication and concerted action demand more sedate sounds. Although that might seem like common sense, on more than one occasion I have observed event coordinators doing the opposite. Nothing brings a spirited protest to a screeching halt faster than making everyone listen to a plaintive folk singer, and nothing makes it harder to deliberate than being surrounded by banging djembes. Awareness of context and purpose is key. Event planning has become a major industry in the corporate world, but grassroots activist organizations are rarely as effective at coordinating message, movement, sound, and image.

Unsolicited, some respondents offered up their own theories about how mainstream popular music functions. A 24-year-old argued that "pop music focuses on lavish lifestyle and sex when there is so much more we'd be outraged and concerned about otherwise." A 63-year-old referred to "mainstream media" as "waste stream media."

Several respondents argued that the full aesthetics of a song matter as much as lyrical content. A song can be about the environment but leave the listener unmoved, bored, or even angry. That sentiment was echoed by Minnesota-based musician Paul Metsa (Pedelty and Racheli 2009, 270–271):

> I don't think the song serves whatever the cause is if it doesn't have all the stuff that a song should have—a good melody and good chord changes, and good lyrics and the ability to harmonize with it. If it doesn't have that it might as well be journalism ... bad songs are one thing, but bad songs about good causes are something completely different, and I run from them like a thief in the night.

Metsa argues that many political songs are like "Kleenex" and should be discarded. His rule might not apply to participatory music, such as the sing-along, but it is a requirement for other performances. I was reminded of his point again at a union rally in the winter of 2011, where the accomplished performer led protesters in a spirited rendition of "This Land Is Your Land" (documented on *YouTube*: see Metsa 2011). Having professional musicians at the helm really does help.

Much more empirical study needs to be done concerning the role of music in the lives of environmental activists and movements. The survey is a good start, but ethnographic fieldwork is needed to develop a richer sense of how music functions within activist networks. The corporate world recognizes event planning, market research, and public aesthetics as essential. Those interested in creating sustainable solutions would do well to learn from the corporate world's ritual specialists. Having taught for several years in a school of journalism and mass communication, the sort of program where corporate public relations, advertising, and event-planning specialists are trained, I have seen the energy and resources paid professionals pour into making the public face of private institutions as seductive, dynamic, inviting, and interesting as possible. PR professionals are the most accomplished ritual specialists of our time, the priests of modern capitalism. A political movement is quite different from a corporation, but the goal is similar: to persuade the public, convince them to take action, and thus change policy. Environmentalists will never command the resources of Archer Daniels Midland, Monsanto, or Dow, but a bit more attention to the aesthetic dimension of public action, including music, would be useful.

That process starts with a better understanding of the sorts of music and musical practices that inspire activists. Having been at many a protest or rally where folk musicians serve as entertainment and inspiration, I was surprised by the survey responses. Activists of all ages tended to cite examples from rock, and punk rock was particularly influential for those under 50. The next section explores genre in relation to American environmental politics.

A Comparative Ecology of Musical Genres

Rock borrowed much more than political themes from the folk tradition. Rock's masculine ethos of radical independence, the American road motif, and other elements can be traced back to its folk roots, through folk-rock interlocutor Bob Dylan on back to Woody Guthrie and even Joe

Hill, who was incorporating those themes into his music long before rock was invented.

The intermingling of folk and rock influences is apparent in Bob Dylan's music. Dylan literally sat at Guthrie's feet in 1961 while the folk icon lay ill from Huntington's disease. Dylan's first complete tune, "Song to Woody" (1962), serves as testament to his appreciation for Guthrie's musical gifts.

Dylan started his musical life in rural Minnesota playing in a rock band. After moving to Minneapolis and then New York City, he became an urban folk artist. As his "finger-pointing" folk gave way to artfully crafted rock years later, folk elements remained, including a strong sense of mystery and an ability to perform the full range of human emotion. Before Dylan, rock had tended toward emotional absolutes: sad breakup songs and happy dance music. Dylan realized that rock, like folk, could do much more. It is hard to imagine pre-Dylan rock incorporating environmental themes. Dylan helped open up rock to folk's more dynamic topical and emotional range.

As folk became increasingly narrow during the 1960s revival, Dylan's interests expanded. Dylan's rock paid homage to deep folk traditions, including a sense of popular impropriety. He continued to poke fun at orthodoxies of both Right and Left. Dylan's new rock, much like old folk, was carnivalesque, polysemic, slippery, and mythic. Meanwhile, folk had narrowed to become a simpler, message-centered, denotative medium. Dylan, like many mid-sixties youths, rejected the simpler poetics and rigid politics of the folk revival (Ingram 2010, 109). He blended folk's more enduring traditions into a new rock idiom (Marqusee 2003).

This artful development had some negative consequences for environmental pop. As folk began to embrace environmentalism, young rockers rejected it. Been there, sung that. Sixties rock, when politically engaged, was more likely to express opposition to the Vietnam war than environmental concerns; other topics seemed less urgent. Moreover, environmental themes did not easily fit the Oedipal framework of rock. Sixties rock expressed generational rage rather than ecological introspection.

In the late 1960s and 1970s, as young rock stars achieved prosperity, they moved from the city to the countryside. As a result, pastoral themes slowly crept back into rock and pop music. In fact, Dylan was one of the few to avoid rock's return to romantic pastoralism: in his music "nature is often an untamed, mysterious force" (Ingram 2010, 116). Most rock acts of the late sixties and early seventies presented nature as a domestic, nurturing force, a protective mother, wounded friend, or innocent child in need of protection. Not so for Dylan. Perhaps his outlook has something to do with growing up in the rural Midwest, where neither climate nor countryside is especially benign.

Folk, blues, and rock share many of the same roots and influences in America. In fact, it was mainly record companies that enforced strict genre divisions, segregating white and black music for the sake of marketing. Rock and roll became viewed as white youth music with a strong debt to blues. Blues became "black music," rather than the transcultural entity it had previously been. As always, musicians were less inclined than audiences to obey genre borders, but the genre work of record companies, critics, and consumers patterned much of what musicians could profitably perform. Many blues musicians performed solo in ragged clothes for white urban "folk" audiences during the day. At night they would don jackets and join bands to play rhythm and blues and rock for racially diverse or mostly black club audiences. Musicians served as the main conduit between these somewhat artificially divided musical styles. American music was segregated not just by Jim Crow but also the prejudices of record companies and critics.

Musical genre divisions in America are not only racial but also conceived of in terms of the rural/urban divide. As primarily an urban sound, rock articulates its immediate environment rather well. From garage bands to stadium tours, rock more authentically reflects how most of the world's population lives: in urban areas (Irvine et al. 2009, 155). Rock recognizes and even celebrates the built environment and advanced technology of the city. If we equate environment to nature and nature to rural life, then rock is not terribly relevant. However, if we think of environment in more literal terms, rock is one of the most honest forms of environmental music available. In American popular music, rock and hip-hop most successfully express the dynamics of urban and suburban life. "Lyrics tended to be urban oriented," explains George Carney, "where the black and white teen-age purchasing power was located" (1994, 20). Rock and hip-hop are urban folk.

All of us are part of metropolitan networks, no matter where we live. As centers of transportation, communication, business, and media, cities are part of nearly everyone's consciousness. Environmental folk tends to look outward, away from the urban environment, while rock embraces it. Ecologically speaking, they are two sides of the same coin.

Hip-hop is even more closely associated with urban environments and urban environmentalism. Debra Rosenthal (2006) argues that hip-hop is an important form of environmental music and literature. She provides several examples, including Mos Def's "New World Water" (1999). The song "reflects the black American experience of being usurped, corrupted, and poisoned," extending the tradition of Langston Hughes's classic poem "The Negro Speaks of Rivers" (Rosenthal 2006, 669).

In putting forth environmental messages, hip-hop artists tend not to look back nostalgically to the rural past. Despite being primarily urban, plenty of rock tunes romanticize America's rural history, equating the countryside with bluer skies and fresher air: consider hits like Lynyrd Skynyrd's "Sweet Home Alabama" (1974) and country rock as a whole. However, it is rare for hip-hop artists to imagine idyllic rural settings. The urban black music tradition retains memories of rural oppression. From Paul Robeson's powerful yet plaintive renditions of traditional Negro spirituals to Billie Holiday's famed club performances and studio recordings of "Strange Fruit" (1972, first recorded 1939), on down to hip-hop's countless allusions to slavery, lynching, and repression, rural life is often equated with terror and repression.

Claudia De Simone has studied Diagnostico, a Brazilian hip-hop collective that is intent on "raising a little hell" to clean up urban watersheds (2008, 7). Diagnostico focuses on neighborhoods neglected by city infrastructure. Environmental hip-hop reminds us that environmentalism is not just about decreasing the impact of human technologies on natural environments. It is also about distributing the benefits of environmental technologies more equitably. With its linguistic depth and topical range, hip-hop is particularly well equipped to deal with environmental matters.

From an ecological standpoint, there is nothing wrong with urban environments. City dwellers, on average, have smaller environmental footprints than their country cousins. Urban life allows for ecologically sound economies of scale, including rationalized delivery of food, consumer goods, and services, public transportation, and more efficient use of fuel for heating and cooling. City dwellers tend to live in boxes, efficiently stacked in columns and ranged into neat rows, whereas rural residents sprawl out onto much greater acreage. Rural people use more fuel to get around, to warm themselves, and even to gain sustenance. The current world population could more easily be sustained if everyone moved to cities and the countryside was left to farmers. Of course, that is not going to happen, and it is an incomplete solution if the goal is to reconnect people with nature. The point stands, however, that rock and hip-hop are not less "environmental" simply because they belong to the city.

In fact, some of the most artful and interesting environmentally relevant music has focused on cities. In *Singing in the Wilderness*, Wilfrid Mellers gives the examples of Aaron Copeland from the United States and

Carlos Chavez from Mexico, classical composers situated in two of the world's largest cities (2001, 105–117). Both embraced the complexity of the urban environments where they lived, bringing city sounds and sensibilities into the more pastoral canon.

In general, classical music has shown some dexterity in moving back and forth across the urban-rural divide. Rock may or may not be able to do that. As soon as rock loses its city associations—high volume dynamics, electronic dissonance, timbral complexity, blunt lyricism, and screaming, high-pitched guitars—it ceases to be rock. That rule isn't written anywhere, but it is applied in practice. Even die-hard rock acts are accused of becoming too "poppy" or "soft rock" when they stray too far from those genre-defining features. As Georg Lukács observed, "every genre has its own objective laws which no artist can ignore without peril" (quoted in Frith 1996, 75). One of those is that rock should be very loud, very fast, and texturally complex.

Classical and folk music incorporate silence more effectively than rock and hip-hop do. Their dynamic range reaches into the lower decibels, a quality that makes them better at evoking natural sound. A classically trained friend asked after attending a recent rock concert: "Don't rock musicians believe in dynamics?"

Granted, wild rivers and hurricanes can produce deafening sound, but most of the nonhuman world is relatively quiet in comparison with human soundscapes. Gordon Hempton's *One Square Inch of Silence* (2009) presents a cogent argument regarding the need for silence in sustaining environments. Making a noble attempt to achieve quiet in protected areas like Olympic National Park, Hempton argues that noise has radically transformed human consciousness. Our adaptation to noise has made it more difficult for us to appreciate the subtler sounds of nature and preserve nonhuman ecosystems. The lack of silent places and moments has damaged us: Hempton calls it chronic sonic urbanitis (CSU).

Quieter styles of music might be better than rock at instilling a sense of environmental awe in the listener. Although there is some pretense involved in classically trained and folk musicians' claim to work in harmony with nature—and admirable honesty in rock's embrace of urban chaos—this may be another reason for the association of environmental music with folk and classical music in many people's minds, and the relative dearth of environmental themes in rock and pop.

Nevertheless, the survey made it clear that a surprising number of young environmentalists find themselves gravitating toward rock, specifically punk. In *The Jukebox in the Garden*, Ingram argues that punk rock prompted an important shift in rock toward dystopian environmental critique, partly in reaction to the hippies' escapist pastoralism. "The nascent environmental critique produced by the [1960s] rock counter-culture was limited and contradictory," he explains, "in that rock culture also stood for hedonism, individualism, egocentricity, escapism and con-sumerist fashion" (2010, 120). The punks had no such contradictions. They turned urban decadence into an art form.

Ingram's point about rock's fetish for "consumerist fashion" is dead on. Clothing is a constant theme in rock biographies, almost to the point of distraction. For example, Jon Savage's *England's Dreaming* (2002), a definitive history of the Sex Pistols and early punk, repeatedly examines not only clothing worn by the Pistols and other bands, but also fan fash-ion. Fashion is clearly central to rock culture. If the avant-garde serves as a research and development department for the culture industries, then rock musicians are their ultimate fashion models. Punk named the game, drawing attention to the consumerist values at the heart of rock music. As the Clash sarcastically proclaimed, *Passion Is a Fashion* (Gilbert 2005).

Yet punk became perhaps the most marketable fashion regime rock ever produced, providing recombinant clothing options for designers and consumers to explore, from Doc Martins to fetish wear. Post-punk pop mainstreamed all of it. Punk fashion went from recycling discarded dregs to inspiring the production of new, discardable clothing. Instead of slow-ing the wasteful fashion cycle, punk accelerated the assembly line.

Although rock's fascination with fashion might seem trivial from an ecological standpoint, it is fairly consequential in marketing and material terms. The punk ethos was, and is, an explicitly ecological ethic: parody consumer excess by conspicuously wearing its rags. Throw the excretory excesses of society back at itself; rub their faces in it. Unfortunately, what seems to resonate instead are cool new combinations of clothes. Buy more clothes, wear them out, and rip 'em up. Better yet, go to a store like Urban Outfitters where they (barely) pay women in Mexican maquilado-ras to do the ripping beforehand. No long-term wearing required.

The concept that clothing should be so quickly replaced is encour-aged by an economy and culture oriented toward high growth. On the runway, at the food court, and inside the store, rock and pop provide the soundtrack for conspicuous consumption of clothes, cars, food, and alcohol. In the total ecology of sound, that function is probably far more important than all others combined.

Punk is problematic for other reasons. Its dystopic urban aesthetic could be viewed as a complete capitulation to environmental decline, the erasure of hope. The Clash sang about punks who "look so sick in the sun" (1979), a phenomenon that is quite literally true. Take a walk in

San Francisco's Haight-Ashbury neighborhood on a rare sunny summer day. The pale skin looks completely out of place against the city's colorful and verdant background, at least until the fog returns. If punks have a natural habitat, it is the concrete, steel, and stenciled environment of the city—anywhere but a green, rural setting. After rock's brief rural retreat in the late sixties and early seventies, punk pulled it back to the city, where rock has continued to thrive.

For all these reasons, bending the urban aesthetic of rock to environmental politics might be difficult. Rock prefers youthful irony, musical eye-rolling, and celebratory cynicism, as opposed to eco-sincerity. Ironic juxtaposition is a mainstay of rock politics, but remains limited and potentially counterproductive as an environmental ethic.

To understand why, we can look at antifascist punk from the late seventies and early eighties. Bands like the Clash and Fear flashed swastikas, donned Doc Martins, and wore military flak jackets in order to play-act fascism. It was political parody, but not everyone got it. Skinhead Oi bands all too easily appropriated punk's left message for their racist, right-wing purposes. All they had to do was drop out the irony. There is a surprisingly thin line between parody and promotion, especially for audiences not in on the joke. Folk's more earnest vibe, no matter how limited artistically, often works better as a medium for political messages.

On the whole, punk has not presented a terribly sophisticated critique of capitalist excess. Punk bands like the Sex Pistols made the most of industrial effluence. Punk fashion, song, and lifestyle revel in urban decay, turning consumer society's castoffs into art. In that sense punks were early adopters of recycling. In an age when "the world soundscape has reached an apex of vulgarity" (Schafer 1994, 3), punk is perhaps the most honest and artful form of musical commentary.

And yet, as was explained earlier, punk is not the opposite of suburban mall shoppers' ecstatic consumerism, but rather its natural complement. Punk's conspicuously excessive after-consumption is every bit as eroticized as mall pop, albeit at the more excretory end of the consumer ecosystem. In an unsustainable system of production, consumption, and waste, punk rockers draw attention to unsustainable excess by reveling in it. But they also tend to live off it, rather than suggesting more positive alternatives.

Much like the hippie movement seventies' punks despised, punk rock has become part and parcel of the American life cycle. The rebellious, critical, and "cool" youth uses music to challenge an older order. Once through with rebellion, the punk, much like the hippie, tends to return to, and dutifully reproduce, the order against which he or she once rebelled.

In other words, punk was, and is, an Oedipal rite of passage, a liminal way out of, and back into, less ironic forms of consumption. While the liminal state represented by hippie, punk, rave and other rock rebellions rarely expands beyond youthful transgression, each generation manages to leave some positive traces in the wider culture. As shown in the survey, music can inspire some people to take action beyond fashion.

Punk amplified the egocentric tendencies of seventies rock, taking them to the point of parody. Punks were both the perfect embodiment and a stinging critique of the me generation. Before punk, rock politics was more of a finger-pointing enterprise: "us" versus "them." Early punk was more of a "me" versus "them" affair, which reached its logical conclusion in the nihilism of Nirvana's apolitical navel gazing, "me" versus "me." We all became stupid and contagious. Punk was planned obsolescence. It came with an expiration date, having "no future" from the very start. While artistically fascinating and a whole lot of fun, it was not the sort of music that could sustain environmental commitment.

Yet somehow, having worked through those early stages, American punk survived. Much of early punk's extreme cynicism faded. Having changed tune, punk bands are now counted among the most politically relevant. Numerous punk influences were cited in the survey, from Canada's Propagandhi to southern California's Rage Against the Machine. A 29-year-old activist stated that "a ton of punk bands" were important in his or her political formation. Another 29-year-old became a human rights lawyer as "a direct outgrowth of the consciousness punk rock gave me."

One of the virtues of punk is that political messages can be piggy-backed onto the cynical sound without seeming overly earnest (uncool) or contradictory. "The Clash may have woken up Midwest teenagers to the terrible things their government was doing in their name in Nicaragua and El Salvador," argues music journalist Pat Gilbert (2005, 364). As a midwesterner who grew up listening to the Clash, I can attest to Gilbert's claim. Several of us found punk attractive and politically interesting, sometimes even using it as an alternative headline service. Mainstream news may have ignored the El Mozote massacre (Danner 1994; Binford 1996), but the Clash's *Sandinista* album (1980) let us know something important was going on beyond our radar. Why else would our favorite bands be screaming about it?

About the environment, punk has had much less to say. However, punk-inspired artists like Billy Bragg and even new country's Steve Earle have taken punk's confrontational ethos and made it more positive, movement-oriented, and effective from a political perspective. Redirected at powerful institutions those predicated on conformity and decorum, punk became political. Earle's "Fuck the FCC" (2004) takes on censor-ship, implicating other acronyms in the process. Earle opposed the Iraq war before it was politically fashionable to do so. Bragg performs folk-punk in support of a range of labor, civil rights, peace, and environmental organizations. Punk helped give rise to the do-it-yourself ethos of indie rock, a genre that has meshed quite nicely with environmental politics since the mid-1990s.

Granted, the politicized musicians mentioned here are rare relative to the mainstream of popular music in America. Most rock, hip-hop, and pop musicians help to make the sell, no matter what is being sold, why, and toward what end. That stands to reason in a consumerist, capitalist society. Environmental ethics are anathema to conspicuous consump-tion, "green consumerism" notwithstanding. However, critical musicians and activist fans repurpose popular styles of music for more environmen-tally friendly ends, much as Joe Hill did with the sacred hymns of his time.

Environmental Music in Contemporary America

Because relatively few North American popular songs are explicitly about environmental issues, the same songs get cited over and over: Marvin Gaye's "Mercy Mercy Me (The Ecology)" (1971), Joni Mitchell's "Big Yel-low Taxi" (1970), a handful of songs by John Denver, and a few others.

Topically, environmental pop songs have much in common, even if the rare examples hail from different sonic genres. Many musicians move away from their typical style and toward a hybrid folk-rock sound when writing and performing environmental songs. Against the wishes of his record label, John Denver became less country when writing and per-forming his environmentally themed music. Similarly, Neil Young's envi-ronmental songs are almost all acoustic and folk-tinged. Other examples include the Beach Boys' "Don't Go Near the Water" (1971), the Eagles' "The Last Resort" (1976), and even Michael Jackson's "Earth Song" (1995). To signal environmental themes, pop musicians tend to use more subdued rhythms than usual, create simpler timbral textures, incorporate acoustic instrumentation (or electronic sampling), and either bring lead vocals up front or drop backup harmonies altogether, thus allowing the lyrics to be more clearly understood and producing a relatively spare, folk-vocal sound. In other words, rock and pop often take on folk quali-ties in order to signal environmental intent.

Perhaps no musician is more associated with environmental causes than John Denver, who first gained fame with country pop songs like

"Take Me Home, Country Roads" (1971) and "Thank God I'm a Country Boy" (1974). Denver leveraged his popular success to produce more overtly environmental statements. Although RCA expected Denver to remain securely in the country camp, he turned to crossover pop for "Rocky Mountain High" (1972), "Calypso" (1975), and other environmentally inflected songs. Whether Denver felt that country was too niche-specific to reach a wider audience or saw it as somehow incompatible with his ecological message, he clearly decided to move away from country when writing environmental music.

Neil Young came to environmental pop from the other direction: rock. His environmental songs include "After the Goldrush" (1970), "Natural Beauty" (1992), and "Be the Rain" (on *Greendale*, 2003). One of his most interesting environmental statements is "After the Garden" (2006), a double-entendre allegory about the Bush administration and environmental degradation. The song celebrates the end of one "garden," representing George W. Bush, then segues into an expression of concern for the future of America itself as a "garden," equating the nation's natural endowment with "Eden." Although many ecocritics would like to move American culture away from pastoralism and images of wilderness—as represented in music by artists like Young and Denver—it is difficult to find another idiom in which to discuss or artfully mediate environmental matters here. Young's music has appeal for good reason. Naturalistic imagery grabs listeners. Wilderness provides not only a mental refuge but also a symbolic language through which to discuss sustainability.

In order to understand environmental music in America, it is important to understand preservationism. Preservationism is a shared ethic in America: even a coal, timber, oil, or real estate developer must speak the language of preservation in order to succeed. Rarely do developers admit that their plans will forever change a cherished landscape. Instead, they tend to argue that a specific development project is uniquely important, that environmental damage will be minimal, and that the major economic benefits of their project outweigh minimal environmental concerns. By using environmental rhetoric, industry demonstrates that there is, in fact, a consensual agreement in public discourse around environmental preservation. The extent and definition of preservation differ— some consider golf courses natural spaces, while others do not—but the ethic is shared, at least rhetorically. Once again, culture is a common stock of symbols, but not necessarily a realm of consensus.

That is not the case for all environmental concerns. There is not even rhetorical consensus regarding global climate change, for example, despite a clear scientific consensus. What's more, there is relatively little public acknowledgment of overconsumption. Profit, growth, and consumption still trump environmental rhetoric, and the typical strategy for dealing with obvious contradictions between sustainability and overconsumption is to deal with them separately, as if they are entirely unrelated. Both the senior George Bush and Bill Clinton made that rhetorical leap in their inaugural speeches, claiming to be environmentally concerned and, practically in the next breath, pledging allegiance to the doctrine of economic growth. Such cognitive dissonance continues to dominate the American mindset, perhaps in part because the American media system is predicated on advertising subsidies and, therefore, is itself committed to the promotion of a high-growth/high-consumption society.

Any slowing or reversal in economic growth strikes terror into the heart of a consumer-oriented economy. The twin ethics of sustainability and biodiversity threaten the ideological underpinnings of corporate growth, governance, and media. Thus, whenever possible, the values of economic growth and sustainability are dealt with separately. When forced together, environmental ethics are generally subordinated to short-term economic exigencies—as illustrated by Barack Obama's inattention to climate change and constant attention to economic growth. When forced to reconcile high-consumption economies and the ethic of sustainability, many Americans envision a world where high energy use and excessive consumption have become fully sustainable through technological innovation. Environmental degradation is to be dealt with after the economy recovers, as if economy and ecology were completely separate. Problems like population growth are almost completely ignored in public discourse, another prerequisite for economic growth. "Rightsizing" population (i.e., having less children and having them consume less) is never considered as a sustainable solution to economic instability, injustice, or unemployment. Economic growth is viewed as the cure for all evils.

Occasionally, environmentalist musicians go beyond consensual preservationism. Neil Young's "Restless Consumer" (2006) is a good example. So is Tracy Chapman's "Mountains o' Things" (1988). Chapman's penetrating lyric and evocative voice connect the listener to a more authentic environment, the world of things that they experience daily, rather than one imagined in the distant past, rural distance, or idyllic future. She draws our attention to the useless commodities for which we work every day, the material excess that surrounds us, and the extreme deprivation of the export processing zone workers who manufacture it all. "Mountains o' Things" is anti-commercial, one of the few counterhegemonic messages found in popular music. We are exposed to between 300 and 3,000 advertising images every day. "Mountains o' Things" is one of the few places where an artist eloquently talks back. The song is the antithesis of most popular music, which promotes accumulation as a pleasurable life goal. From Elvis to Ke$ha, millions simply give in to the simplest, most unsustainable version of the American dream. Mainstream rock and pop are America's apocalyptic party music. They inspire the worst sort of ritual catharsis; laugh, dance, and look away. Fun stuff, and culturally significant. However, in terms of ecological function, mainstream rock and pop tend to be less liberating than commonly claimed, and more patterned by the interests of dominant institutions than typically admitted.

Conversely, rare songs like Ani DiFranco's "Your Next Bold Move" (2001) encourage introspective reflection. Her song speaks directly to frustrated environmental activists, describing the sense of political paralysis that has gripped much of the American movement. The lyric is worth reading in full (and is used here with paid permission from Hall Leonard Publishers):

Your Next Bold Move

Coming of age during the plague of Reagan and Bush
Watching capitalism gun down democracy
It had this funny effect on me, I guess

I am cancer, I am HIV
And I'm down at the Blue Jesus
Blue Cross hospital
Just lookin' up from my pillow feeling blessed

And the mighty multinationals
Have monopolized the oxygen
So it's as easy as breathing
For us all to participate

Yes they're buying and selling off shares of air
And you know it's all around you, but it's hard to point
    and say "there"
So you just sit on your hands and quietly contemplate

Your next bold move
The next thing you're gonna need to prove to yourself

What a waste of thumbs that are opposable
To make machines that are disposable

And sell them to seagulls flying in circles
Around one big right wing

Yes, the left wing was broken long ago
By the slingshot of COINTELPRO
And now it's so hard to have faith in anything

Especially your next bold move
Or the next thing you're gonna need to prove to yourself

You want to track each trickle back to its source
And then scream up the faucet 'til your face is hoarse
Cuz you're surrounded by a world's worth of things you
    just can't excuse

But you've got the hard cough of a chain smoker
And you're at the arctic circle playing strip poker
And it's getting colder and colder every time you lose

So go ahead, make your next bold move
Tell us what's the next thing you're gonna need to prove
    to yourself

    DiFranco's self-reflective song artfully expresses the sense of helplessness felt by many American environmentalists. The enormity of major ecological challenges—rapidly declining biodiversity, soil depletion, water pollution, anthropogenic climate change, increasing environmental health threats, and so on—combined with a lack of serious attention to these problems in mainstream politics, news, and popular culture, can often lead to a sense of paralysis. It is easy to see how one would be tempted to "just sit on your hands and quietly contemplate" or perhaps be drawn to popular culture's more seductive rites of denial.

    Of course, giving up and giving in are not the only options. Chapters 3 and 4 will present examples of more optimistic strategies. Meanwhile, having discussed American musicians, audiences, and activists, it is fitting to end this chapter on American popular music with a look into the insights of musical researchers and ecocritics.

The "Nature" Debate: Do Coal Pits Sound Like Canyons?

As Timothy Morton points out, Americans have a tendency to put "something called nature on a pedestal" and admire it "from afar" (2007, 5).

Imagining an ecological system as external to ourselves, something exclusively nonhuman, inhibits our ability to think about environmental matters more critically and creatively. Morton raises several excellent points. However, I am not yet ready to give up on "nature."

To understand Morton's deconstructive impulse, it is useful to compare two fields of environmental inquiry: biological ecology (science) versus ecocriticism (humanities). Ecologists aim for synthesis. They seek to discover and describe relationships between organisms as well as relationships between organic and inorganic systems.

Conversely, the humanities are predicated on taking things apart—on analysis—with "deconstruction" the most common contemporary thread. Much ecocriticism is driven by the need to point out theoretical limitations and ideological biases of science. "Nature" is a favorite target (Morton 2007), but others have taken apart the concepts of "climate" (Hulme 2009), "the animal," "sustainability," and so on. Climate scientists and others would benefit from reading these critiques. They lay bare ideological assumptions and help us escape from paradigmatic pitfalls.

But, like science, humanistic deconstruction is limited. Terms like "nature" may be problematic, but we probably do not have time to create a new language from whole cloth. Even if we did, our new, improved, more accurate, and more truthful terminology would soon become equally corrupted. If the "proper relationship" Morton calls for were called "Bob," then Bob would soon be under attack as well, sullied by the pragmatics of practice.

If we have learned nothing else after decades of identity politics, we know that changing words only goes so far toward solving social problems (N. Klein 2010, 107–125). Morton recognizes that fact when, paraphrasing Derrida, he asserts that language "is never really *yours*" (2007, 200). As Christopher Manes reminds us, "all language both reveals and conceals" (1996, 17). I reject Morton's call to abandon "nature" precisely because, like Morton, I would like to broaden the discussion and "open it up" (2007, 5). That will not happen if we simply start over with an entirely new language. We have to work with what we have, not wish it away as if culture, nature, and entire environmental discourses were only words on the seminarian's desk. Morton points out that "nature" was "practically a synonym for evil in the Middle Ages" and "the basis for good" in the Romantic period. Therefore, the term has enough plasticity to be reconceptualized, made more useful for today's purposes (ibid., 15).

A more careful and nuanced reading of any term, culture, or historical period will show that language is always in flux and contested, no matter how hegemonic it appears. Morton himself shows that "nature has been used to support the capitalist theory of value and to undermine it; to point out what is intrinsically human, and to exclude the human; to inspire kindness and compassion, and to justify competition and cruelty" (ibid., 19). Many applications of "nature" that I encountered during fieldwork differ remarkably from the meanings Morton identifies in the Romantic literature. The use of "nature" in environmental discourse has not "put a stop to argument or rational inquiry" (16), and its abandonment will not solve much either.

Musicologists have shown less interest in ecocritical debate, until fairly recently (Allen 2011). "In the English-speaking world," Alexander Rehding points out, "the cultural study of nature has become a burgeoning industry in other humanistic disciplines, but has hardly hit musicology" (2002, 305). Hopefully we will not get bogged down in a similarly circular debate over specific word choices. One way to avoid semantic dead ends is to keep "semioethics" in mind (Petrilli and Ponzio 2003). Susan Petrilli and Augusto Ponzio suggest that theorists recognize "the implications, perspectives, risks, and responsibilities involved in semiosis" (Petrilli 2009, 344). It is not enough to pull language apart, as interesting as that is. "A major issue for semioethics," argues Petrilli, "is 'care for life' from a global perspective" (ibid.). Semioethics reminds us that attention to pragmatic applications, critical reflexivity, and creativity are just as important as discursive deconstruction.

Ultimately, the environmental impacts of environmental ideologies are more important than theoretical debates over the their internal logics. "Americans confronted with a natural landscape have either exploited it or designated it a wilderness area" observes Frederick Turner. "The polluter and the ecology freak are two faces of the same coin; they both perpetuate a theory about nature that allows no alternative to raping it or tying it up in a plastic bag to protect it from contamination" (1996, 45). Turner moves us closer to understanding the most important meanings of American nature discourses: the actual behaviors and institutions they inspire, facilitate, and legitimate.

Turner's observation is true, to a degree. As is so often the case in ecocritical scholarship, however, Turner's dichotomous critique is almost as absolute as the orthodoxy he challenges. True, Americans do have a firm and somewhat simple belief that a given place is either virgin territory or despoiled land. It would be good for us to gain more nuance, but that does not mean that everything connected to American environmental ideology has to be thrown out. Culture, including American culture, is never that simple.

In fact, the American outlook on nature has many positive aspects. Frankly, I prefer America's national parks to the more carefully groomed spaces in much of Europe, for example. I do not find the garden metaphor Turner promotes to be a universal human good, any more than the wilderness trope is. As a matter of environmental preference, I would rather not see everything turned into a "garden." Granted, it would be good to have a whole lot less environmental "raping" (Turner 1996, 45) and a clearer sense of ecology in all that we do, but thank goodness our extreme fear of despoliation has kept so much North American land from development. I am reminded of an encounter with a man from Britain's Lake District, who was on holiday at Vancouver Island's Botanical Beach Provincial Park. He was ecstatic at being able to walk in such a biodiverse wilderness: "You are so lucky," he said. "We have many pretty places back home in England, but nothing like this." Then he added, rather humorously, "Are those bear warnings for real?" Perhaps North Americans do put nature on a pedestal, but as a result there are still plenty of bears walking around the continent.

The more horticultural metaphor Turner promotes would undo much of what American preservationists have struggled to accomplish. In fact, one could imagine garden language assisting mining, logging, and real estate development companies who seek to "cultivate" public wilderness lands. It is best to understand each perspective in its ethnographic context and complexity rather than in a philosophical, theoretical, ideological, or literary distillation. Gardens are great, but they are not enough. Granted, American national parks and wilderness areas are more radically managed than most realize, but there is danger in seeking too much middle ground as a starting point. Once a natural space enters fully into development, horticultural or otherwise, biodiversity suffers considerably (Pitt-Brooke 2004).

Turner's provocative question (1996, 40) is: would the Grand Canyon "still be a national park" if made by man? I would answer no. Other than in science fiction (D. Adams 1984), the Grand Canyon, with all of its biological and geological complexity, could not be created artificially. Take a walk in new-growth woods and then in an old-growth forest and you will immediately understand the difference. Climb down the cliffs of the Grand Canyon and then visit a coal pit. They are different spaces, empirically and otherwise. The greatest problem with the metaphoric challenge is the same error made by those who believe that technology can solve everything or that carbon offsets undo all impacts. Human creation is energy-intensive: the grander the work, the greater the extraction.

If the Grand Canyon were made by human beings, there would probably have been an equal or larger area decimated to make it. It is better to work with ecosystems than try to replicate them. Our gardens are great, but hardly a replacement for more natural landscapes, especially on a large scale.

The reason we think of canyons and coal pits as very different places is that they are very different spaces—and not solely because they are culturally conceived. That is the hubris of humanity, a species-centric solipsism that believes the world exists only because we imagine it into existence. Coal pits and canyons are different in material terms. That is brought home in Hunter Hensley's moving *Requiem for the Mountains*, a chant and video exposition illustrating the difference between landscapes destroyed by mountaintop removal and others less impacted by mining. The ecocritic might suggest that it is Hensley's art that makes these places so radically different for the listener. I would not deny that his moving piece adds to one's appreciation for the mountain and distaste for the coal pit; that is the whole point of the performance. It is a privilege to hear and see *Requiem for the Mountains* performed live; Hensley's *YouTube* recording (2010) also provides a sense of the performance's profound impact. However, and this is Hensley's point, the mountains play an active role in creating meaning as well. The ecosystem has agency, as do coal companies when they blast off beautiful mountaintops. Each element and actor communicates something different, and we make meaning of our environment through our encounters with each one.

Quite simply, the beautiful and biodiverse mountains move one to song in a different way than do coal pits. Neither type of place prescribes a specific song—there is no essential and singular meaning in either—but they evoke different human reactions. They are truly different places to start with. Perhaps a Peabody Coal CEO could see beauty in the coal pit, but that takes a lot more cultural work than finding aesthetic pleasure in a less disturbed ecosystem. The CEO's home walls are probably lined with landscapes, not pictures of mining pits.

Several musicians have advocated for an end to mountaintop removal. In 2010 the Natural Resources Defense Council (NRDC) organized a concert featuring Allison Krause, Emmylou Harris, Kathy Mattea, and others to raise awareness about the destructive practice. The performers raised $60,000 for the NRDC to advocate for more sustainable mining techniques, mountain preservation, and greener energy sources. "The Appalachians have inspired countless country, folk, bluegrass, gospel, and Americana songs," explained Emmylou Harris. "Now those sources of inspiration are being secretly destroyed" (quoted in Webster 2010). If musicians like

Hensley and Harris were to give in to Turner's argument that there is no such thing as a natural environment, then it is hard to imagine them making the inspiring music they do, or using their music to preserve biodiversity in Appalachia. Every conception of nature may ultimately be myth, but not all mythologies are created equal, and each story we tell ourselves about our world inspires a different set of actions within it.

Katherine Irvine and her colleagues (2009) provide further evidence that soundscapes are made up of more than semiotic associations. Quite simply, there are sounds that work better or worse for us as a species. Irvine et al. determined that the variables of green space, biodiversity, and sound levels co-vary in urban spaces. Without consciously accounting for those variables, the residents they interviewed showed a strong preference for sounds associated with greater biodiversity and a strong negative reaction to anthropogenic or "mechanical noise," despite living among those sounds all the time (2009, 167). The study strongly affirms that increasing biodiversity in urban green spaces is not just an arbitrary aesthetic preference on the part of the critic, scientist, or environmental activist. Humans subconsciously prefer to be surrounded by the sounds of nature.

Theoretically, people could make any environment pleasurable, but in empirical reality preserving biodiversity and green space is much more pleasant than being surrounded by purely human constructs. Those of us who make music in simulated caves—dingy clubs, bars, and backrooms—might learn a thing or two from the Tuva, who perform "in natural acoustic environments," including real caves (Levin 2006, 31). These are the places where Tuvan songs "were meant to be performed" (ibid.). In a way, these are the sorts of soundscapes to which we might want to aspire, or at least protect with our music.

I may be practicing strategic essentialism here, or at the very least betraying an American preference for preservationism. However, the point is probably best made in terms of balance: balance between recognizing present predicaments and imagining future possibilities, between realizing the constructed nature of human consciousness and the need to value nonhuman life, between enacting pragmatics and appreciating art, between the sciences and the arts. I find it useful to keep returning to the touchstone term "sustainability." It is hard to imagine a sustainable world where mountains become coal pits and Grand Canyons are made by man, no matter how useful such juxtapositions are in the ecocritical imagination.

That is not to say that heavily modified landscapes are unworthy of preservation. All places are worthy of stewardship, but not all conceptions of place are equally worthy. Just because the culture/nature distinction fails us, we do not want to fall into another absolute—the untenable claim that the world around us is nothing more than what we subjectively imagine it to be, a claim that renders all things—Grand Canyon, garden, and coal pit—objectively the same.

Yet the ecocritics' basic point remains: whether we are new age musicians, scientists, or theosophists, we are never simply part of nature. We are the "naked ape," able and obligated to make meaning in order to sustain ourselves (Morris 1984). We make the world our home, in part through song. Therefore, one way to assess and appreciate our musical creations is to interpret what sound does or does not do to sustain us and the world of life around us.

That includes songs of nationhood and place. Is this land "made for you and me" or is America a patchwork of private interests? Which "America the Beautiful" do we want, and how much of it should be fruited plain, forests, or parking lots? Such questions are more relevant than ever in an era when public sovereignty over land, water, and resources is increasingly called into question. Our songs will help shape future debates over the environment. In turn, the places we preserve or create will result in new soundscapes, and new music. We have just begun exploring the ecological functions of musical sound. However, it is clear that music plays some role in expressing and influencing what we do in, with, and to the nation as physical space. In the next chapter we will take a closer look at how music works in relation to place, as the focus narrows to regional soundscapes.

3

Regional Geography in Song

Music Makes Place

Musicians transform geographic regions into living myths. For example, Greek lyricists provided mythic histories for ancient Mediterranean landscapes. Homer's sung poetry gave the Mediterranean world new meaning, rooting contemporaneous imaginations in lyrical histories that seemed to reach back to the beginning of time. His songs connected people to place, and still do. The soundscape has changed, and the ancient Greek's musical sound is largely lost (Ingalls 1999, 392), but Homer's words have remained to take on new meanings in very old places.

During the medieval period, itinerant minstrels sang playful ballads of epic battles, leaders, edicts, and natural disasters, paralleling contemporary journalism in function if not form. The invention of the printing press did little to diminish ancient traditions of making meaning through music. From the fifteenth through the seventeenth century, printed broadsides assisted balladeers as they continued to deliver the news of the day in song (Stephens 1988, 100). The invention of the newspaper in the seventeenth century and the spread of literacy gradually did away with the balladeers, but that process took many centuries.

As late as the twentieth century, Mexican balladeers continued to practice the ancient tradition of telling musical stories of place. As war ravaged the Mexican countryside, cutting off rural villagers from metropolitan news sources, guitarists traveled from town to town to perform songs about battles, generals, presidents, and *Yanqui* interventions. Even through the late post-Revolutionary period, these *corridos* (literally, "that which is current") served as the "newspaper of the folk" for many rural people (Redfield 1930, 186). Although corridos have lost their central role as news organs, *corridistas* continue to provide critical commentary on current events in contemporary Mexico (Wald 2001). In doing so, they provide listeners with a sense of regional identification, much as ancient Greek lyricists made tangible spaces into mythical places. Music peoples our places with characters, stories, and sounds. Those sounds resonate because they so profoundly reflect our living sense of place. Through stories, music, art and other cultural magic, we feel a collective sense of belonging.

Although regions are also imagined places, never fully knowable spaces, space becomes increasingly tangible as we move from global and national abstractions down to specific regions. One need not randomly draw upon generic "mountain majesties," "amber waves of grain," or "shining seas"—there are specific land and water forms to invoke. A citizen of Washington State might never experience the Everglades for herself, but that distant ecosystem has nevertheless become part of her "imagined community," the nation-state (Anderson 1983). However, nearly all Washingtonians have at some point in their lives directly experienced the sight, sound, texture, and taste of the Columbia River basin for themselves. It feels more tangible, part of the material reality of one's actual existence and shared space. All human connections to the natural world take cultural work, but experiencing the river running at one's feet is different, more visceral, than imagining another river half a world away. The Blue Danube means less to a Minnesotan than Ol' Muddy. Societies focus cultural work on the places that matter the most to them.

Homer, balladeers, and corridistas present a romantic vision of place-making music. However, musical place-making is not always positive, from the point of sustaining healthy ecosystems. The following history describes one such case: when Woody Guthrie helped the Bonneville Power Administration manufacture a new sense of place in the Columbia River Valley. Guthrie's Columbia River songs gave the citizens of that region a new sense of identity. In that sense, his music was a place-making success. However, with his music Guthrie unwittingly supported large companies, banks, and landowners, the same institutions he so steadfastly opposed for most of his musical life. He also aided a river's ruin and replaced relatively sustainable soundscapes with the sound of false progress.

In some ways this chapter is the tale of two rivers, Woody Guthrie's Columbia and Pete Seeger's Hudson. If I linger on Woody's river, it is because I believe the story has much to teach us. If a musical magician like Woody Guthrie could go this wrong, then surely the rest of us can as well. There was bound to be a misstep or two in Guthrie's storied career, and despite all that follows, I hesitate to call even his Columbia River adventure a mistake. The story is by no means finished. His music lives on and continues to create new meaning in the Pacific Northwest. Meanwhile, Pete Seeger's Hudson River Valley gets cleaner each year, giving us hope that Woody Guthrie's Columbia can be restored as well.

To end the chapter, I go to middle ground, Minnesota. Above the headwaters of another great river, Cloud Cult presents a modest alternative to the epic songs and dramatic plans that marked America's Century. This comparison of contrasting cases serves to illustrate some of the varied roles music plays in relation to regional ecosystems.

A River Gone Wrong

The previous chapters were focused on rock and pop. In focusing on rock, I may have made folk music seem like rock's opposite, a more natural and sustainable cultural practice. However, as will be shown here, there is nothing intrinsically environmentalist about folk music. This chapter is about folk gone wrong, environmentally speaking. It is about the smallest music imaginable, a guy and his guitar, who together helped ruin a river.

That statement was a bit hyperbolic, much like Guthrie's music. Critiquing America's most lauded folk icon for his collaboration in damming a river and extinguishing species is unfair, unless balanced by mention of his incredible accomplishments. Woody Guthrie was perhaps the greatest socially engaged musician in American history. He did much, much more good than harm.

Yet that is what makes this story so tragic and worth telling. We tend to assume that socially conscious music, well-intentioned interventions, can do no harm. Music might not change the world, but at least it won't add to the earth's burdens. Unfortunately, that is not always true. As Lawrence Grossberg reminds us, there is nothing intrinsically good, bad, left, or right, about music (1993). Furthermore, the utopian schemes of one era can become the dystopian realities of the next. Nothing illustrates that better than Woody Guthrie's effort to promote rural utopia in the Pacific Northwest.

In 1941 the Bonneville Power Administration (BPA) offered Guthrie a job in public relations. With a family to support and mounting debts to pay, Guthrie accepted a one-month contract. In that short period, he penned at least 26 songs to promote dam construction along the Columbia River. Biographer Ed Cray refers to Guthrie's month in Portland as "probably the most productive of his life" (2004, 212). Mary Katherine Aldin calls Guthrie's BPA work a "breakthrough" (1999, 8). Most of his Columbia River songs, all written in 1941, are available on *Roll On Columbia* (Guthrie 1991).

By accepting the post, Guthrie entered into a public battle between private utilities and the BPA. In the thirties and forties, BPA agents worked with local granges throughout the Columbia River watershed to create People's Utility Districts (PUDs). One of their goals was to contest the power of private utilities, large landowners, banks, and insurance companies. It might seem that the BPA won the battle, given that today 14 dams line the Columbia while 214 others block its tributaries. However, the agribusinesses and bankers that once opposed BPA's dams are now their biggest advocates.

New debates swirl around the dams. Environmentalists, local tribes, and scientists claim that the BPA's grand projects have decimated fish populations and damaged watershed habitats (Knickerbocker 1997; Mann and Plummer 2000; Montaigne 2001; Wissmar and Craig 2004). Biologists have demonstrated that the dams impede salmon migration, impound harmful chemicals (Feist et al. 2005), and alter "temperature regimes," thus affecting fish health and reproductive success throughout the region (Naughton et al. 2005). Several species have been extinguished as a result, including the Snake River coho salmon, the last of which was seen in 1984. It is estimated that the current salmon population in the Columbia River system represents less than 3 percent of their original numbers (Montaigne 2001, 2). Extinction is imminent for many of the remaining fish species if several dams are not removed.

The science is piling up. Even many lifelong supporters of the dams have come to recognize the negative effects of erecting massive barriers along the river. Although overly rapid reclamation of the river might have unintended ill effects, most research indicates a need to dismantle at least some of the dams soon. There is a particularly strong consensus among biologists that unless four dams on the Snake River, a Columbia tributary, are removed, additional species will soon join the Snake River coho. As of 2010 the federal government continued to argue that technologically advanced alternatives to dam removal would eventually allow salmon and dams to coexist. William Yardley's headline says it all: "Obama Follows Bush on Salmon Recovery" (2009). Despite over two billion dollars spent on dam-salmon coexistence programs, they have failed to produce sustainable salmon populations.

It is not simply a matter of jobs versus fish. Advocates for the fishing and tourist industries have lobbied to breach dams along the Snake River. That has angered farmers, barge owners, and conservative citizens throughout eastern Oregon, Washington, Idaho, and Montana, who see dam removal as yet another *cause célèbre* of urban environmentalists. The same conservative forces that once fought the BPA dam-building campaign are now fighting to keep the dams intact.

The irony is even greater on the Left. How has it come to pass that a national icon of musical dissent, Woody Guthrie, and the dams he championed, have become rallying points for captains of industry, corporate landowners, bankers, and insurance companies? How is it that this treasured figure of both the Old and the New Left advocated for an environmental intervention that now serves as a sign of industrial excess and decadence for activists throughout the region? More importantly, what can we learn from Guthrie's experience?

To answer those questions, I began with a range of materials made available by the Woody Guthrie Archives, including BPA films and recordings, videotaped interviews with Guthrie's colleagues and contemporaries, and his personal notes, diaries, and lyric sheets. Unless otherwise noted, all materials cited here are housed in the Woody Guthrie Archives (currently in transit between their previous home in New York City and a new site in Oklahoma). In addition to those materials, some of which had not previously been accessed by academics, I drew upon published work by Guthrie himself, biographers, journalists, and historians. My goal was to better understand the time, place, debate, and, above all, Guthrie's orientation to the BPA.

Guthrie's status as a BPA contractor greatly influenced his musical work. On the plus side, BPA sponsorship allowed him to produce several unforgettable songs. However, by putting himself in the position of a PR man, Guthrie empowered the very forces he so effectively opposed in the rest of his musical life. Although he preferred political art to propaganda, his work for the BPA crossed that line. He would never allow his art to be used that way again.

A Soundtrack for Industrial Development

Guthrie was contracted to produce movie music. The BPA had already produced a promotional documentary named *Hydro* in 1939, two years before Guthrie arrived on the scene. After playing in a theater near New York's Times Square, *Hydro* was distributed nationally. The success of that effort led Stephen Kahn, BPA official and film producer, to begin production on a more ambitious project, *The Columbia*. His original intent was to produce a feature-length, semifictional film touting the benefits of hydroelectric power. Instead, the result was a picturesque documentary. *Hydro* footage was reused in *The Columbia*, but many of the technical details were edited out for the sake of narrative flow. More importantly, Kahn added to the soundtrack several Guthrie songs commissioned and written specifically for the new film. Originally, Guthrie was hired to act and provide folksy narration, not just music, which occupies a mere subclause in the detailed job description in Guthrie's BPA contract. The singer was also clearly intended to be a central character and voice throughout the film. Not long after meeting and hiring Guthrie, however, Kahn decided to have him focus on music alone. In the end, the film included only three Guthrie songs.

Both *Hydro* and *The Columbia* are typical propaganda pieces, touting the unquestionable benefits of dams to workers, consumers, and industry. *Hydro* goes into very specific detail about the potential economic benefits of the dams, documenting projected savings for individual households. Kahn and his director, Gunther von Fritsch, recognized that audiences would prefer a good story to an accounting lesson and made *The Columbia* more of a Hollywood-style production and marketing pitch, with a dramatic storyline, breathtaking images, and Guthrie's compelling music.

The Columbia is part of a series of Depression-era, government-sponsored films designed to document troubled times while promoting technological solutions. Its closest kin and immediate ancestor was Pare Lorentz's *The River*, released in 1937, which dramatically illustrates the Mississippi River's role in the economic development of the United States as well as the high costs of its use and abuse. "We built one hundred cities and one thousand towns," states the narrator, before asking, "but at what cost?" *The River*'s answer to erosion, pollution, poverty, and flooding in the Mississippi River Valley is, of course, dams. The dams "will transform into freshwater pools" the Upper Mississippi as well as its tributaries. Today, river advocates use the term "freshwater pools" with derision, but in mid-century it seemed like a utopian solution to the wild, destructive force of the river.

As in *The Columbia*, *The River*'s positive punch line is heralded with uplifting music and images of busy workmen and miles of power lines bringing prosperity to far-flung hamlets. To save society as well as watersheds, wild rivers needed to be controlled.

The Columbia starts with the image of an electrical tower, a symbol of mid-century modernity. Next, we watch the river roll by to the tune of Guthrie's "Roll On, Columbia." The narration begins: "Freedom and liberty . . . a century and a half ago Thomas Jefferson envisioned an empire of freedom and opportunity in the extreme Northwest." The narrator bemoans the wasted power of the Columbia and the fact that "only salmon" could freely travel its length. Native Americans are shown fishing as the narrator continues to argue that the river is woefully underutilized.

As in Guthrie's "Pastures of Plenty," a song written for the BPA, the film's storyline and narration draw a direct comparison between the desert environs of the Upper Columbia and the Dust Bowl of the Great Plains. Both parched lands are contrasted with the potential paradise that Columbia's diverted water and power could someday produce in a "land full of promise, the Pacific Northwest" (a line from "Pastures of Plenty"). On cue, the more upbeat "Roll On, Columbia" returns to herald a brighter future under the BPA.

The Columbia narrator presents a series of arguments for damming the Columbia. Dams are compared to natural features, including a glacial dam that blocked the river's flow during the most recent ice age. The BPA wants to "build an industrial empire from the wasted water of the Columbia." To do so, "they moved mountains."

Next we hear a bit of Guthrie's "The Grand Coulee Dam," before segueing into the film's most patriotic segment. The narrator argues that the BPA dams aided the U.S. war effort: "almost magically, the atom bomb was born" (the film was not released until 1948). However, the connection between BPA's hydrological power and nuclear weapons was more material than magical. The enriched plutonium used in the bomb that destroyed Nagasaki, Japan, on August 9, 1945, came from the Hanford "B" reactor on the banks of the Columbia (Alvarez 2003, 31). That fact is alluded to obliquely in the film because it was still a state secret at the time of the film's release.

The patriotic elements of *The Columbia* show how BPA officials were appealing to audiences beyond the Pacific Northwest. They would have to impress federal legislators and regulators. Moreover, they saw themselves as presenting a new model for regional development, not just for the Columbia River Valley. Similarly, Guthrie saw the BPA project as a potential solution to problems of national and even international scope, from solving Dust Bowl displacement to ending the exploitation of agricultural labor worldwide.

The Columbia argues that dams must be built to control catastrophic flooding and to cure a "grave electric shortage." But it follows that argument with a global appeal, suggesting that the BPA project will help feed the planet's starving masses as a "hungry world cries out." Guthrie's haunting "Pastures of Plenty" provides musical texture and tone, including a sobering reminder that migrant workers bring "light sparkling wine" to consumers' tables. The film and its music link the fate of migrant workers to the BPA's dams.

The Columbia ends by articulating the BPA with "democracy," a model "for other nations to follow." In other words, the film implies that the BPA model is a democratic answer to socialist models of development. This was clearly a response to the detractors who painted the BPA and its projects as a communist experiment. Ironically, free market advocates and capitalists are now the dams' greatest protectors and have been their main beneficiaries for decades. Despite the patriotic turn from *Hydro* to *The Columbia*, Guthrie privately expressed doubt that "Washington DC" would authorize the second film's release. In a letter to Elizabeth and Harold Ambellan, sent from Portland, he worried that censors at the Department of the Interior would shelve the film. Like Kahn and others involved in the project, Guthrie knew they needed to walk a fine line in order to get their message out. It must have been a frustrating experience for a musician who had controlled most of his own artistic output up to that point. However, as Guthrie explained in song, getting anything done requires a steady supply of the "Do-Re-Mi." Access to larger audiences, and the cash they provide, depends on pleasing institutional gatekeepers.

Near the end, *The Columbia* argues for further dam construction, complaining that only 10 percent of the river had been developed, sending "30 million horsepower wasting to the sea . . . a tremendous force for good or evil." The implication is that the "wasted" power went toward evil. The numbers changed from one film to the next. *Hydro*, released in 1939, claimed that the Columbia contained the potential for 10 million horsepower, if properly developed. In other words, the filmmakers had discovered more than 20 million "wasted" horsepower in the 10 years between films. PR is rarely a friend to science. In this case, neither was art.

The Columbia included much less emphasis on the plight of workers and a much more patriotic pitch. *Hydro* emphasized technology and its promise for workers, the ability to empower "chemical weapons to subdue an encroaching army of weeds," and the "power to push the city to the furthest county line." By the mid- and late 1940s, technological and social arguments needed to be folded more cleverly into arguments for national development and patriotism. World War II and the incipient red scare had changed the ideological climate.

The project's demands largely determined the content of Guthrie's songs. However, he believed in the project. The BPA's intended goals were very much in line with Guthrie's worldview. Guthrie also believed in the power of song to change minds. He believed that his songs about lynching "had the potential to change public perception on the emotionally charged issue" (Jackson 2005, 663). Similarly, he believed that songs in favor of the BPA project would help their cause.

Environmental Art and Propaganda

Guthrie spent little time explaining his music. His songs were written to stand on their own merits. On the denotative level, the lyrics tell simple stories, communicating basic meanings. The subjects central to the Columbia River cycle are: (1) technological awe and optimism, (2) concern for working people, and (3) an appreciation for the natural environment of the Pacific Northwest. There is little evidence that Guthrie saw a contradiction between aggressive economic development and conserving the natural environment. In fact, the following verse from "Lumber Is King" presents one of the few direct arguments for sustainable development (the text is taken verbatim from a lyric sheet rediscovered by the BPA's Bill Murlin in 1983, now housed at the Woody Guthrie Archives):

> King lumber might live for 100 years, too,
> If when you cut one tree, you stop to plant 2;
> But, Boys, if you don't, he's on his way down;
> Cause Lumber's just King in a Lumbering town.

Coming out of the Great Depression, most people were less concerned with environmental preservation than with economic development growth. Resources appeared inexhaustible, especially in the vast wilderness of the Pacific Northwest. Guthrie showed incredible insight in noting the need for sustainable forestry.

If we read between the lines, there is much greater complexity to Guthrie's lyrics than often acknowledged. His keen sense of critical irony and polysemic play is evident in the Columbia River songs. To start with the most enduring song of the cycle, there is irony in the title and content of "Roll On, Columbia." Guthrie was paid to promote a project intended to dam the wild river—tame it, so to speak. The song's title and theme are antithetical to those of "We Fought the Old Columbia," a song Stephen Kahn penned as a model to inspire Guthrie. Somehow, Guthrie's musical river just keeps on rolling, despite the dams.

Guthrie was extremely intelligent, a thoughtful and painstaking lyricist, changing the words to his songs constantly, spending days on single words and phrases until a song worked. He would have known that dams stop a river from "rolling on." Did he craft the song's title, refrain, and theme in recognition of the propagandistic power of a wilder river image (good PR) or as a tongue-in-cheek stab at his sponsor (interesting art)? Perhaps a bit of both. As will be shown below, Guthrie's BPA boss wanted him to write a song about fighting the Columbia, not one that let it "roll on."

Guthrie's lyrics demonstrate a somewhat bookish familiarity with hydrological engineering, the kind of technical knowledge he displayed later in his atom bomb songs. Guthrie knew what he was singing about, at least from an intellectual standpoint. Therefore, he surely knew that the great dams would make the Columbia do anything but "roll on." The verses used in the film, those typically sung as part of Washington's state folk song, present a fairly innocuous description of the river's beauty, its major tributaries, and its potential to turn the "darkness to dawn." After those verses, however, the song becomes an ode to Manifest Destiny, including a description of how "(w)e hung every Indian with smoke in his gun" and other references to Indian removal, before Guthrie returns to the dams' potential benefits.

Since Guthrie believed in anything but Manifest Destiny and hanging Indians, those incongruous verses are quite possibly evidence of intentional parody. They give an all-too-honest account of how the Northwest came to be under white control in the first place. It would have been out of character for Guthrie to view such events in a positive or even neutral light. Guthrie expressed strong interest in observing Indian fishermen along the Columbia. According to his BPA driver, Elmer Buehler, indigenous fishermen and the natural environment were about all Guthrie seemed curious about during the chauffeured tour. "He was very much interested in the Indians up there," said Buehler in a filmed interview. "He looked upon them as the common people too" (Murlin 2005). It is difficult to imagine the last few lines about hanging Indians being anything but a critical intervention. As is true of "This Land Is Your Land," leaving out Guthrie's punch-line stanzas is tantamount to presenting a different, perhaps even antithetical, song.

Other evidence of tongue-in-cheek wordplay in "Roll On, Columbia" includes a line about the Grand Coulee Dam, which Guthrie calls:

> The mightiest thing ever built by a man,
> To run the great factories for old Uncle Sam.

As if Uncle Sam's "great factories" were not enough to raise our suspicions, it appears that these lines became the basis for another song with a more overtly critical take on technology: "The Biggest Thing That Man Has Ever Done (The Great Historical Bum)," another lyric penned for the Columbia project. Over the following years, each version of "The Biggest Thing" became increasingly critical of major state projects, from the "Tower of Babel" to the U.S. atom bomb, while lauding the workers who sell their labor to produce such follies. Guthrie's Everyman protagonist was a "straw boss on the pyramids, the Tower of Babel, too." The song presents the Grand Coulee Dam as just one of many "biggest things" man has done, albeit one that makes the Tower of Babel look like "a plaything for a kid."

It does not take a lot of imagination to get the ultimate point: man's greatest accomplishments become symbols of his greatest failures. Conversely, Guthrie ends another tune, "Song of the Grand Coulee Dam," with the statement: "I wish we had a lot more Grand Coulee Dams." Was it a changed mood, a changed perspective, or the influence of Stephen Kahn's censorious gaze? There is no way to know for certain, but it is worth noting that "The Biggest Thing" went on to be a staple in Guthrie's repertoire, while "Song of the Grand Coulee Dam" died an early and well-deserved death.

Like many Guthrie songs, "The Biggest Thing That Man Has Ever Done" evolved over time. The original ends with a call to beat down Hitler, to "blow his soul to hell." The next version, from 1945, makes only a glancing, indirect reference to Hitler in the form of the "Kaiser" and "Hun." The later lyric is much more of an ode to arrogance than a celebration of technology. It ends:

> Next I took to farming on the great Midwestern plain;
> The dust it blowed a thousand years, but never come a rain;
> Me and a million other folks we left there on the run
> And that was about the biggest thing that man had ever done.

Ten years later the song becomes a cry for world peace as "the biggest thing" man will have ever done. What began as patriotic propaganda becomes a critical reflection on the potential hubris of all major undertakings. Was it the passing of time or the conditions of Guthrie's employment that made for the apparent changes in the writer's outlook? Did he bury his critical reflections in ironic juxtaposition while writing under BPA sponsorship, or did the artist become more critical of technology in subsequent years?

Fen Montaigne wrote the following assessment of the Grand Coulee: "Five hundred feet tall and with no fish ladders Grand Coulee was an engineering marvel and a salmon exterminator" (2001, 15). Although there is no evidence that Guthrie foresaw the dam's destructive effects on fish populations, he was perhaps the first to recognize its potential as a symbol of hubris.

Only "Roll On, Columbia," "Pastures of Plenty," and "Columbia Talkin' Blues" were used in *The Columbia*. "Pastures of Plenty" presents a compelling portrait of Dust Bowl refugees making their way to the Pacific Northwest, a paradise where dust fields could be traded for pastures of plenty. Although they are missing from the original BPA manuscripts, later commercial recordings and printed lyrics end with a set of verses that include Guthrie's haunting, artful, and enigmatic line: "We come with the dust and we're gone with the wind." He uses that line only once in the BPA version, but repeats it twice near the end of later versions.

"Pastures of Plenty" would seem to be a song of economic hope and earthly redemption, especially in the context of the BPA film project, but it becomes more of a funeral dirge in performance. Guthrie's vocal presentation is pensive, perhaps even a bit angry, yet ultimately resigned to fate. "Pastures of Plenty" comes across as more of a warning or admonition about institutional power and neglect than a celebration of technological promise. In using it, Kahn emphasized musical quality over denotative content.

"Pastures of Plenty" is a powerful example of interpellation. The second-person subject of the song is "you," the rich man who owns the hops, crops, and land. "I" and "us," the migrants, do all the work for "you." Nevertheless, "our" day will come:

> I think of the dust and the days that are gone,
> And the day that's to come on a farm of our own;
> One turn of the wheel and the waters will flow
> 'Cross the growing field, down the hot thirsty row.

Guthrie had already written dozens of commentaries for socialist newspapers before his arrival in Portland. Clearly, he believed in the need for working people, including family farmers, to gain control of the means of production. He was not enough of an ideologue to believe such a moment was imminent, but he viewed the BPA as a step in the right direction. "Pastures of Plenty" adds critical depth to the BPA film, but it has become much more important than the film, and rightfully so. It has been recorded and performed by Dave Van Ronk, Harry Belafonte, the Alarm, Lila Downs, Alison Krauss and Union Station, and many others.

Despite the critical interventions listed above, and perhaps because of Guthrie's conditions of employment, his "radicalism is vague and contained" in the Columbia cycle (Garman 2000, 184). For the most part, he put aside his typical critical commentary. Guthrie seemed to recognize that he was being paid to produce propaganda, not art. He was willing to make that trade, not just for pay, but because he believed in the cause.

On the whole, Guthrie's songs present powerful propaganda in support of the BPA project. That project was about more than dams and
hydroelectric power; it was about who would benefit. Private companies
had controlled the entire power grid, leaving 47 percent of Oregonians
without power. Extending power lines to their rural hamlets would not
produce sufficient profit for the private utilities. Fueled by that unmet
demand, BPA agents became effective organizers, arguing for the creation
of People's Utility Districts (PUDs), co-ops that would manage power on
a local level, and in a democratic fashion (most Oregon PUDs remain
People's Utility Districts, while most Washington PUDs are now referred
to as Public Utility Districts). BPA officials also recognized the need for
propaganda to contest the private utilities' PR. Guthrie entered into that
fight willingly and with an honest interest in promoting the BPA's dam
project.

In hindsight, the results were mixed, at best. Many of the PUDs with-
ered away; most of the surviving PUDs failed to become the progressive
institutions BPA officials originally envisioned. One battle over naming
rights symbolizes the PUDs' failure to ignite the locals' progressive spirit.
In 1966 Guthrie was honored by the BPA and Secretary of the Interior
Stewart Udall with the Conservation Service Award "Yours was not a passing comment on the beauties of nature, but a living, breathing, singing
force in our struggle to use our land and save it too" (quoted in Guthrie
1983, xi). As part of that honor, the BPA named a local power substation
after Guthrie. Biographer Bryan Garman argues that the award marked a
key moment in the cultural revision of Guthrie's legacy, changing Guthrie
from a political radical to pastoral patriot (2000, 165). Many locals dis-
agreed with Udall's assessment of Guthrie, finding it offensive to name
their power station after "a 1930-vintage beatnik who was lately idolized
by the folk singing set" (Johnson 1968, 10). When the BPA sold the
Woody Guthrie substation to a PUD along the Hood River in 2000, the
PUD's first act was to change its name.

Simply putting power in the hands of locals does not automatically
promote progressive action. The reflective and ironic wink that runs
through many of Guthrie's lyrics indicates that he recognized the complexities of power and human agency. Perhaps that is one of the reasons
he never succumbed to the sort of disillusionment experienced by so
much of the Left in the 1940s. He never fully bought in to the program,
remaining a free radical, largely self-taught and self-directed.

Perhaps the closest Guthrie ever got to full institutional buy-in came
during his month with the BPA. It would appear from his lyrics, diaries, and letters that he thought very little, if at all, about the potential

environmental and human costs of damming a river. But although there is little environmental reflection there, he clearly thought a great deal about the travails of sponsorship. In 1942, soon after completing his work for the BPA, Guthrie wrote in his diary that "the good art of good music and good singing is used like a weapon by the politicians to mix up, keep down, divide, keep poor, confuse, keep ignorant, the people." Such an artist, thinker, and critic would never enter into the production of propaganda lightly. In equating the Tower of Babel and the Grand Coulee Dam, Guthrie poked a bit of fun but refrained from biting the hand that fed him. However, it is worth noting that Guthrie never again accepted an offer of institutional sponsorship.

One Guitar Was Abused

The Columbia and Guthrie's songs represent the public face of Guthrie's BPA experience. Interviews and documents in the Woody Guthrie Archives (WGA) provide additional clues, giving us a fairly clear picture of what he actually did during his month in the Pacific Northwest. That picture is distinctly different from the popular image of the rambling songwriter rubbing shoulders with workers. The WGA contains extensive recorded interviews with Stephen Kahn, chief of the BPA Information Office, Elmer Buehler, Guthrie's driver, and construction workers who saw Guthrie at the Coulee Dam construction site. Bill Murlin, BPA administrator and Guthrie historian, conducted interviews with Buehler (2005). Denise Matthews and Mike Madjic interviewed Buehler and Kahn for a documentary entitled *Roll On Columbia*, a retrospective of Guthrie's BPA experience. The full, unpublished videotaped interviews (1999a, 1999b) are available in the WGA, along with contracts, letters, and other documentation.

These records indicate that Guthrie was not a farmer, manual laborer, or labor activist with a side interest in song, as commonly represented, but rather a professional songwriter and artist with a passionate interest in labor struggles, the dispossessed, and small farmers. Like most working artists of his or any era, Guthrie spent more time with musicians, urban audiences, supporters, and sponsors than with the subjects of his songs.

To get Guthrie hired, Kahn had him audition for his own boss, Dr. Paul J. Raver. He instructed Guthrie just to play a song or two to win Raver over. "Don't talk," Kahn advised, fearing that Guthrie would ruin his chances by critiquing "capitalism." Although he had just met the singer, it was already apparent to Kahn that Guthrie was a political radical. Guthrie wowed the boss with his music and got the job.

Kahn had been looking for someone with the "common touch" and felt that he had found his man in Guthrie. On the other hand, Kahn didn't trust Guthrie with a government car, so he procured a driver for him. The itinerant musician wanted to try his hand at acting as well, but Kahn, who wanted more of a leading-man type, decided to have the thin, sickly Guthrie stick to making music and have an actor lip-synch Guthrie's tunes. World War II interrupted that plan, leaving Kahn with Guthrie's songs but no money for actors or dialogue. Instead of a Hollywood-style musical, Kahn was forced to produce another documentary.

After securing the job, Guthrie asked Kahn what sort of songs he wanted. Kahn asked for songs about the river and BPA dam projects and handed Guthrie a song he had written as a model, "We Fought the Old Columbia":

> We face Columbia's fury
> From the Rockies to the sea
> And we brought to life a vision
> Of a land that was to be
>
> Of a land that men had dreamed of
> From the Grecian days 'til now
> Where true democracy is realized
> Can Columbia show us how?

"That ain't my style," Guthrie told Kahn. Although the stiff phrasing and rigid rhyme are much less poetic than Guthrie's more artful lyrics, there is a similar geographic and temporal sweep in the musician's songs, which also refer to democracy and a romantic vision of the western landscape. Lines like "From the Canadian Rockies to the ocean of the settin' sun" ("Ramblin' Blues") capture the spirit of Kahn's example. Guthrie was clearly writing for his boss.

After Kahn sent Guthrie and Buehler on the road for seven to nine days, he required the musician to sit in an adjoining room and type at least three pages per day. He later joked that he was "whipping" Guthrie to get the work done: he considered a song a day to be "about par." He asked Guthrie to double-space so that he could write in editorial comments and "black out the bad stuff"—clearly irksome for the independent artist. Kahn's New Deal politics were not so far from Guthrie's as to require a great deal of censorship. His inclusion of "Pastures of Plenty" on *The Columbia* and mentions of the condition of migrants in both films demonstrate Kahn's progressive politics. The difference is that Kahn was much more skilled at actualizing his politics within an institutional structure, and more inclined to do so.

"I didn't want to film anything that would incriminate me," Kahn admitted (quoted in Cray 2004, 209). As the interviews indicate, this merely demonstrates the man's political savvy. "If Guthrie's voice was to be heard," argues Cray, "it would only be on the sound track, singing songs Kahn had carefully sanitized" (ibid.). Kahn's inclusion of "Pastures of Plenty" in *The Columbia* may contradict that claim. Kahn had to carefully consider both promise and possibility in his work, and he did so expertly. Further on down the chain of command, Guthrie clearly recognized that he was being paid to produce a certain set of messages, and that the conditions of employment and the propagandistic task at hand would require him to omit, ensconce, or sublimate some of his core values and musical themes. As Mary Guthrie confirmed, the BPA "didn't want any politics" (quoted ibid., 211).

Kahn's request for Guthrie to "bring in three pages" per day, "like in Hollywood," however, demonstrates a misunderstanding of the songwriter's craft and may also explain the uneven quality of the Columbia River songs. Guthrie was out of his element. Despite the subsequent valorization of his BPA songs and the categorical transformation of his quickly drafted lyrics into a venerated "cycle," most of the songs, Kahn noted, are "pretty poor." A songwriter, even a great one like Woody Guthrie, can turn out only so many good songs on demand and in such a short period. What is truly remarkable is that Guthrie was able to compose a couple of memorable songs during his month in Portland.

Probably no one helped Guthrie more than his BPA chauffeur, Elmer Buehler, who provided quick and easy entry into the Pacific Northwest. Capturing a region in song without any prior experience was a daunting task. Guthrie wrote directly about what he was shown in that whirlwind tour across Oregon and Washington. If the better songs read like travelogues, it is because they reflect Guthrie's actual experience as a harried tourist. A magnificent countryside and massive construction projects were flashed before Guthrie in quick succession as Buehler shepherded him from site to site. The itinerant guitarist jotted down notes and wrote music in the back seat of the car, entertained by a parade of mountains, cliffs, and cascades.

Buehler saw Guthrie perform twice during his month of service with the BPA. The first time was an impromptu performance at a hotel. People walked in from the street when they heard the music, and Buehler was impressed with Guthrie's abilities as a performer, while noting that no one in the appreciative audience knew his name. Buehler himself arranged the other performance, which took place at a grange meeting and was also a big hit. Guthrie chose his audiences with care. Asked by the Inland Empire Chamber of Commerce to play "background music" for a local event, he replied, "I wouldn't play any background music, let alone in the foreground" (in Matthews and Madjic 1999a)—further evidence that he worked for the BPA because he believed in its goals and vision.

As with any artist, it is sometimes hard to separate out history, biography, and legend. Subsequent descriptions of the folk icon's Pacific Northwest experience, based mainly on Guthrie's dramatic self-presentation, show him as an itinerant songsmith, playing for the people and rubbing shoulders with workers. He wasn't. The legend illustrates a fundamental misunderstanding of what professional musicians do for a living, even a politicized musician like Guthrie. Professional musicians write and perform music, a consuming career that leaves little or no time for other activities. It is no accident that the most productive month in Guthrie's career took place while on the BPA payroll, probably because he was finally afforded the space, per diem fee, driver, home, salary, and resources to write songs full time. Guthrie was able to write music *because* he was not out working on the dams, riding the rails, or living in the shanties portrayed in his Dust Bowl songs. Past work as a commentator for communist dailies in Los Angeles and as a radio personality, for example, did not afford the same level of time and financial support for his art. He was doing other work: writing and talking. Composing and performing high-quality music is not something one does in one's spare time; it is a time-consuming commitment.

Interviewed in 2005, Buehler claimed that Guthrie never met with BPA construction workers, even when he was given the opportunity to do so. Nor did he rub shoulders with small farmers and PUD members. Asked by Bill Murlin if Guthrie talked with his audience after the grange performance, Buehler replied: "I can't remember him mingling with the crowd, I don't think he did." About Guthrie's interactions with others, he said: "I can't recall him talking to the average person . . . like at Bonneville Dam. . . . I know he didn't talk to anybody." Or at the Grand Coulee: "I don't think that at the dam site he did. They were mostly blue-collar workers. They were on the go and whatever else." When Matthews and Madjic asked Buehler if Guthrie visited any "Hoovervilles," Buehler noted that they crossed a bridge over one such encampment, but the songwriter did not want to stop, saying, "This is something you see everywhere. . . . I've been through that myself," as they drove past (1999a). In 1966 Kahn told freelance reporter Dave Johnson that Guthrie mingled with many BPA workers. That is the only such claim by anyone who worked directly with Guthrie in Oregon, and it was mouthed by the man in charge of BPA's PR. In truth, there would have been little time for Guthrie to gain such grassroots experience. Soon after arriving in Portland, he and Buehler left for their tour of Washington and Oregon, and Buehler took him to meet only "people who are friendly to Bonneville" (Murlin 2005). There is no evidence that Guthrie ever spoke directly to a BPA construction worker.

And then there is the question of the shantytowns, including those constructed by Dust Bowl migrants. After returning to Portland from the whirlwind car tour, Guthrie "poured it all out onto paper" under Kahn's watchful eye. Between his wife, three children, and an insistent boss, it is hard to imagine Guthrie having time to write 26 songs while engaging in conversations with workers, shanty dwellers, and the common people. He was by all accounts a fairly reclusive individual. His songs were the result of keen observation, imagination, and projection, the raw materials for great music.

In a letter from Portland to "Pete, Mill, and Lee" (Pete Seeger, Millard Lampell, and Lee Hays, the Almanac Singers), Guthrie claims: "I made it my business to go into lots of the tents and shacks this trip that I didn't make on the other trips" (Guthrie 1990, 54). That would appear to be more than a little stretch. Guthrie, like any good performer, promoted his stage persona regardless of how well it matched the backstage practice. There was little time to visit the shantytowns in Portland and little evidence that he did so, apart from Kahn's claim to have told Buehler and Guthrie to start their car tour five blocks from BPA headquarters at "Sullivan's Gulch" (Cray 2004, 209; Matthews and Madjic 1999b). "What's that?" asked Guthrie, and Kahn explained that it was a "Hooverville" (ibid.). The shantytown that Buehler offered to stop at, and that Guthrie declined to visit, fits the description of Sullivan's Gulch. At the very least Guthrie's Hooverville experiences in the Pacific Northwest have been amplified far beyond what would have been possible for a one month work trip that required constant writing. His claim to past traveling companions that he had visited more "tents and shacks" than before calls into question whether he had ever spent significant time among migrants. His magical and clearly fictitious "autobiography," *Bound for Glory* (1983), presents numerous Hooverville experiences. However, the timing of these events, the dialogue, and the assessments of people who were familiar with Guthrie indicate that those stories were composites, at best.

Photographs in the Woody Guthrie Archives of the singer visiting at least one encampment show him being escorted by officials, hardly evidence that Guthrie was himself a shanty dweller, and more of an indication that he functioned like many "cultural workers" of his time. His knowledge of the West Coast shantytowns was possibly derived as much from intertextual engagement—reading Steinbeck's *The Grapes of Wrath* (1939) and watching the subsequent film—as from direct experience. Steinbeck's tale provided intertextual depth to the life he lived and, perhaps more importantly, presented in his songs. Although he loved the book, Guthrie also wanted to "pick stones about Dust Bowl people that John Steinbeck did not write about" (quoted in Garman 1996, 69).

Artists are empathetic outsiders. Guthrie's Dust Bowl upbringing did not just make him aware of the plight of the Oklahoma migrants; it added subjective depth to his art. However, he was hardly a farmer or laborer, by birth, upbringing, or chosen profession. As an accomplished writer, composer, musician, and performer, Guthrie spent most of his time writing lyrics, modifying musical compositions, rehearsing, and performing, as well as writing for local and national publications.

The romantic notion that Guthrie spent a great deal of time living in shanties and logging towns is part of his performance persona. It is also what his audiences in New York City, Los Angeles, and other urban centers wanted to hear. For them, Guthrie was "a model to be emulated," a fact that drove him to "deliberately play down his early middle class upbringing and stress his later years of poverty and cross-country ramblings" (Reuss and Reuss 2000, 161).

As Richard and JoAnne Reuss explain, "he had spent most of his life among workers, dust bowlers, hoboes, and the rural peoples of America, and he was the most suffused with their worldview and vernacular—or so most of the Almanacs believed" (ibid.). In fact, what made an observer like Guthrie such a great artist was his lifelong separation from the norm, the sense of marginal detachment that helps an artist to understand the normative "worldview" and "vernacular" from an outsider's vantage point. Guthrie served as a musical foil for urban folk musicians and audiences who adored him, not to mention academic collectors like Alan Lomax and Charles Seeger. They wanted Woody Guthrie, the man, to be identical to Woody Guthrie, the performer and legend. To point out the disjuncture between Guthrie's musical persona and his life as a working writer, performer, and musician is not to take anything away from his art. It was Guthrie's unwavering dedication to music and working people that made a real impact, allowing him to serve both much more effectively than a lifetime of conversations and cohabitation in and among the people would have.

Guthrie's superhuman status has been supported by a host of academics and other promoters. The mythologizing started with Guthrie
himself. Take the following (Guthrie 1991, 12):

> These Pacific Northwest songs and ballads have got all of these
> personal feelings for me because I was there on these very spots
> and very grounds before, when the rockwall canyon stood there
> laughing around at me, and while the crazybug machines, jeeps,
> jacks, dozers, mixers, trucks, cars, lifts, chains and pulleys and all
> of us beat ourselves down every day yelling and singing little
> snatches of songs we was too hot and too busy and too tired to set
> down with our pen and pencil right then while the thing was
> being built. This is the main thing I tried to get at here in these
> Pacific Northwest songs.

Part of that description is literally true. Guthrie did spend a month in the
Pacific Northwest, and he did take in the panoply of images and sounds
described in his songs. The implicit claim that he was deeply connected
to the place as a long-term construction worker is factually false. However, it is artistically true. Guthrie had plenty of time to use his "pen and
pencil" in the short month he was there. He had a salary, a driver, a hotel
room, and warm bed each night. The assumption that Guthrie spent
much of his time during the BPA project rubbing elbows with workers is
a romantic myth that the itinerant folk singer did all he could to promote. Musicians are mythmakers in the best sense of the word. It is when
myth becomes propaganda that art starts to lose its way.

Joe Klein's landmark biography states that Guthrie "loved to com-
mune with the thousands of construction workers" (1980, 202). Klein
takes at face value a claim by Guthrie in the letter to the Almanac Singers
that he went into a tent city full of migrant workers, who greeted him
with lines like "Say mister, you don't happen to be Mister Jesus do you?"
(Guthrie 1990, 204). Similar dialogues appear throughout *Bound for Glory*
and Guthrie's notes, probably representing the artist's hoped-for role in
the workers' future. In self-parody, Guthrie typed up a humorous note
intended for the "Folksay Album #1" (1944) in which he insists that he
truly was at all of the places described in "The Biggest Thing," including
Babylon, Egypt, Rome, and the Boston Tea Party. In humorous recognition of the impossibility of one man's accomplishing all of the things
others ascribed to him, he ends with the note: "One guitar is abused."

Guthrie's art and profession demanded that he play the assigned
roles: artistic representative of all workers, chronicler of migrants' lives,

and champion of the underclass. Not only his songs but also his letters and notes can be viewed as extensions of a well-crafted performance. That does not make Guthrie a fraud; it makes him a musician. In liner notes, Guthrie's close friend Millard Lampell described him as "Contrary, irresponsible. He couldn't show up anywhere on time. Couldn't hammer a nail straight" (Guthrie and Lampell 1972). That's not the description of a worker; it is the portrait of an artist, a bohemian, and a performer. A division of labor is necessary in all work and all movements. The performer requires time to think, create, explore, and perform. You cannot be a performer at Guthrie's level and also have a day job. He seems to indicate as much in his private diaries:

> Mostly we need to publicize our own works more and more, the same as a merchant spends most of his money not for goods, but by telling the world that he has the goods, and what the goods are good for.

The success of any performance or ritual requires that the artist and audience maintain a shared mythic imagination. It is not surprising that Guthrie would promote that perception, nor is it surprising that an "enormous amount of mythology has been perpetuated by idolaters and popular writers" in order to extend Guthrie's myth into the present (Reuss 1968, i).

The Columbia River Valley as Workers' Paradise

Although there is little evidence that Guthrie's depiction of BPA workers came from direct experience, it is clear that he enjoyed his travels to the region's natural areas. Buehler told Bill Murlin in 2005 that Guthrie looked out at the scenery of Lost Lake, Oregon, and said to himself: "This has to be paradise," repeating the final word several times. Guthrie "never had too many words about anything," Buehler recalled (Murlin 2005). It was Buehler who later rescued *The Columbia* from incineration. He had been demoted to janitor, essentially blacklisted, as punishment, he believes, for years of organizing local PUDs. Buehler is convinced that the film's destruction (like his demotion) was ordered by Secretary of the Interior Douglas McKay, former governor of Oregon, a "son of a bitch" who had a vendetta against the BPA. McKay, in turn, reportedly referred to Buehler as a "carnival barker" (Murlin 2005). Kahn added support for Buehler's claim, arguing that McKay was indebted to private utilities for their support of his election campaigns.

An internal federal investigation in 1980 was unable to determine whether the order for incineration came from Washington. Almost all of McKay's former staff had died by then, but one of the few surviving staffers, Nelson Hazeltine, remembered receiving orders to weed out card-carrying communists from the BPA. Hazeltine said that he did not carry out the order, but his statement provides evidence that McKay did, in fact, have an ideological interest in firing BPA staff.

We are indebted to the blacklisted Buehler. Although at least one other copy of *The Columbia* was preserved, Buehler's copy was the one selected by the National Archives. "I believed in what they were doing," he explains (Murlin 2005) regarding his sacrifices for the BPA. "That makes your job a lot easier." In many ways, Buehler, Kahn, and the BPA together made Guthrie's work a lot easier, allowing him to focus solely on writing songs. Sacrifices were made all around.

Guthrie may not have been a card-carrying member of any party, but his thinking consistently followed that of the Old Left. Guthrie wrote numerous columns for *People's World*, the *Daily Worker*, *New Masses*, *Worker Magazine*, and *Worker Sunday Magazine*. He favorably reviewed books like *Marxism and Poetry* and championed the interests of labor (Reuss 1968, 66–70). The Old Left promoted a fairly straightforward Marxist model of social relations. Labor was, and would always be, the heroic protagonist, fighting and one day defeating the capitalist class. The internal contradictions of capitalism would inevitably lead to its demise. Such a model emphasizes certain social goals while precluding others. Environmental degradation is one of the most significant omissions from that model, an oversight that has rendered both capitalist and socialist models of development unsustainable.

Guthrie looked at the river and saw beauty. He looked at the blasters, jackhammers, and dams and saw jobs. He believed that the PUDs would distribute the irrigated land's bounty equitably. For Guthrie and most leftists of his era, there was no contradiction between development predicated on rapid growth and love for the land. The land seemed boundless. The struggle was over who would profit from nature's bounty, not who would be its best steward. Except for a few marginal radicals, the day's debate did not encompass environmental matters. In 1941 Left and Right alike worshiped economic growth and demonstrated unquestioned faith in technology to solve social problems.

In a letter to the Almanac Singers, Guthrie argued that folk songs should be brought up to date. He tells the young musicians to write songs about their reality in New York City, emphasizing modern technology, because "these are the things that arm the workers and these are the source

of the final victory of Public Ownership" (Guthrie 1990, 55). The technological optimism of the BPA appealed to him. *Bound for Glory*, too, represents the technological optimism of the time, with several passages trum-
peting the promise of new construction projects, and with conspicuous
mention of dams (1943, 251).

No verse more clearly illustrates the evolution of environmental
awareness among the American Left in the last 65 years than this one
from Guthrie's "Columbia Talkin' Blues," also known as "Talking Columbia" (Guthrie 1991, 56):

> Fellers back east they done a lot of talking,
> Some of them a-balking, some of them a-squawking,
> But with all of their figures and all their books,
> Them boys didn't know their Royal Chinooks.
> (Salmons . . . that's a) Good River.
> Needs some more (a couple more dozen) big (power) dams
> on (scattered up and down) it. (Keepin' folks busy.)

Politicians did not understand the need for more dams—they did not
know "their Royal Chinooks"—but Guthrie, as champion of the worker
and public control over electricity, contested those who would limit the
growth of the BPA and stop the federally sponsored damming of the river.
Little did conservatives know that the federal subsidy would eventually
provide their businesses with electricity at a cost that remains, on average,
half that paid by other Americans. Nor did Guthrie know that the dams
he championed would threaten the "Royal Chinooks" and drive entire
salmon species into extinction.

Guthrie was a true believer in the concept of public control over natural resources. In a letter to "Eliz and Harold" Ambellan, he argues for the
BPA on the grounds that it will lead to "Public Ownership" through the
creation of "Peoples Utility Districts" (1941). "The main job," he argued,
"is to force the private owned concerns to sell out to the government."

Guthrie and the BPA won the day in their argument for more dams,
but their fight for public control was much less successful. Today, vested
private interests argue for the maintenance of those same dams, having
benefited from their bounty. Many if not most in eastern Washington and
rural Oregon seem to support that position. In other words, many of the
children of the farmers and workers whom Guthrie championed have
since allied themselves with the large landowners, private utilities, and
conservative politicians against the scientists, environmental activists,
and urban liberals who have called for dismantling the dams. Meanwhile,

the dams have decimated fish populations and greatly degraded the environment Guthrie celebrated in song.

There are only a few indications that Guthrie stopped to question the dams or other technological marvels until the atom bomb was unleashed on Japan. After that horrendous milestone, he changed his tune. His mostly unpublished atom bomb songs demonstrate a shift away from chronicling and lauding technological change toward explicit critique of the dangers it presented. He was well ahead of his time in doing so. When it came to BPA's hydrological projects, however, Guthrie had much less foresight.

Musical Lessons for All the "Greenies"
Who "Hate Hydroelectric Projects"

The polysemic power of folk music sometimes allows folk songs to outlive their original purpose, to find new meaning in new eras. That power exists in much of Guthrie's work, one of his greatest strengths as a writer, as we saw in the case of "This Land Is Your Land" in Chapter 2. Unfortunately, most of his BPA songs are too directly connected to the dam projects to transcend their time. The unusually explicit policy support Guthrie lent to the BPA is now used to counter progressive change along the river. In an article for *Forbes* entitled "Cruising with Woody Guthrie," Lawrence Minard throws Guthrie's lyrics at the "greenies" who "hate hydroelectric projects" (1992, 192–193). Much like the BPA itself, Guthrie's music has been appropriated all too easily for the conservative cause.

As was discussed in the previous chapter, even a song like "The Land Is Your Land" can be appropriated for conservative purposes—all one needs to do is delete the final verses. The Columbia songs, with their explicit appeal for a very specific policy, illustrate one of the great dangers of art for the sake of propaganda. Propaganda presents a deceptively clear articulation of specific policies to universal truths. And so, in the *Forbes* article, Guthrie becomes the unwitting ally of the Right as Minard argues against river reclamation and in favor of family houseboat vacations on the river-turned-reservoir, vacations that require "seven or eight gallons [of gasoline] per hour of cruising time" (1992, 193).

Countering Minard's use of the songs, teacher and musician Peter DuBois demonstrates how Guthrie's work can be remade to work for, not against, the river. DuBois, having made a trip down the Columbia along with 30 other teachers, explains: "Woody did not foresee . . . that the Coulee Dam would cut off one-third of the River's salmon spawning grounds and overnight make the mighty Canadian spring Chinook salmon extinct"

(2006, 1). DuBois has updated several of the songs in order to present a more critical understanding of the river, the fish, and the people most directly impacted by the BPA projects:

> I used Woody's song *Ramblin' Blues* to honor the Native people who lived off runs of up to 10 million adult salmon. This century's decline in wild salmon runs mirrors the plight of the Salmon Nations as they were moved onto reservations and sacred fishing grounds were flooded by reservoirs. Kettle Falls, the second largest gathering area for tribes after Celilo Falls, was washed away by Lake Roosevelt when the Grand Coulee Dam was built. (Ibid.)

DuBois turns "Pastures of Plenty" into a protest against oversubscribed water rights on the Columbia and the exposure of migrant workers to dangerous pesticides and chemicals from the polluted river (ibid., 3). "The Biggest Thing That Man Has Ever Done" is updated to include Hanford's dumping of radioactive waste into the watershed (ibid., 2), and "Roll On, Columbia" gets the following treatment: "Now the river's not a river at all / It's slack water lakes formed by concrete walls" (ibid.).

As DuBois illustrates, one has to dramatically rewrite the pro-dam songs to turn them into anthems for breaching dams. These were not the concerns of Guthrie's time. He had plenty to say about worker's lives, the travails of migrants, and the excesses of power, but little of value to tell us about stewardship of the environment. However, DuBois demonstrates that Guthrie's vivid descriptions of the land can still be put to good use.

John Gold notes that Guthrie is most often thought of as a folklorist and radical minstrel. He argues for the adoption of a third category to explain Guthrie's musicianship: social documentarian (1998). Gold makes an excellent point. Thinking of Guthrie's music solely as a form of strategic communication undervalues his role as a musical observer and documentarian.

I have already alluded to a fourth category: propagandist. This is not to denigrate Guthrie's Columbia songs: the word "propaganda" is not necessarily pejorative. People tend to assume that propaganda is the lie others tell. Communication is not that simple. Propaganda tends to consist of selective truths, not outright lies, arguments for an assumed good crafted out of axiom and fact. Propaganda is often an act of narrative omission rather than an outright lie. As the saying goes, "Two half truths can add up to one big lie." Polysemic, contradictory, and subversive realities are expunged from propaganda. Propaganda is anathema to art, but it is the soul of politics. There is little doubt that when it came to his BPA work, Guthrie was both documentarian and propagandist. In much of his other music, he was more of an artist.

Few question the use of propaganda in opposition to terror and oppression. Many engage in propaganda without recognizing it, conveniently adopting an organizational ideology as their own. Subtle daily disciplines reinforce our obedience to institutional mandates and propaganda. Others are more self-reflexive in their production of propaganda, deliberately occluding complexity for the sake of what they believe to be a greater good or goal: strategic essentialism. Guthrie seems to have been among the latter: a selective and conscious propagandist who refused simply to sell out to the highest bidder, he chose an institution, the BPA, that was aligned with his own beliefs as a political artist. Guthrie would make the same choice during World War II, putting aside his beef with Uncle Sam, the rich, and imperialism to fight what he saw as a noble war. Many participate in propaganda, but only a select few, like Guthrie, do so in such a conscious and purposeful fashion.

Yet musical propagandist was an uneasy role for Guthrie. It is doubtful that his thoughts on the dam project paralleled the BPA's as closely as his Columbia River songs would indicate. Throughout his life, Guthrie was constantly in trouble for failing to serve as a company man, whether the company in question was the Communist party or one of the singing groups he temporarily participated in. He got himself fired on New Year's Day, 1941, from a show called "Pipe Smoking Time" for refusing to comply with the demands of the Model Tobacco Company. When Guthrie engaged in propaganda, it was on his own terms. Still, it is fair to distinguish the propagandistic songs of the Columbia cycle from Guthrie's other work. In reference to "Roll On, Columbia," Lance Morrow and Nathan Thornburgh note: "Instead of his usual hobo's plainsong, Guthrie broke into an anthem that might have been written by the National Association of Manufacturers" (2002, 78).

We can learn from this example as we make more modest artistic interventions into environmental debates. In an essay entitled "The Historical Roots of Our Ecological Crisis," Lynn White Jr. advises: "Unless we think about fundamentals, our specific measures may produce new backlashes more serious than those they are designed to remedy" (1996, 5).

History is useful for thinking through "fundamentals" and proceeding with humility. Consider the images of electrical towers in the logos, pictures, and documentary films of the late Depression era—symbols of progress that clearly held great aesthetic value, not to mention ideological power. As unimaginable as it is to us today, people viewed the towers as beautiful. Today environmentalists drive through southern Minnesota and northern Iowa with a similar sense of pride in the giant wind turbines dotting the fields. One can imagine our grandchildren one day cursing us for having crowded the horizon with them. I am all for wind power, but the point is that anything we do requires humble recognition that our solutions are more likely to fail than to succeed. One generation's moral triumph is often the next generation's ethical indictment.

Hero worship fails as scholarship and ultimately diminishes the complex humanity of the subject. Unquestioned devotion is often shown to musicians like Woody Guthrie, artists like Frida Kahlo, and others who, in their own time, refused to accept the sorts of reductive identities we now foist upon them. All artists occupy prior archetypes, and Woody Guthrie was no different. He had to negotiate the demands of his art, audience, and heart while trying to make a living.

What Would Woody Do?

"If we hired Woody Guthrie today, we'd have him singing about saving salmon and conserving energy instead of using him to sell power," argues Bill Murlin, a recently retired BPA administrator who collected Guthrie's 1941 song sheets and records (quoted by Timothy Egan, in Carriker 2001, 36). Stephen Kahn, Guthrie's BPA boss, went through the sort of transformation Murlin describes. Having learned the damage dams can do, Kahn supported a political candidate in Idaho who wanted to save Hells Canyon from the same fate as the Columbia River Gorge. I was fortunate enough to interview Kahn on the phone in July 2006. Mr. Kahn, age 96, was living in Carmel, California, and incredibly sharp. In later correspondence (letter to author, 2006), he enclosed a lyrical tribute to Woody that he had written in 2005. The poem, "This Land Was Your Land," warned that land was being lost to private interests and poor environmental stewardship.

Kahn recognized Guthrie as "something of a poet." "He'd written a lot of junk," he said of Guthrie's BPA songs, "but every once in a while you get something that gets to you" (interview, 2006). Comparing Guthrie with *The Columbia*'s director, Kahn said that von Fritsch "had the talent, but not the heart," whereas "Woody had both the talent and the heart." Von Fritsch went on to direct a film for the White House and eventually accepted a position making "March of Time" newsreels, but Guthrie "never lost the indomitable spirit of rebellion" (ibid.). Perhaps there is no higher praise for an artist.

Kahn continued to see promise in the public ownership model. He argued that "even though ultimately they had environmental consequences we may not like," the BPA and PUDs presented an ownership "model we might want to consider again" rather than relying on "the market" for everything. Perhaps Guthrie would have made the same assessment. We will never know, and ultimately it does not matter. The truth is, we will never know what Woody would do, and we do not want to commit "the sin of anachronism" by projecting our own values onto past heroes (Morrow and Thornburgh 2002, 78). In fact, Guthrie is more myth than man in the contemporary consciousness. Myths serve their purpose, but it is people who make music. Guthrie was a man who made music, a brave act in any context. He took the additional step of making music for social aims. The lyrics and other documents he left behind provide us with a sketch of a man who used his art to teach, persuade, and entertain. Guthrie also used his music to think through the problems of his day. The fact that some of his thinking was conditioned by employment does not make him less heroic; it simply shows us that he was human.

To say that Guthrie redefined the region through music is inaccurate on two counts. First, as has been made clear, the composer's original intentions mattered less than how other people and institutions selectively employed the songs. As songs like "Roll On, Columbia" achieved official state sanction, they became something other than what Guthrie or his BPA bosses originally intended. The second, more important point is that no single singer or song represents an entire region. Others compete to be heard. For example, the Nez Perce create a very different soundscape in the Columbia watershed than does Guthrie's Columbia River repertoire. Bernie Krause spent many years among the Nez Perce of central Washington, listening to and recording the music of the region (2001). The Nez Perce's musical Columbia is far different from Woody Guthrie's— less itinerant, less triumphant, and more deeply infused with a sense of daily life in situ. Same place, different soundscape.

An Old Left icon advocated the construction of dams that the current Left struggles to dismantle. There is a lesson in there somewhere. Is it one of humility? That even the best of us make mistakes? That times change? That we should constantly be aware of sponsorship? That we should be wary of transforming politicized art into propaganda?

What is perhaps most remarkable about the BPA case is that it shows a very human Guthrie struggling to find a working balance between art and propaganda, between institutional efficacy and individual agency, while remaining true to his core beliefs. Music for Guthrie was not just a personal passion or commodity, but rather a sacred act with the potential to transform the world. That was equally true for Guthrie's protégé, Pete Seeger, whose musical movement to clean up the Hudson River provides a much more hopeful example.

Pete Seeger's Hudson

Seeger launched the Hudson River experiment after reading William Verplanck and Moses Wakeman Collyer's *The Sloops of the Hudson* (1908). He came up with the idea of building a modern replica of the old sloops, a visible and working reminder that the Hudson had once been a beautiful river, and could become one again. The Scenic Hudson Group, the Hudson River Fisherman's Association, and other activists had already banded together to clean up the polluted river and watershed. The "Riverkeeper" program they started spread across the country and remains one of the most active river stewardship organizations today (riverkeeper.org). A member of the Hudson Scenic Board of Directors liked Seeger's concept and suggested a kickoff concert to raise funds for the new sloop.

For publicity reasons, the wider coalition was wary of being directly connected to Seeger, and many did not want a fundraising concert involving the controversial singer. However, they too liked the sloop idea, and a majority of members voted to support the concert. The first concert was held in 1966: 160 people showed up, and $160 was raised (Forbes 2004, 517). The same group has hosted a yearly concert ever since, netting, on average, about $50,000 for the cause, largely through the sale of merchandise.

The original $160 was hardly enough to build a sloop, but the stalwarts and mainstays were all there at that first concert, excited and ready to build something bigger. One never knows whether a small audience is the beginning, middle, or end of something. In hindsight, we can say that the first Clearwater Concert was the start of a very big thing. Three years later, the *Clearwater* was sailing the river and changing minds, behaviors, laws, and policies.

As an indicator of just how much things have changed since the 1960s, the boat's name was at first considered controversial, even among environmental activists. Many preferred a less confrontational name, like *Heritage. Clearwater* won by a slim margin of votes, mainly supplied by younger members.

The first hurdle was coming up with the capital to build the sloop; the next was drumming up enough business to keep it afloat, mainly through school excursions and tour groups. The program became so successful that another sloop was added: the *Woody Guthrie.* Forty years later people swim in the Hudson Highlands section of the river. That would have been unimaginable when Seeger and his friends started their long campaign. Generations of musicians have been influenced by Seeger's Hudson River project, including Sharon Abreu, who performed at the Turtleback Mountain event featured in Chapter 1. I asked Sharon to write about her origins as an environmental artist and educator:

> I became an environmental educator because of a fun festival that had good music. Going to that festival really changed my life. I was studying classical singing in New York City when I attended a Pumpkin Festival in the West Village sponsored by the Hudson River Sloop Clearwater environmental group. It was a really fun event. They had a half-price membership offer so I joined. I was invited to a meeting in lower Manhattan at which I started learning about my drinking water, the history of the Hudson River, just a few blocks from the apartment where I lived, and the connection between politics, the environment, and human health and well-being. I got inspired to use my voice and songwriting for environmental education, and I continued learning about more environmental issues, like deforestation and climate change. (Email to author, 2011)

Another Orcas Island folk artist, Carolyn Cruso, who is featured in Chapter 4, sailed the *Clearwater* as a youth, an experience that had a strong influence on her views toward nature and music alike.

At the start of the Hudson River effort it would have been difficult to imagine the influence Seeger's project would eventually have on the watershed, water policy, activists, and artists involved. Equally unimaginable would be the influence of *God Bless the Grass* (1966), an album Seeger made in collaboration with Malvina Reynolds. Folk was not yet the environmentally tinged genre we think of today. Seeger and Reynolds were two of the first folk singers to make the somewhat controversial move into environmental themes.

The traditional Left criticized Seeger's environmental turn, as did many young, rock-oriented leftists who were coming of age in the 1960s (Ingram 2008). The Old Left felt that Seeger had abandoned labor-centered politics, a folk music mainstay that had seen them through the dark days of the fifties. On the other side of the generational divide, some New Left youths viewed *God Bless the Grass* as an example of "artistic conservatism" in an age that demanded new approaches, and new music. As Ingram explains, Bob Dylan's "going electric" was much more than a signal of generational shift; it represented the exhaustion of traditional folk sensibilities as young people moved away from proletarian collectivism and toward New Left artistic and cultural interests. Unfortunately, critics from the Old and New Left alike missed the fact that Seeger and Reynolds were actually ahead of the curve, not behind it. Seeger's inclusion of environmental matters was a necessary corrective to traditional progressive politics and a reminder to the New Left that political action is often most effective when connected to place.

Although *God Bless the Grass* may have lacked the sonic originality younger audiences sought in the mid-sixties, Ingram hears echoes of Seeger's environmental music in the songs of contemporary "Americana" artists like David Rovics. He argues that Seeger's Clearwater project did much to set the tone for subsequent environmental movements, while Seeger's environmental art and advocacy greatly influenced subsequent developments in folk music. Yet, Seeger's turn to environmental politics represented something of a lost opportunity for musicians and movements alike in the mid-sixties. The Left tended to see environmentalism as a liberal cause, and one much less urgent than stopping the Vietnam war. Clearly, Guthrie's and Seeger's river music and movements were oceans apart. The explanation is partly a matter of era: few musicians or activists were focused on environmental issues before World War II. The fact that Guthrie wrote and sang in the shadow of the Great Depression somewhat dictated his emphasis on labor politics. Seeger was ahead of his time in emphasizing environmental preservation in the mid-sixties. For Guthrie to incorporate environmentalism into his songwriting during the forties would have been practically unthinkable.

Guthrie's times were not completely unlike the current period. In the shadow of the worst economic downturn since the Depression, environmental concerns have again taken a back seat to worries about jobs, prosperity, and economic growth. Rather than face the unsustainability of a high-growth economy, many Americans view environmental concerns as antithetical to economic progress. Difficult decisions about high-consumption economies and ecologies are put off.

Unfortunately, any system bereft of regulatory feedback will eventually destroy itself. The warning signs of recession are interpreted ideologically, as evidence that we need to forget about ecology for now and focus on producing more things, faster. In the strange world we inhabit, that is considered a "conservative" economic philosophy.

Seeger bucked both liberal and conservative tendencies in the sixties by focusing on environmental issues. His radical refusal to accept institutional sponsorship guaranteed Seeger the artistic freedom to ignore dominant trends. Perhaps he learned from Guthrie's example. Seeger is fond of quoting an Arabic proverb about the king who hires a poet so that he can cut out his tongue (Forbes 2004, 516). Thanks to his radical sense of independence from institutional influences, Seeger played a central role in bringing environmental concerns into American popular music. Meanwhile, the Hudson River, once one of the most polluted in the nation, has become a more positive model of river stewardship than the Columbia. Seeger's musical activism played an important role in making the Hudson River Valley what it is today. The closer we get to actual ecosystems and locales, the easier it is to see how music works in relation to place and how it functions in relation to cultural ecologies (e.g., political ideologies, institutions, movements) and material ecosystems (e.g., hydrological cycling, resource management, environmental regulation).

Music's "Modern Muir"

Classical composer John Luther Adams is one of the best examples of musicianship related to bioregion. Although neither rock nor folk, his music is worth examining in this comparative chapter. Many of the dynamics identified above are illustrated in Adams's work: the complexities of sponsorship, the ways in which a composer's experiences within a region influence musical compositions about that region, and the importance of choosing performance contexts where creation can be translated into action. Those elements transcend genre or, perhaps, demonstrate that "environmental music" is a coherent subgenre in and of itself.

On the other hand, there is nothing truly equivalent in rock and folk to Adams's environmental compositions. No well-known, critically acclaimed composers in rock, or even folk, have intentionally and almost exclusively focused on environmental questions. Popular music disfavors intense exploration of singular themes outside rock's genre staples: romance, parties, and intoxication. All the more reason to study the work of classical composers like Adams; there is much to learn from musicians who have advanced environmentally themed music, regardless of genre, style, or tradition.

Adams initially moved to Alaska in the 1970s to explore and advocate for preservation of the Arctic Wildlife Refuge. Unlike many musicians, he has never been afraid to marry art and activism. A January 2011 entry on his website (johnlutheradams.com) reads:

The disaster in the Gulf of Mexico is a call for all of us to search our souls about the way we live, and to demand that our elected officials take real action to fight climate change and move our economy to sustainable energy sources.

Nor has Adams's environmental activism hampered his reputation in the art music world. *Earth and the Great Weather* (1993) and *In the White Silence* (1998) were both critical successes. Both are remarkable collaborations with indigenous artists, environmental organizations, and others with a stake in the Alaskan environment (Feisst 2010).

In *The Place Where You Go to Listen* (2009), Adams opens a window into the creative process through which an artist is informed by the natural world. For the Museum of the North in Fairbanks, Alaska, he created a sound-and-light exhibit that encourages listeners and viewers to form their own interpretations, drawing on their personal relationship with the local environment. He placed his work in a performance context where the intersubjective relationship between artist and environment could more fully envelop and involve the audience. Tyler Kinnear describes how Adams's installation encourages environmental contemplation and even action (2010,13):

Adams's installation not only creates a sense of place through its sonic properties, but also puts forth a gesture of environmental advocacy. Through the translation of geophysical data into music, the composer invites listeners to reawaken to the geophysical activities around them, paying closer attention to the "voices" (heard and unheard) of nature. *The Place* may be viewed in light of a growing cultural awareness of the relationship between humans and the environment. This is perhaps influenced most strongly by concerns over climate change.

By placing his music in a local museum, Adams makes it more immediately relevant to the lives of the people who develop, destroy, or sustain the Alaskan environment. An evocative and subtle play of lights completes the musical installation encouraging environmental contemplation. In other words, Adams interpellates the listener as an active environmental agent, rather than telling them what to think or do.

In his journal entry for May 24, 2004, published in *The Place Where You Go to Listen: In Search of an Ecology of Music* (2009), Adams conveys a sense of how difficult it is to find musical models, given the scarcity of environmental music in the West:

There are few musical models for my current work, few influences that seem directly pertinent. Most of my influences have long been assimilated into my music. I'm on my own now. Most of the time I feel as though I'm working (as Richard Serra says) from out of my previous work.

From time to time I've turned to Native cultures for inspiration. In recent years I've also turned to visual art, searching for musical equivalents of color and texture, space and presence. But it seems that, sooner or later, everything leads me back to nature as my primary source. Nature is geography and geology. Nature is biology and ecology. Nature is physics. More specifically for a composer, nature is acoustics—the physics of sound. Nature is inexhaustible. (2009, 21)

A critic might recognize a frontier narrative in Adams's journal entry—not to mention discourses of consumption (nature as musical use-value) and perhaps appropriation of "Native cultures." However, those elements make Adams's work all the more compelling. It is easy to see his struggle as our own. Each of us wants to be in nature, to use nature, while preserving it at the same time. A wilderness inhabited is no longer wilderness. Contemporary composers cannot escape that environmental conundrum, nor can bird watchers, conservationists, developers, ecotourists, or anyone else who wants to be in, use, and preserve natural environments at the same time. Adams is artfully struggling through ecological conundrums, rather than avoiding them in the pastoral music tradition.

Adams believes that museum visitors have made his installation "their own" (2009, 141). It is reasonable to assume that those who visit the museum will be moved to listen to, experience, and appreciate the spectacular environment of Alaska in new ways. One would hope that such awareness might translate into sustainable lifeways, but as in all things musical, it is mostly an act of faith. Sabine Feisst's forthcoming ecomusicological study of Adams's work promises to greatly advance our understanding of Adams, the "John Muir of Music" (Feisst 2010), as will Tyler Kinnear's forthcoming dissertation on the topic (2010).

Listening to Nature

In a chapter about bioregions, it seems appropriate to deal with the question of whether animals make music. How we answer that question might influence how we listen to the life around us and manage ecosystems. "Nature produces noises, not musical sounds," Claude Levi-Strauss argued (quoted in J. L. Adams 2009, 114). Levi-Strauss was weighing in on a debate "over the presence and extent of music-making in the wider animal kingdom" (Roper 2007, 59). That debate continues. Some draw a strict line between human musicality and the relatively limited, naturally selected vocalizations of animals. For example, Ian Cross argues that music is intrinsically human: "Musics are those temporally patterned human activities, individual and social, that involve the production and perception of sound and have no evident and immediate efficacy or fixed consensual reference" (2001, 98).

The discussion parallels the anthropological debate over whether nonhuman primates have "culture." I would argue that they do not. Take language: the protolinguistic skills of nonhuman primates are by no means synonymous with human language, let alone indicative of the level of symbolic logic required for the development of culture. Nor are the beautiful soundworks of birds and whales the same thing as the human, cultural phenomena we call music (Sacks 2007, x). Birds and whales are among many creatures that make "organized sound," and perhaps are, therefore, also music makers. However, their music is to ours what the signing of Koko the gorilla is to human language.

It is unclear which is more anthropocentric: to appreciate other species for how well they represent human-like characteristics or to appreciate them for their own distinct qualities? Does thinking of birdsong as music advance or inhibit our understanding of the human phenomenon of music? Probably a bit of both.

Among those arguing for animal musicality is Emma Rose Roper, whose study of the Australian magpie presents compelling evidence of sonic improvisation, invention, and melodic imitation (2007, 72). David Rothenberg agrees, finding music in birdsong (2005) as well as whale communication (2008). A clarinetist and electronic musician, Rothenberg works with natural soundscapes and animal sounds to produce musical pieces, letting whalesong and birdsong create the structures around which his music takes form.

In a sense, much of environmental musicianship represents a tamed, anthropomorphic nature that serves human musical interests. Yet anthropomorphizing is inevitable, and so is environmental management. Human groups actively manage their environments no matter who they are or where they live. Hunting and gathering bands burn prairies to make them more productive; they create elaborate rituals and myths to regulate food supplies. Our populations and prosthetics have advanced and multiplied, but the truth is that all humans modify their environments and always have. From !Kung hunters stalking game to astronauts practicing hydroponic gardening, human beings survive by intentionally and radically managing their surroundings. White reminds us: "For 6 millennia, at least, the banks of the lower Nile have been a human artifact rather than the swampy jungle which nature, apart from man, would have made it" (1996, 3). The same can be said of every environment on Earth. The traces of human interventions are everywhere. Meanwhile, our closest relatives, the other great apes in the family Hominidae, remain restricted to specific biomes and habitats, those in which they first evolved, environments for which they are more specifically adapted. Conversely, humans evolved the biological prerequisites for culture, allowing for creative adaptation to virtually all known biomes. Clearly, the ability to produce and interpret music is part of that bio-cultural endowment. We are just beginning to understand the connections between music, human evolution, and culture (Cross 2001; Levitin 2006; Sacks, 2007; McDermott 2008).

Therefore, the question is not whether humans have or have not managed a given environment, but how and to what degree (Johnson and Earle 2000; Diamond 2005). For example, although both are the result of carbon emissions, global climate change is potentially much worse than the more localized smog people experienced in thirteenth-century London (White 1996, 5). So too, different anthropogenic ecosystems produce dramatically different soundscapes. As is evidenced through the cases provided above, how we make music is related to how we interact with the rest of the living world. As in all things ecological, it is not a matter of simple, linear cause and effect, but rather complex, reciprocal, and systemic relationships among social, cultural, and material factors. In other words, the most important question is not "Do birds and whales make music?" but, rather, how does our music relate to theirs? Adams's compositions artfully explore that question, as do those of David Rothenberg (2005, 2008).

Cloud Cult and Music at the Mississippi River Headwaters

Like Seeger's New York State and Guthrie's Pacific Northwest, Minnesota is bisected by a great river. The state gains its sense of regional identity in part from being the source of the Mississippi River. However, America's main artery has been abused for over a century—put to work, polluted, and then neglected. Meanwhile, musicians have sung its praises, from "Ol' Man River" (1927, 1941) to "Proud Mary" (1968, 1989). Ferde Grofé's *Mississippi River Suite* (1947) is among the best-known tributes.

Although Grofé created his *Grand Canyon Suite* (1932) as a moving call for preservation, no such work was done with his *Mississippi River Suite*. Perhaps that is because Grofé had deeper connections to the Grand Canyon and less reverence for America's working river.

In an insightful essay about Grofé's masterwork, Brooks Toliver (2004) explains how the *Grand Canyon Suite* (1932), composed in the picturesque tradition, assisted in the movement to preserve the Grand Canyon. Preservationist art, especially the "aesthetic of the picturesque," argues Toliver, "offered an environmentally sensitive way of appreciating nature" and "allowed Americans a means of 'acting out' the conquering of wilderness without acting out policies that would ensure its disappearance" (2004, 339). Toliver goes on to show how the *Grand Canyon Suite* also retains "remnants of the ideology it opposes" by evoking a frontier mentality that was, and is, about the conquest and control of nature (ibid., 338). Nevertheless, Grofé's Grand Canyon is infinitely more majestic and natural than the domesticated river of the *Mississippi River Suite*.

Maybe the difference is a matter of geography. The Grand Canyon is more comprehensible geographically. It fits into the picturesque frame more easily than the meandering and massive Mississippi River. The Grand Canyon is a more specific location, more encompassing and definitive than a river. Rivers are often invoked in poetry and song to represent the passage of time, fleeting, quickly moving through space, evading holistic representation. Conversely, dramatic landscapes like the Grand Canyon are represented as timeless entities, infinitely fixed in past, present, and future. To treat them otherwise is viewed as an abomination against nature. Grofé's *Mississippi River Suite* takes the listener from the "Father of Waters" (first movement) to "Mardi Gras" (fourth movement). It is like a family member or an old friend, part of the human landscape. Like the *Hudson River Suite* (1955), Grofé's tour starts with timeless nature but ends in a more urban, managed, human world. Perhaps less populated sites like the Grand Canyon represent the pastoralists' hope for maintaining at least a few relatively untouched places, to remind us what much of this land once looked and sounded like (Hempton 2009).

Denise Von Glahn provides further clues to explain the dramatic difference in tone between Grofé's *Grand Canyon Suite* (1932) and his *Mississippi River Suite* (1947). One clue might be found in the *Hudson River Suite* (1955). Originally, the *Hudson River Suite* was similar to the *Grand Canyon Suite* in that it largely ignored human presence. There was little in the work to suggest a human soundscape along the river. However, at the request of his sponsors, Grofé added an ending that would capture "the din of New York" (Von Glahn 2003, 211).

Similarly, after accepting a commission from Robert Moses and the New York State Power Authority in 1961, Grofé produced the *Niagara Falls Suite*. In the fourth movement, "Power of Niagara" (1961), he painted a musical picture of the great falls as one might actually experience them, replete with "sirens, factory whistles, and all the jarring, clanking noises that might be associated with modern, industrial America" (Von Glahn 2003, 214). The final movement "recognized the utter capitulation of nature to mankind at Niagara." "The music may not be his most appealing," writes Von Glahn (ibid.), "but it is perhaps his most honest."

It is not clear to what extent "Power of Niagara" reflects the views of the artist or his sponsor (ibid., 211). What's more, the lack of lyrical content makes symphonic composition less denotative in nature than popular song, providing fewer explicit clues as to the composer's intentions. The difference between the suites might be a result of sponsorship, how Grofé felt about each geographic feature, or a reflection of differing levels of human presence at the Grand Canyon (little), Mississippi River (much more), Hudson River (relatively bucolic until it touches Manhattan), and Niagara Falls (a noisy cacophony). In other words, in addition to asking how and why Grofé crafted the compositions in the way that he did—the composer's intent—we can examine the creative agency of the places themselves.

The documentary *Mississippi, River of Song* takes the viewer on a trip that is reminiscent of Grofé's *Mississippi River Suite* (Filmmakers Collaborative et al. 1998). Narrated by Ani DiFranco, the tour begins in Minnesota with Ojibwa drummers, Scandinavian polka bands, and punk rockers, among others. It ends three hours later in the jazz culture of New Orleans. The documentary reminds viewers that there are still regional differences in America, differences reflected and reproduced through music. Wonderful as it is, however, *Mississippi, River of Song* presents a problem for ecomusicologists. Throughout the film's musical tour, there is no mention of the river's environmental health. The river is used for transportation and commerce, and as a symbolic means of musical identification, but the river itself, as an ecosystem and entity, seems not to matter. In *Mississippi, River of Song*, the river is not a real, material entity facing severe threats to its biodiversity and water quality, it is a cultural metaphor and transportation corridor serving human needs. Are environmental problems ephemeral from a musical perspective? Too mundane for music?

There were many such threats a decade ago when the film was made, including pollution caused by urban and agricultural runoff. New ones have come along since, including invasive species like the "flying" silver carp, *Hypophthalmichthys molitrix*, a huge fish that crowds out native species and radically alters the ecosystem. Likewise, Ol' Man River carries an increasing range of excreted human medicines and chemicals that wastewater cleaning processes cannot filter out, including endocrine disruptors that impede fish and reptile reproduction.

For much of the twentieth century, people were willing to do just about everything to the Mississippi River but protect it. So far, music has reflected that tendency, rather than helping us to sustain life in and along the river. Yet, as environmentalists, scientists, and others seek to restore and sustain the river and watershed, many of the same songs are becoming useful pedagogically and organizationally, resonating with listeners in a way that dry lectures on endocrine disruptors or hydrological cycling simply cannot. As a deeply polysemic, intertextual, and emotional phenomenon, music effectively bolsters whatever medium and movement it is performed within, as was demonstrated above in DuBois's creative use of Guthrie's Columbia River songs (2006). Along the Mississippi River as well, songs that once celebrated the river's human exploration, exploitation, and neglect are now serving as a soundtrack for environmental restoration.

To return briefly to a point raised in Chapter 2, *Mississippi, River of Song* demonstrates how closely rock and pop are linked to the urban environment. Rock and pop are featured during the film tour's city dockings. The film reflects how every major American city, whether along the Mississippi River or elsewhere, is identified with a regionalized rock "sound," such as the Austin sound (alt Americana rock), the Athens sound (new wave), the Seattle sound (grunge), the Minneapolis sound (punk and Prince), and the Miami sound (Latin pop, Curtis and Rose 1994)—although other cities are defined more by rhythm and blues, like Detroit (Motown), jazz, as in the case of New Orleans, or hip-hop, as is now the case for Brooklyn. Sounds define not only cities but also moments in time. Each city and sound experiences brief periods of chart-topping national fame, a series of sound explosions that continue to reverberate as part of a city's identity, long after the music reaches its national zenith.

Southern rock is perhaps the closest we get to rock regionalism. As Richard Butler demonstrates in "The Geography of Rock: 1954–1970," rock's spatial identifications exist mainly at a subregional level, the city (1994). Rock is less likely to define entire bioregions; it is rare for an entire region to be closely identified with a singular rock style. Even when it tries to take on the more pastoralist impulse of environmental folk or classical music, rock tends to make a mess of things. Rock festivals like

Woodstock call forth images of muddied fields, garbage, and Dionysian disregard for the local environment. In other words, rock turns everything it touches into the city. Therefore, rock is not the type of music one associates with a larger bioregion. That might be changing. For example, Cloud Cult is a popular rock band with strong environmental connections. The band is from a rural area and regionally identified with the Upper Midwest as a whole.

As is true of many enterprises in the digital age, it is hard to know whether to refer to Cloud Cult in the singular or plural. The band began in 1995 as a solo project created by Craig Minowa. As a student of environmental science, Minowa quite naturally melded his two passions into Cloud Cult. Discontented with traditional look-at-me rock concerts, he recruited musicians and painters to expand his act beyond traditional rock theatrics. At the end of each set, paintings created on stage are auctioned off to the audience. The art provides tangible connections to Cloud Cult beyond the typical "merch," like T-shirts, CDs, and bumper stickers. Environmental organizations are encouraged to set up tables and distribute information at shows.

Minowa created Earthology Records, one of the first labels designed to reduce rock's impact on the planet. From reduced and recycled packaging to sustainable energy sources, Earthology was engineered to integrate message and medium. Cloud Cult's base of operation is an organic farm powered by solar and geothermal energy, built largely out of reclaimed wood and recycled plastics.

While grieving for the death of his son in 2002, Minowa returned to songwriting, experiencing his most painful and prolific period as a composer. Cloud Cult released *Light Chasers*, their seventh album, in 2010. During the release tour the band played sold-out shows at Minneapolis's First Avenue and throughout the country. In 1995 Minowa had a hard time imagining that his music would matter to so many people, but it is a concept whose time has come.

I was fortunate enough to catch a Cloud Cult show in the spring of 2010. Cloud Cult appears to be pulling together two unlikely audiences: rockers and ravers. Just as hip-hop managed to marry rap, pop, punk, and metal, Cloud Cult is creating an interesting mélange of ambient rock with rave inflections and more than a little classical influence. That hybridity is reflected in its eclectic yet very devoted following. Genre classifications are important to audiences, critics, music journalists, and scholars, but artists seem to be at their most creative in the margins and borders between genres. Although this indeterminate quality makes bands like Cloud Cult hard to "place" for booking agents, clubs, marketers, and music distributors, artistically it works well. Cloud Cult is among the bands that many now refer to as "post-rock."

I asked Minowa how his music relates to place, specifically northern Minnesota—a leading question, but one that Cloud Cult's founder has thought about a lot. "Writing in rural locations is perfect for the type of music we do," he answered. "The world slows down a lot, which allows you to catch up with your own ghosts and thoughts." He added, "The inspiration of the stars and of the natural universe is a big part of what makes us tick." As much as some ecocritics would like to kill off pastoralism and replace it with something else, Thoreau's tradition of rural contemplation is a deep and meaningful part of American culture. As Cloud Cult and previous examples show, it leads to some of the most interesting environmental music.

Cloud Cult is very different from the "eco-friendly" rockers on *Rolling Stone*'s list (Chapter 1). Ecological themes are infused throughout Cloud Cult's musical repertoire. Minowa, however, has moved from explicit attention to ecological problems toward more general environmental themes: "I used to write directly about the environmental problems around us, but I found it to be ineffective." This mirrored what local musicians told Desdamona Racheli and me during an interview-based field project (2009). Topical pop often fails to sit well with local audiences. "People felt like they were being preached to," explained Minowa. "I think the better alternative for me is to work on getting people in touch with their souls. I think when we are balanced on the inside, it's natural for us to live our external lives in more of a balance."

Yet Cloud Cult does a lot of work on the "outside" as well, creating community contexts where music can be translated into collective action. Earthology is a good example. Minowa characterized that endeavor as a model and prototype for others:

> At the time, there weren't any environmentally friendly CD-manufacturing companies, so I started Earthology to create a model for green CD production. I think that has been our best success to date, because over the years we worked closely with conventional CD-manufacturing companies to develop product lines that could be as green as ours but on a bigger and more economical scale. We don't do the replication anymore, because these companies are now doing it more affordably, but they still come to us for advice.

As an illustration of Minowa's point, I was struck by the ways in which one CD-printing executive spoke about his company's production process. Ron Barghini of the ADS Group gave me a tour of one of the largest printing factories in the Midwest. His company has made environmentally friendly packaging a priority. Although that might seem like a practical business decision—given threats from digital distribution—I got the sense that the management and staff at ADS were genuinely proud of having "greened" their operations. Environmental concerns were a central part of the factory tour, and it was quite clear that the spiel was not just rehearsed, but heartfelt.

Starting with pressure from bands like Cloud Cult and Guster, elements of the industry have responded. To a certain extent the move toward a more sustainable musical infrastructure has been driven by supply-side interests, especially pressure from bands. However, digital downloading will continue to threaten (from an industry perspective) or promise (from an ecological perspective) to make the biggest difference yet to popular music's business model.

Minowa's musical inspiration has changed over time: "I don't actually listen to a lot of contemporary music," he explained. "I'm the least hip person in our band, when it comes to knowing who is who in the modern world of rock stars." Judging from the small sample of songwriters I encountered during my fieldwork, Minowa's relative indifference to contemporary popular music seems to be fairly common. Whereas instrumentalists speak constantly about the famous musicians who inspire them, songwriters tend to be somewhat less interested in well-known musicians. Their influences tend to be more eclectic and idiosyncratic. They are as likely to find inspiration in literature, landscape, or sculpture as in each other's songs. "My influences tend to be philosophers and spiritual seeking authors," Minowa said. "I also listen to a lot of old-time music."

Songwriters are often more solitary than instrumentalists as well. While some bands write songs together, the more typical model is that songwriters craft words and charts (sheets with chords, melodies, and very basic arrangements) and record rough demos that bandmates can use to learn the basic "form" of a new song. Then the band gets involved creatively, adding their instrumental signatures. Composers of popular music rarely define full arrangements beforehand. While much of that is an ensemble process, the first bit, basic songwriting, is not. "I'm a solitary kind of person," explained Minowa. "I'm spending a lot of time with my family and with nature." He continued:

When it comes to music composition, I'm very particular about what I want to hear. It's very spiritual for me, and is a part of my soul's growth and learning process. I find a lot of answers in my personal life by listening to what comes out of the music. Since it's so personal, it loses personal value for me when I write as part of a group, and since I do it first and foremost as a spiritual learning tool, I feel it's more important for me to take the time to sit and wait for the answers to come, rather than work it out quickly as a group. But the music has a lot of layers in it, so when it comes time to perform it live, the full instrumentation can only be done by a large group. Still, the people I choose to work with on that level are also very spiritually centered, which makes the live show replicate the sacredness of what can sometimes be felt in the creation process.

As represented by Thoreau's solitary explorations of nature, there is a long tradition in America of seeking out solitude in the wilderness, escaping social distraction in order to gain more intimate immersion into a natural landscape, and then writing about it. That tradition is reflected in Cloud Cult's creative process.

The potential tension between the solo and ensemble processes explains why songwriters tend to "choose to work with" people who share their basic outlook. Bands that lack a core identification tend to break up quickly, especially if the songwriter is pushing messages with a specific topical or ideological bent. Cloud Cult's longevity appears to represent a healthy balance between individual inspiration, effective leadership, and collective buy-in.

Like many songwriters, Minowa prefers to have his music speak for itself. He was hesitant to share details about specific songs. When I asked him to explain the genesis of "Running with the Wolves" from *Light Chasers* (2010), he politely declined. Moving back toward more general themes, Minowa summarized his work as a whole:

I think music is a sacred ceremony and one of the languages of the soul. I think it allows us to communicate with each other on levels beyond talk. I think it also allows us to get in touch with deeper elements of the universe and listen to messages from that side. All of these communication benefits are an essential part of building true sustainability and community.

Ray Pratt argues that by "affectively empowering emotional changes, music promotes establishment of sustaining relations of community and subculture," conditions "that are fundamental to creation of an alternative public realm" (1994, 14). Cloud Cult's music has demonstrated a potential for creating more positive rock ecologies, an "alternative public realm" to more common rock models.

Cloud Cult is not the first band to establish musical communities oriented around sustainability, but it may be one of the most successful. The Grateful Dead, among others, founded and supported communes focused on sustainable land use. Most such experiments flashed and faded. Cloud Cult is less dramatic in its proclamations and perhaps more realistic in drawing environmental connections between the band, the land, and the local community. Theirs is a more modest, recognizable, transferable, and sustainable effort to live and perform together, based on free association. It is a very American model. By not reducing their musical efforts to homogenizing manifestos, Cloud Cult is much more in line with "eco-cosmopolitan environmentalism," a philosophy that encourages "individuals to think beyond the boundaries of their own cultures, ethnicities, or nations" in order to consider the needs of other communities and the health of the "more-than-human" world (Heise 2008, 60–61). That includes serious attention to place, whether in local contexts or conceptions of the "global biosphere" (ibid., 62). No easy task, but another reason why art is just as important as science in the struggle to create and maintain sustainable communities.

The story of Cloud Cult may not be the best way to end a chapter about regional identification. Cloud Cult's music does not yet color the popular imagination of the region in the way "Roll On, Columbia" has defined the Pacific Northwest, for example, or Seeger's music has impacted the Hudson River watershed. However, Cloud Cult is in the forefront of a movement to re-territorialize rock, in part through making music in, and about, place. That is something of a historical change for rock. The Beatles, apart from being British, had no strong anchor in the geographic imagination; they are identified with several places at the same time— Liverpool, London, India, New York, a little bit of everywhere. Cloud Cult is potentially re-placing rock, articulating it to specific forests, streams, and lakes. Having been inspired by and connected to a specific ecosystem in northern Minnesota, Cloud Cult's music has ecological resonance far beyond the region. Reggae, ranchera, and reggaeton have gained global appeal precisely because of specific local associations. Relatively placeless meta-genres like rock and pop may begin to find greater ecological relevance when generated in specific environmental contexts as well.

In truth, it is hard to match the earlier Columbia or Hudson River examples, especially in rock and pop. References to place were once very common in American music. As Heise reminds us, "rootedness in place

has long been valued as an ideal counterweight to the mobility, restless-
ness, rootlessness, and nomadism that Americans themselves as well as
observers from outside have often construed as paradigmatic of American
national character" (2008, 9). Increasingly, traveling road motifs and
generic settings (bedroom, club, crib) take the place of specific regional
and local metaphors. "Americans are less inclined than they once were
to seek the cachet of topographical uniqueness to craft an identity," Von
Glahn argues (2003, 272).

Fewer and fewer lyrics refer to local places, regions, and natural features. Perhaps it is because "Americans now feel more at home," as Von
Glahn optimistically suggests (ibid.). There is less need to musically express
our connection to the places where we live, because such connections are
assumed. I hope she is correct but have my doubts. The lack of local reference may instead reflect the fact that less attention is being paid to
specific physical environments. Such sonic disconnections could have
important ecological ramifications. Music does not have to reference specific environments to be environmental, but one of the most important
ways for music to do environmental work is to connect listeners to the
places where they live, to create sustainable soundscapes. The lack of
specific environmental references in popular music may be emblematic
of a wider problem.

On the other hand, music, especially topical music, follows broader
cultural trends. It takes a lot of time to conceive, produce, and distribute
it. Musicians see themselves more as documentarians than activists, reacting to the world rather than trying to shape it. The music of the bioregion
may be coming back, starting with bands like Cloud Cult.

People are just beginning to think seriously about themselves and
their communities in terms of biomes and watersheds, as opposed to
political geography. Leading that movement are activists, including school-
children who stencil storm drain signs that let people know which watershed they belong to. Another model comes from the Cascadia project
(discovery.org/cascadia/), which encourages the residents of western
Washington and Oregon to imagine themselves as part of a shared bioregion: Cascadia. The goal is to more effectively define political boundaries in accord with the needs of a bioregion, especially in terms of "commerce, community, and conservation." Regional public transportation is
central to such efforts, but music could play a role in encouraging such
identifications to take hold in people's imaginations as well.

Illustrating the current limits of bioregional thinking, the Cascadia
project does not reach into British Columbia, even though the bioregion does. National political boundaries, grant funding guidelines, and

infrastructural logistics still trump bioregion, even at the conceptual level and the planning stage. A truly radical bioregional conception would transcend political boundaries, recognizing the Rio Grande Valley as a bioregion shared by the United States and Mexico, the Boundary Waters/Quetico region as the domain of northern Minnesotans and western Ontarians, and so on. Similarly, Guthrie's musical Columbia failed to reach back into eastern British Columbia, where the river finds its head-waters. In other words, musical regions tend to be circumscribed by the nation-state. National identity still trumps regional identification.

As the movement toward bioregional identification advances, it would not be surprising to see regional conceptions more directly reflected in music once again. One day, perhaps, "Cascadia" or the northern boreal forest will be celebrated in song. Songs like "Roll On, Columbia" may start to instill 'a very different pride of place than they did in the twentieth century, fostering a sense of shared stewardship within bioregional eco-systems. Maybe, as Von Glahn optimistically opines, we now "feel more at home," and maybe that will translate into better environmental stewardship.

But what would it look and sound like if we did take local places and local music more seriously? How might we go about that? So far I have dealt with the question of music and place as an observer, looking at regional, national, and global musical ecologies—fairly safe stuff, from a methodological perspective. In the next chapter I leap off the observation platform to see what it is like to make environmentally themed music on the local level. Please do try this at home.

4

Local Music

A Tonic for the Troops?

Previous chapters described music and musicians who have influenced people across the globe and nation. But what are the rest of us to do? What about local music, the kind that anyone can make? Theoretically, this is where music matters most, at least from an ecological perspective. It is where we live.

Local music connects local people to local places, places in need of protection and stewardship. Music coheres and enlivens face-to-face communities, and it can inspire a shared sense of stewardship. There are countless ethnographic examples of music connecting small-scale communities to the world of life around them. Rather than an aberration, it has been universal practice for bands, tribes, and villagers to use musical rites to understand and venerate their surrounding environment.

The situation is more complicated in large, hierarchical, and socially complex societies. Theoretically, local communities and subcultures could still experience a deep orientation to place, but empirically that is not the case for many people. Therefore, renewing community connections to local place is essential if our lives and societies are to become more sustainable.

That is more easily said than done. As an ethnographer and ecomusicologist, I have just started to discover the sorts of profound and hopeful examples I had initially imagined and set out to find. I thought that community would simply spring forth as a result of shared musical activity in the local area. But it was not that simple. Like all worthwhile endeavors, it has taken a great deal of work to cultivate ecologically meaningful musical relationships within the local community.

The starting premise for this fieldwork was simple: make music with friends, family, and neighbors in order to foster a stronger sense of community (Mattern 1998, 9–23). Nothing terribly new or uncommon there. An additional goal took the experiment into fairly new territory for ethnographic fieldwork: to make music that might encourage environmental stewardship.

I was never so naïve as to believe that music would magically inspire audiences to action. The act of making music does not, by itself, make us more environmentally aware or active. If that were the case, the problem would be solved. Music does not automatically set the world right, no matter how it is performed. Making music matter requires a great deal of individual and collective effort in addition to art.

Nor is music necessarily a social good. In fact, becoming a truly accomplished musician requires one to be somewhat selfish, to engage in an obsessive, all-consuming neglect of other social activities and people. That includes taking time away from family and friends in order to make music, at least in the learning stage. That is why musicians typically do not make the best models for creating more sustainable lifeways.

The field research began with another basic premise: anyone can make music, and more people should be doing so. People should be getting together in backyards, parks, and dumpsites, and not just to remove invasive species, restore streams, and educate students. Hard work is not enough to sustain a community or a biodiverse environment. People should be doing pleasurable, cultural labor as well, educating each other, celebrating the landscape, and building sustainable communities. Music is clearly an essential part of that, and anyone can do it. "Anyone" includes me. If we—musicologists, ethnomusicologists, and ecomusicologists— keep asking others to make music that builds communities and sustain ecologies, we should see how that actually works first hand. Physicians, heal thyselves.

Granted, there is also value in writing about music, or no one would write books about music or read them. Not everyone needs to be making music all the time for music to matter. However, the musicological literature places a high value on musical participation. We tend to think that more people should make music, because when they do, good things happen. That is part of the premise here: that if more people made music in, and about, cherished and threatened local places, there would be a strong ecological net benefit. With that in mind, I decided to learn what it would take for the average person, an anthropologist, to just go out and start making environmental music. If not, I would at least learn something from musical failure. Either way, I would learn. That is what ethnographers do.

Therefore, I became a musician. That differentiates this study from most. "Within cultural and media studies the emphasis is often on musical texts and representations," notes ethnographer Sara Cohen (2007, 20). Ethnography is an "alternative approach" that "grounds music practice and theory in the specifics, social dynamics, and materiality of physical and geographic locations" (ibid., 21). Ellen Waterman reminds us (2007, 114) that "the interdiscipline of acoustic ecology," especially R. Murray Schafer's soundscape studies (1977, 1994), included ethnographic research from the outset. Ethnography has been somewhat less emphasized in popular music studies, which is odd, because popular music is ostensibly about participation.

Participant observation is a central component of ethnography: one needs to spend significant time with cultural experts, fieldwork "informants." That involvement can take any number of forms. In this project, participation meant becoming a musician.

It is important to define what I mean by "musician." In a sense, we are all musicians. We all make music, whether by pounding out a rudimentary beat (Koko can't do that) or humming a melody (Koko won't even try). Therefore, there was nothing to "become." Humans are musicians from birth. Like everyone else, I was already a musician before this research began.

In a sociolinguistic sense, however, "musician" connotes something more specific than "member of a music-making species." That became clear whenever I explained this research to a colleague or acquaintance. Without fail, my inquirer would shift into show-and-tell mode, describing someone they know who is "an incredible musician." Some would even proudly self-report their own musical status, as in: "I am a classically trained musician," or: "I used to play in a band."

In other words, to be considered a musician seems to require more than recognition of the universal human capacity for music making. Sociolinguistically speaking, to be a musician means successful completion of a sanctioned training regimen, the ability to perform in public, the recognition by others of musical talent, or all of these. "Talent" may be expressed in music that audiences enjoy or achievement of a genre-specific threshold for musicality or both.

Typically, whenever I explain this research or, for that matter, whenever I now perform in public, people tell me about other musicians they know, lauding a friend or acquaintance for his or her musical skills. "My friend Jon is a professional musician," they explain, "incredible keyboard skills . . . plays at the Dakota sometimes." Of course, playing at local clubs only "sometimes" means that one makes a living that way. However, such scripts indicate that professionalism is an important factor in the socio-linguistic algorithm of what defines someone as a "musician."

Although we are all music makers, one must go through a process of enculturation and performances to gain the social status of "musician." In the popular imagination, there are musicians and then there are the rest of us. That is perhaps what most needs to change: our conception of musicianship. In fact, one of my main goals is to encourage others to play music with friends and family. Enough spectatorship already! Let's quit watching and do something. For now, however, the cultural prem-ise remains that there are musicians (a few) and listeners (the rest). In order to do this fieldwork I had to become one of the few, a performing musician.

My field site would be "wherever the music is" (Levin 2006, xii), including rehearsal spaces, recording studios, and, most of all, concert venues. Ethnographer Stacy Holman Jones explained that in order to study women's music, it would become her "work to make—to be— women's music" (1999, 217). For ethnographers, becoming part of the music could mean entering the audience, backstage, onstage, or at the studio. For me it meant becoming a musician and becoming competent enough to perform alongside more accomplished musician-informants. On the participant-observation spectrum, I participated more directly than most ethnographers. That is not bragging. In the process, I relearned an important lesson: the more you participate, the less you observe.

As a musical ethnographer, I never fooled myself into thinking I had become a bona fide professional. Similarly, just because an anthropol-ogist plants corn alongside the Maya, that does not make her a *milpa* farmer, and it certainly doesn't make her Mayan. Nor was I so deluded as to believe my music would do anything environmentally speaking. If we cannot prove that the music of Neil Young, Steve Earle, Billy Bragg, and Ani DiFranco makes a difference, ecologically speaking, what chance does a proto-professional musician like me have? In some ways, that is the research question.

In other words, the goal was more investigational than applied. The corn-planting ethnographer described above might not become an expert farmer, but even a rudimentary apprenticeship in the field should allow for a much better understanding of Maya culture and agriculture than simply interviewing Maya farmers or forming a Maya focus group.

These eight years of becoming a musician have given me useful in-sights into the environmental and political potential of popular music, as well as the struggles involved in making music. I would have learned a lot by interviewing musicians, watching them from the audience, and analyzing their songs, but there are plenty of people already doing that. It seemed as if it might be useful to do some participant observation as well.

For those not accustomed to reading ethnographic work, please forgive the use of the first person throughout this chapter. I need the "I" in order to present this fieldwork accurately and honestly. It is the opposite of what American readers are used to. For example, *New York Times* reporters go to ridiculous lengths to avoid the first person, using awkward phrases like "A reporter was told that . . ." to convey information that they were told directly. Thanks to the positivistic tradition in the United States, one is not supposed to use "I" in nonfiction narrative and should even limit the first person plural. As ethnographers, we can't help ourselves. Often, the only way to accurately, honestly, and reflexively write about field experience is to use the first person. To do otherwise would be false and inaccurate. As ethnographers, we do not send in remote drones to do our fieldwork for us.

On the other hand, I often cringe when reading ethnographic accounts that turn out to be more about anthropologists than informants and their cultures. The informants are usually much more interesting. Unfortunately, the only access we have to informants and their cultural worlds is through our individual field experiences, so consider yourself forewarned.

As Theodore Levin argues, "The only sensible way to do ethnographic research is collaboratively" (2006, xiii). I view my fellow musicians, bandmates, audience members, venue managers, and sound engineers as collaborators rather than research subjects. When I use "we" in this chapter I am generally referring to all of the above, without whom none of this would matter or even make sense.

Becoming a Musician

To be honest, I did not start from scratch. As is true of most people, my childhood was filled with informal musical training. Informally, I learned by listening to my mother, Jane, play organ and piano. She is an accomplished sight-reader with the ability to perform any piece that is set in front of her. That sounds like hyperbole, but it is true. When she accompanies the *Messiah,* for example, Jane does not drop a single note. Few human musicians can honestly make that claim.

To grow up around that kind of talent and musical accomplishment is very different from starting formal music training at the age of 40, my age when this project began. Most learning is informal, and singing around a piano with professional accompaniment teaches one a great deal. As the youngest, I learned a great deal from listening to talented older siblings as well.

As for formal training, I spent my school years learning and performing chorale music, including a very good high school choir led by an extraordinary director, Stanley Wold. Dr. Wold is now artistic director of the Arrowhead Chorale of the University of Minnesota, Duluth. Few high school singers receive that kind of training. I appreciated it then, and appreciate it even more now.

Three years of piano lessons were particularly valuable to me as a songwriter. School band and choir taught me how to follow musical notation, but learning piano taught me how to really read it. I have mostly forgotten how to play piano, but the basic lessons were retained. Throwing a heavily rehearsed keyboard track onto a recording is not completely beyond me. My guess is that such experiences early in life are typical for musicians. One thing that separates musicians from the rest of us is that they have the good sense to keep playing into their adult years.

Although it is valuable, classically trained musicians need to unlearn quite a bit of their formal training in order to become rock, folk, blues, or hip-hop performers. Classical music is far from a universal standard. It is, instead, one genre among many, with a particular set of aesthetic values. Rare rock acts perform operatic vocals, but most classical vocal techniques fail to deliver the character of voice that rock standards require. Just as the Bosavi, Mayan, or American rock singer fails miserably when judged according to Western classical norms, so too a choirboy tends to fare poorly in a metal band. I know that from firsthand experience; during my teenage years I was a choirboy who fared poorly in metal bands.

Whenever one applies the genre standard of one style to another, the other type of music necessarily comes off as inferior. Tom Waits's lyrics are far more interesting than Bach's, and his voice has much more of a human, theatrical, and social-realist character than Renée Fleming's classically trained voice. Reversing things, Waits's compositions would fail to impress at the Met, and his voice would be judged less than ideal for opera. I like both Waits and Fleming, a lot, but their musical genres, goals, and qualities are incomparable.

Pardon a short detour while I explain a bit further, because this is an important point for ecomusicology. Because music is culturally and temporally specific, looking for universal or "nomothetic" principles is a losing game. While certain harmonic capacities, pitch recognitions, and rhythmic abilities are part of our human endowment (Phillips-Silver, Aktipis, and Bryant 2010), most musical qualities are difficult to translate from culture to culture. For example, Steven Feld (1982, 231) found that the Bosavi of Papua New Guinea could only relate to certain sounds from foreign recordings: those that resonated with their own musical sign system. The timbre of the clarinet and saxophone, when relatively isolated, matched the sound of local fruit doves, a sound the Bosavi cherish. Japanese koto music reminded them of water sounds and their own water-related music. However, the frenetic pace of the blues and the timbre of many Western instruments and voices grated on them.

Similarly, Levin found that at least one Tuvan musician "couldn't stand the sound of the violin" (2006, 223). For him, it makes an "unnatural sound" (ibid.); for many Westerners, on the other hand, no instrument has a more "natural" intonation. In our band, the Hypoxic Punks, Leon Hsu's violin signals a sense of natural beauty within the otherwise decadent rock sound. Similarly, cellist Sarah Young and violinist Shannon Frid help Cloud Cult develop a more natural sound than the typical rock band. For the Tuvan musician, however, Western strings are grating and unnatural.

Tuvans pay much less attention to melody than either Bosavi or Western listeners. Tuvan musicians and listeners focus on precise manipulation of overtones to produce what they consider pleasurable timbres (Levin 2006, 47). For the Tuva, pitch is "subordinate to timbre" (ibid.). To understand this, it is important to remember what timbre is. What distinguish any two sounds at the same pitch and volume are overtones. Musical sounds contain a fundamental, the pitch at which the loudest vibration is taking place. Take the note we call "A." Thanks to the International Standards Organization (ISO), we call any note whose fundamental is 440 hertz (Hz) an "A." Overtones are integer multiples of the fundamental. For "A," therefore, the overtones are 880 (first harmonic), 1320 (second harmonic), 1760 (third harmonic), and so on. While all musicians are concerned about overtones, often subconsciously, Tuvan musicians are preoccupied with them, consciously.

Tuvan vocalists violate several principles of Western classical music, including their relative lack of concern for pitch. Classical musicians, practicing the human universal of ethnocentrism, are trained to believe that their particular use of the vocal instrument has achieved a universal standard for excellence. In truth, the classical model is one among many, and one that violates others' standards. Just as the young rock aficionado might find *bel canto* off-putting, so too would many listeners unaccustomed to the Western musical tradition. Listeners tend to prefer the sound textures and timbres they grew up hearing. Even adults who are trained to appreciate new styles of music do not necessarily find pleasure in listening to them. There is a difference between appreciation and pleasure.

Beyond certain wide parameters for what constitutes music for all humans, one society's music is often another society's noise. Spanish conquistadors interpreted the highly coordinated and trained musicianship of the Mexica as nothing more than noise, although they seemed to be able to respond to Mexica percussion. It frightened them. In fact, it might be more than coincidence that Pedro de Alvarado ordered his men to hack off the Aztec drummers' arms during the *Noche Triste* massacre of June 30, 1520. Mesoamerican music seemed like an affront, an abomination.

Individuals can be enculturated into the appreciation of many types of music and taught to understand the internal rules of aesthetic judgment. However, the idea that one cultural tradition has captured universal principles is simply not true. While Western rock and classical music are close enough to be mutually comprehensible, that does not mean that they work according to the same rules, or can be judged as if they did.

That brings us back around to the original point, the rock musician has to unlearn certain classical conventions and proscriptions. Take Jesse Mandell-McClinton, a pianist who played with the Hypoxic Punks for about a year. When he was 12, having already reached a level of excellence as a classically trained musician, Jesse called a halt to further classical instruction. Formal sight training was taking him away from the improvisational skills he wanted to learn. Or, to reframe the point in affirmative terms, Jesse sought to learn the harmonic and rhythmic nuances of popular music, such as jazz, rock, and hip-hop.

In doing research for *How Popular Musicians Learn*, Lucy Green discovered that formal "music education has had relatively little to do with the development of the majority of those musicians who have produced the vast proportion of the music which the global population listens to, dances to, identifies with and enjoys" (2002, 5). Similarly, Daniel Levitin argues that "expressivity" is rarely learned in music schools (2006, 208). Jesse is infinitely more talented than I am, and thus more adept at crossing genre lines. Yet I have also had to unlearn much of my earlier classical training in order to compose and perform rock and folk music. It is a matter of moving between two very different musical cultures.

The word "training" is used conspicuously in classical music, and classical musicians often invoke the term when bragging about their musical learning. It is quite the opposite in rock and folk. It would be embarrassing for a rock musician to speak of his or her "training." Rarely does one read a biography of a popular musician who even mentions formal training. It is not that popular musicians lack formal classical training—they are often introduced to music the same way Jesse and I were. However, rock's ethos of authenticity and collectivity encourages popular musicians to downplay formal education.

The rock musician is supposed to be born, not made, a natural, unwashed talent from the back roads or barroom. The rock musician cannot be seen as having sat through hours, days, and years of lessons as a child. That is part of rock's folk heritage. Just as Allen Lomax imagined Woody Guthrie to be an untutored, natural musician from the hinterland, rock audiences like to imagine that their guitar heroes were born for the business.

The second reason formal training is de-emphasized in rock is that popular musicians learn collaboratively (L. Green 2002), often from an early age. In contrast to formal instruction, their development is less likely to be directed by an authority figure. Instead, musical recordings perform that role. Rock musicians' lessons tend to take the form of listening to popular recordings alone and together with fellow learners. The neophyte rocker listens to favorite songs over and over, plays along until he or she gets it right, and advances by "jamming" with peers and through endless, unsupervised experimentation.

Some readers might protest that collaborative learning is important in classical training as well. Indeed, it is more a matter of degree than absolute difference: classical musicians learn together, but on the whole classical training is more hierarchical and programmed. The ideal end result is much more predefined, and the rules are more clearly spelled out. In both genres, however, what starts with replication often ends in innovation, at least for the virtuoso.

I have performed with several virtuoso instrumentalists but certainly did not become one myself. I did not put in my ten thousand hours of practice early enough in life; even if I had, I might never have achieved their level of dexterity. Instead, I learned guitar well enough not to embarrass myself. I learned rhythm guitar so that I could contribute chord support while playing harmonica or singing on stage; it is also useful for writing songs.

For full disclosure, I was in a band back in high school as well, but only as a singer. The band was called "Omen" (the drummer's name was Pete Oulman). We performed cover tunes. Our repertoire mixed pop metal and punk. Then, as now, I found myself negotiating with musicians who preferred hard rock to punk. The negotiation usually ended, and ends, with a satisfactory hybrid sound, or at least a satisfactory détente. In the case of Omen, the rest of the band got to play progressive rock and metal while I got to perform some Jim Carroll or Ramones. With the Hypoxic Punks, however, the result is more of a hybrid folk rock with punk tinge (see ecomusicology.net).

Band breakups are often blamed on "artistic differences," but difference is also productive. Having musicians with different genre inclinations can produce interesting new sounds. Despite legal definitions of authorship, popular composition is a collective process. I write the melodies, lyrics, and chords, and then put together a chart and rough demo recording, but the band turns my solo sample into a new song. Each musician adds his or her stamp, developing a part that no chart or demo could predetermine. That is typical practice, and part of the magic of popular music. I could write everything out in full notation, and did so at the beginning, but I found the typical, collaborative process more effective and fun. For example, Leon comes up with violin parts I could never imagine. He listens to the existing melody, chords, and rhythms, then creates a violin part to complement it. It is truly a collaborative process.

Before moving further into the collaborative process, a few more details are necessary about my training as an ethnographer and musician. Ten years after high school, I had my first contact with the guitar while doing research in El Salvador. I bought a guitar from a local luthier, who made and sold instruments from his garage. During my fieldwork downtime I enjoyed picking through some folk songs from Pete Seeger's songbooks, a method of learning that colors my music to the present. Arpeggios came easily, thanks to piano lessons, and repetitive lines were not terribly challenging. Conversely, forming chords took a lot more work at first, and I have yet to become truly adept at using a pick. I remain, at best, a mediocre rhythm guitarist.

"One guitar is abused," Guthrie wrote in an unpublished note for Folksay Album #1 (1944). My first guitar was indeed abused and started falling apart after being dragged through Central America and Mexico on various forms of public transportation. I did not learn much with that guitar, but it was a start. The idea of turning musical performance into a formal ethnographic study did not develop for another decade, and I still knew practically nothing about playing guitar when this project started taking shape.

In 2002 I completed field research for *Musical Ritual in Mexico City* (2004). After watching musicians for years, becoming one seemed like the next logical step. I bought a Taylor 310 guitar and started learning.

Without caveat, I would say that Lucy Green got it right (2002): popular music is learned through collaboration with peers. However, there are many types of musicians, including cover musicians, improvisers, and composers. Cover musicians seek to duplicate popular recordings as faithfully as possible. They tend to be music aficionados who idolize a famous instrumentalist (or two) and aim to duplicate the work of a master musician. To the untrained ear, their playing may become indistinguishable from that of their idol. Of all local musicians, cover artists tend to make the most secure living, thanks to weddings and corporate events.

Improvisers tend to be cover musicians who take it to the next level. As Green explains, duplication is something of a training stage and may be followed by improvisation. Often improvisation begins by accident, as subtle variations make their way into cover songs with positive effect. Most mistakes, like the great majority of genetic mutations, fail. However, some musical accidents, like fortuitous changes in DNA, add something new, useful, and interesting. That is how music remains vital and how virtuoso instrumentalists make their mark. They master traditional patterns of play and then add their distinctive signature.

Composers tend to be known less for their instrumental artistry and more for their musical innovations. They may not master others' songs, as cover musicians do, or become virtuoso instrumentalists. Instead, their goal is to use an instrument as a means for creating entirely new songs. Some composers belong to all three groups: Mark Knopfler, for example, is a virtuoso guitarist as well as a great songwriter. Other songwriters play down instrumental learning to focus instead on composition. Whereas improvisation stresses instrumental mastery and innovation—in the sense of variations on a predetermined theme—composition produces wholly new songs in a more intentional fashion. Some bands "jam" to produce new songs from scratch, but most rock and pop songs are first composed by songwriters, at least in rough form, before entering into the collaborative process.

Rather than learning guitar to play existing songs, my orientation was that of a songwriter, from the start. I may have made a virtue out of necessity; I don't have the talent or time to become a virtuoso guitarist. Or, it may have been a matter of preference and emphasis. Regardless, with the limited time at my disposal I have used guitar, voice, and harmonica to write and perform music rather than seeking to become an expert instrumentalist. Frankly, the fact that I can pound out rhythms and chords at all still surprises me. When I first started, it seemed like an impossible dream.

As for my songwriting method, melody and words tend to come first. That may have to do with the fact that I sang long before I played an instrument. I then place these inside a basic chord structure. By the time I have auditioned hundreds of variant lines and words for a lyric, even my poorly trained left hand can automatically follow the song's chord progression on guitar. As I move up the neck, things get iffy. Major barre chords are fine, and I have written whole songs based mainly on them. However, I am still not terribly adept at moving up the fret board while playing lots of different chord variants. I leave the serious noodling to bandmates. That is making a virtue of necessity.

Gradually, additional verses, chorus/refrain, bridge, and/or outro sections form. The chords of each are programmed into muscle memory as I play them over and over during the songwriting process. Working with words and melodies takes my focus away from the otherwise tedious process of learning to form chord patterns and transitions on the guitar. If taking lessons and running scales bores you to death, and all you care about is learning basic rhythm guitar, I strongly recommend writing music as a method for learning guitar. The British fanzine *Sideburns* was on to something in 1976 when its cover proclaimed: "This is a chord, this is another, this is a third. Now form a band." The traditional model assumes years of training before composition and performance. That is not how most popular music works. It is an iterative process where learning, collaboration, performance, composition, and proficiency feed off each other.

As discussed earlier, writing about music is almost as difficult as learning to play it. Music surrounds us yet often escapes conscious recognition. It is deeply felt, yet hard to articulate. As opposed to the study of supernovae or atomic nuclei, written descriptions and visual diagrams are highly inadequate for communicating the meanings of music. Music is as much about emotion as meaning, and much more about meaning than function. Therefore, ethnographic methodology is useful, because it is designed to gain immersive access into cultural experience. Ethnography incorporates all of the senses. In other words, ethnography is an art as much as an empirical science.

Translating the immersive experience of music into cold text remains difficult, however, regardless of the method used to gather information (Goodall 2000, 76). The website *Ecomusicology.net* provides audio and visual recordings of some of the music described in this chapter as well as some of the music referenced in previous chapters. It also provides a snapshot of the fieldwork learning process.

I am glad that no such website or audiovisual record accompanied my previous fieldwork in Mexico and Central America. Ethnographers are usually accorded some amount of trust that the things they write about really happened. Although there is plenty of second-guessing about what Margaret Mead or Clifford Geertz really did in the field, it is usually assumed that they did it with a certain degree of cultural competence. I am not sure if that is the case here, but please give a look and listen to *Ecomusicology.net* and follow that site's link to the Hypoxic Punks' site (hypoxicpunks.org) so you can judge for yourself. My hope is that appending the words "local" and "punk" to music ensures that all sins will be forgiven. Having surrounded myself with professionals and advanced amateur musicians, I have no doubt that the listener will appreciate my bandmates' talent, if nothing else.

Making Music Matter:
An Expensive and Time-Consuming Struggle

Learning an instrument, composing songs, joining a band, recording music, and performing live music provided me with a richer sense of the challenges and potential of popular music, including its potential as an environmental force. More importantly, I became aware of the implicit disciplines, structures, conventions, and customs that govern the production, distribution, and consumption of music on the local level. While this may sound like an "action research" approach (Stringer 2007)—and maybe it is—I became a performing musician to gain privileged access to informants and learn from them.

My fieldwork mainly took place in Minneapolis, Minnesota, and Orcas Island, Washington. My prior fieldwork in Mexico City informed the project as well, although I did not perform in Mexico, apart from a few impromptu mariachi sing-alongs or evenings at the piano bar. Through learning to play an instrument, composing music, rehearsing with other musicians, recording, and performing live, I hoped to learn more about music as an environmental phenomenon. As stated from the outset, I was guided by the belief that political pop would be able to inform and motivate individuals while helping to organize and sustain communities and movements. However, I was never so deluded as to believe that my music could do all of that. In fact, I quickly learned how relatively useless most overtly topical music is, or at least how difficult it is to do well. As Simon Frith cautioned, music can become "too didactic to be used by anyone" (1984, 68). If that is the case for the famous musicians Frith studied, it is doubly true for local beginners.

In addition to didacticism, there is the problem of coming off as accusatory. Bob Dylan complained about "finger-pointing songs" and cited that folk tendency as one of the main reasons he switched to rock (Marqusee 2003). For many, music is not the place for righteous condemnation. On the other hand, Dylan's professed love for Joe Hill's music does not square with his distaste for finger pointing. Perhaps Hill's humor and antiquity saved him from Dylan's rebuke.

My songs about the environment tend to inhabit a character. I do that in part to keep from looking as if I am pointing fingers. Only one of my songs attacks specific institutions: "Boneyards," written from the point of view of a farmer who is himself implicated. That is my most autobiographical song. During my childhood I worked in a cattle auction market, and I have no qualms about pointing fingers in that case, because the finger is pointing at me as well. In addition to citing "Archer Daniels Midland, Monsanto, and Dow," the finger in "Boneyards" points to all of us involved in industrial agriculture, from the feedlot to the consumer. We've all made a mess of things, quite literally, and have to find a way to work ourselves out it.

The ecological heroine of "Ride" is a "little girl on a bike." "River's Getting Dirty" presents the opposite allegory, a bunch of people polluting a river in their daily struggles to get by. "Allegory" may be too strong a word. Rather than a clear narrative, the song presents a confused set of relationships to the river. The characters could be anyone and are practically everyone.

Another song I wrote about the environment, "Dead Zone," is told from the point of view of a man whose way of life extracts a great deal from his local environment. I wrote that song with myself in mind, but some listeners have taken it as an accusation against others. More than one has asked, "So what's wrong with Costco?" The big-box store is mentioned as part of the man's complicated life, but frankly I just used it for the rhyme. The listeners' "mistaken" reaction (it is just as valid as mine) brought home a point made by folk singer Carolyn Cruso: people will tend to assume that a singer-songwriter is accusing others while exempting him- or herself. That tendency makes it hard to write critical music, even about institutions. On the other hand, fear of finger pointing can make one so musically introspective that one's songs take on a sickeningly confessional tone. What's more, when the songwriter starts focusing on creating reasonably coherent, interesting, and aesthetically pleasing pieces of music, the message is often lost altogether. Composing topical music is one big balancing act.

I am not sure that lyrics matter all that much in local music, however. I learned early on that people do not attend local concerts to listen to words. Performing at a beer garden during the 1976 National Hobo Festival, I started making up words to J. J. Cale's "Cocaine." "If you want to eat fish, just make a wish, Cocaine." Nonsensical stuff like that. Only my bandmates noticed; the grizzled, intoxicated motorcyclists who made up most of our audience just kept right on dancing.

It is partly a matter of genre. Unlike rock, folk is assumed to be personal and completely free of artifice, the words and music pouring directly from the singer's heart. Even folk narratives about other people are assumed to represent the singer-songwriter's real experience and true feelings. Rock, pop, and hip-hop allow the singer to be much more playful and shape-shifting, making the composer's vantage point much harder to pin down. In some ways, it is artistically liberating. On the other hand, words can become somewhat superfluous in rock, not only less central to a song's meaning and feel, but harder to hear over all of the instruments. Folk is more likely to allow for serious messages and more likely to be taken seriously. Conversely, the perceived distance between a rocker's stage persona and the person behind it allows the songwriter to insert ideas indirectly and thus seem less preachy. Folk festivals are dripping with earnest emotion, while rock's collective catharsis is more about taking a mental vacation. Both have value.

Although it took me many years to become competent enough to perform in public, in some ways learning to play rhythm guitar was the easy part. The next step would be more stressful, not to mention expensive. Expense is rarely mentioned in popular music research or, for that matter, musicians' autobiographies. One wonders how poor kids ever make it in rock. Some of the basic accoutrements are hard to come by. Guitars are not cheap. Neither is all of the other equipment. For example, a PA is essential for rehearsal. Without it you cannot match volume and mix the various instruments and voices together effectively. Popular musicians do not have the luxury of occupying acoustically sculpted rehearsal spaces, technological marvels in their own right. At some point in the twentieth century, people realized that electronics made it unnecessary to struggle with ancient acoustic equations: a trumpet added to the ensemble here means three more violins over here, and so on. Now we can simply push the violin feed up a bit more on the PA rather than go out and hire two more musicians.

Classical musicians pride themselves on producing unamplified sound in multi-million-dollar, acoustically engineered concert halls where they perform for captive audiences. Popular musicians need to find other ways to balance their instruments. They too want audiences to hear intricate timbral textures without undue loss of quality, but achieve it in different ways. Many rock and folk musicians prefer the more naturalistic voicing allowed by a microphone. They spend years perfecting vocal techniques that require microphone amplification to achieve full effect. Conversely, classically trained vocalists spend years learning how to project sound, using their bodies as resonating chambers. However, even the best opera singer would be drowned out by rock instruments, sans PA, and, once again, one should not forget the role played by advanced concert hall acoustics and the expectation of quiet audiences listening intently. Rock bands hope to see their audiences dancing, talking, laughing, and moving. Conversely, classical musicians expect their audiences to remain seated but raptly attentive for the duration of a concert.

Some rock and pop vocalists use PAs as a digital prosthetic. Rather than using a microphone to deliver the sound of their natural singing voice to distant ears, they have digital filters doing everything from pitch correction to timbral "enhancement." Many in the current generation of pop stars (Ke$ha, for one) have taken the practice to such an extreme that only their closest confidants know what their singing voices really sound like. That is not a terribly common practice for local bands, at least not in the kinds of shows we play, although a good sound system and sound board operator tend to apply a certain degree of naturalistic reverb and compression. That is necessary in order for an audience member to hear something akin to what they would hear if their ears were inches from the singer's mouth. That is, assuming the singer's mouth remains an inch or two from the microphone. My microphone technique is crap.

As for other expenses, guitar strings run from 5 to 20 dollars per set, depending on the brand and quality. Replacement parts and overhauls add up as well. Moving equipment around is equally difficult, time-consuming, and expensive. As the Sierra Club and U2 stories in the Introduction illustrate, moving equipment is not only costly but environmentally problematic as well. Despite many scholars' belief that home recording is inexpensive and easy, a high-quality recording is still expensive to produce.

We recorded at Atomic K Studios, with sound engineers Karl Demer, Merritt Benton, and Brandon Eiynck. Atomic K is a wonderful place to work. Musicians often claim that studios' surrounding environments affect musical sound. They do not mean that literally: studios are virtually soundproof. They are referring to the "vibe" musicians get in a given geographic location (S. Cohen 2007, 8). Having recorded briefly at two other locations, I believe it. Atomic K is comfortable, close to good, inexpensive restaurants, and not as aggressively edgy as most downtown studios. It enabled us to focus on our work. It was easier for us to work there than in the more frenetic art spaces across the river.

We used a few long weekends to do our recordings. Sometimes referred to as a "lockout," this kind of schedule is common for local musicians working on tight budgets. As rock fans know, the recording studio is a site of musical innovation rather than a place where live performance is simply reproduced. Whereas classical ensembles enter the studio seeking to preserve what has been perfected outside it, the rock band rarely emerges with the same sound they brought in. Each new track changes the overall equation, and by the end a recorded song has become something new altogether. The recording starts with a strong live performance, but something new comes out in the end. A band then works to recapture the studio sound in subsequent live performances. That process is time-consuming and expensive.

In her ethnography of Liverpool's Parr Street Studios, Cohen notes that "popular and urban music making tends to be hidden from the view of those that are not involved" (2007, 5). As part of this fieldwork, recording and performing music opened up a new world of professional networks, musical communities, and sound locations. What struck me more than anything else was how nice everyone was to us. Each city's music scene has a collective identity. Minneapolis's reputation—"Minnesota nice"—is part of what brings musicians here to record. Likewise, touring bands from Minnesota take the city's reputation with them and are clearly marked as Minnesotans even when performing in Chicago, New York, or London. There is a strong cultural ethos of civility in the Minnesota music scene. I have been told other cities are not always like that, that even in small local studios and clubs, people can get very nasty with each other.

That is not to say that the Minnesota music scene is completely egalitarian. Matthew Stahl's description of the "independent" rock community of San Francisco fits certain aspects of the Minneapolis music scene fairly well, although far fewer Minnesotans share the illusory (and art-killing) aim of making it to the big time (2003, 140):

> Even at the level of small-capacity bars and cafés, home-burned CDs, short-run seven inches, and word-of-mouth promotion of local bands supported primarily by day jobs, processes of hierarchization are carried out by local music infrastructures and business institutions. These processes not only produce differences between ranks of musicians in the world of indie rock, they also structure the kinds of sociality that are possible in that world.

This observation led Stahl to critique the "limited usability of ultimately hierarchical indie rock institutions and conventions for the production of a community" (ibid., 141). Mark Mattern argues that music can serve as either "social cement or social solvent" (1998, 144). Stahl's ethnography indicates that it can be both at the same time, cementing vertical relationships while dissolving more equitable, community-oriented formations. This does not bode well for rock music's political potential at the local level, if community is a prerequisite for meaningful political action. Nevertheless, the social dynamics Stahl describes might be less the case as one moves away from industrial nerve centers like New York and Los Angeles. The Twin Cities club scene is far from a utopian community, but it is not as bad as the one Stahl describes in San Francisco, especially in our little corner of the local music scene.

In fact, I have been surprised by how welcoming Minneapolis's musical community is to the uninitiated. Most bar owners and managers were nice to work with, even if we did not bring them much business. One exception proved the rule. Referred to as "a raging prick" by another, normally soft-spoken musician, the venue owner was held up as an example of how one should *not* act in the Minneapolis music scene. "Oh yeah, I dealt with that asshole," said another local. We brought him an excellent crowd on a Thursday night, and a very good bar take, but we won't go back.

"Music makers produce and characterize place not only by inhabiting the urban environment," Cohen writes, "but by interpreting and experiencing it" (2007, 6). I am lucky to have chosen Minneapolis, a scene that is incredibly welcoming.

Our first CD cost $4,000. That seemed like a lot of money to someone who imagined making music locally could be a break-even proposition. However, breaking even or coming out ahead happens for only the hardest-working and most entrepreneurial bands. It is a game for the young and, ideally, a game for young people with financial backing. The typical demo recording costs between $4,000 and $8,000 per song. Try affording that while waiting tables.

Making music is also expensive in terms of time. Ethnographic fieldwork, too, like any act of enculturation, is very time-consuming. One goal of ethnography is to conduct research in "naturalistic settings" closely approximating the normal lives of informants (when they are not being bothered by us). Ethnographers never fully duplicate the informants' experience, but we do our best attempt to simulate those conditions. We watch our informants, work with them, ask questions, and get things wrong, buoyed by occasional triumphs and moments of personal achievement. Ethnographers are like children, learning through trial and error. It is the intersubjective encounter between ethnographers and informants that matters most: the moments that provide the ethnographic "Aha's!"

My field research paralleled my informants' experience to a remarkable degree. It all took an incredibly long time and cost me a fair amount
of money as well. My projects in Central America and Mexico each took
a year in the field. This one required much more than that, partly because
it takes so long for musicians to reach the performance stage.

When it came to time and expense, my toolkit resembled the American
middle-class norm. Since I worked in a professional position, my musical
learning took place mostly at night and on the weekends. That is what the
average person has to deal with when jumping into a local music community, and is something that must be assumed if the goal is to think
about participatory music making. It is different from the professional
musician's situation, but similar to what most local amateur and semi-
professional musicians encounter. As for expense, I started in a slightly
better position than most local musicians. A few small, community-oriented grants helped fund the purchase of equipment, but I used my own
money for personal instruments and expenses, such as my own guitars
and harmonicas. I probably did not deserve a Taylor 310 guitar as a
starter instrument, but if I have learned one thing it is that technical merit
does not always match instrumentation. Some of the 19-year-olds who
played before and after our band had the most amazing tech. Despite
rock's street pretenses, it tends to represent wealth. Rock, like almost
everything else in America, is the art of conspicuous consumption.

Songwriting

Popular conceptions about how popular music is conceived, written, and
recorded fail to match the actual evidence. Take songwriting. People often
ask what a given pop song is about, trying to locate its singular meaning
in the author's original intent. It is assumed that the songwriter had a
fully conceived idea from day one, which he or she then translated into
notation, performance, and, finally, a recording. I have yet to meet a
songwriter who works that way. Songwriting is rarely a linear process
(Webb 1998).

Take the matter of lyrics and melody. Lyrics are very different from
poetry. As both David Boucher (2004) and Simon Frith (1996, 158–182)
have explained, the lyricist faces a range of constraints that authors of
poetry, prose, and spoken word do not. Meter is more strictly defined in
music. The lyricist has to work in concert with a stricter sense of rhythm
than the poet. The expectation of rhyme is also greater, and so is the
assumption of simplicity. Audiences are quick to sanction popular musicians, with the possible exception of rappers, for verbosity.

Lyrics should not get in the way of the music. Whereas the world of the poem is almost entirely textual, words are just a small part of most pop songs. The lyricist supplements and propels textual meanings with music, whereas the poet does so by scaffolding each word and phrase with additional words and phrases. For poets, text is context.

Furthermore, vocalized lyrics are part and parcel of musical sound, rather than something outside it. Words are often chosen because of the way they sound, musically speaking, rather than what they literally mean. That can be the case with poetry, to a degree, but it is an absolute and practical requirement in song, where even the sound of words must be musical.

Conversely, narrative conventions are generally less strict in song, as evidenced by songs built entirely on sense impressions. Even the most abstract poem tends to have some narrative thread holding it together. Not so with song lyrics, which is why some can seem downright nonsensical when taken out of their musical context. Lyrics and poetry have much in common, but writing lyrics and writing poetry present different challenges and opportunities.

The polysemic and even nonsensical nature of many rock lyrics is described nicely by *New Yorker* critic Alex Ross in his essay "The Pavement Tapes" (1997, 85):

> At least one long and winding road to hell is paved with interpretations of rock lyrics. Writing on the subject tends to fall apart because lyrics make less sense to the eye than to the ear. Words are blurred and bent by the music that swirls around them.

Ross goes so far as to claim that "rock loves nonsense" (ibid.). Meaning in rock tends to be communicated via sound and context rather than manifested primarily through lyrics. Politically speaking, rock can be employed to build community, provide emotional coloring to political events (e.g., a protest), enhance other media (e.g., a documentary film), fund organizations, and allow people to blow off steam, but it rarely communicates political meanings directly through lyrics.

Long before he was Sir Bob Geldof, the new wave composer entitled an album *A Tonic for the Troops* (Boomtown Rats 1979). Early on, Geldof had a strong sense of what rock music does and does not do. One thing music can do is provide a spark for audiences who need a chance to collectively recharge.

Unfortunately, in a consumer society, weariness and relief often come from the same place. In *Culture against Man* (1963), Jules Henry described

America as a sort of cruel Rube Goldberg machine. We are obedient subjects of a corporatized culture, providing unquestioning labor by day and
becoming obedient consumers at night. Many imagine fun to be the
opposite of work, but Henry argues that they are two sides of the same
coin: hamsters on a big wheel, more or less, chasing the illusory fun of
consumer goods and entertainment. Henry describes "fun" in America as
a superficial "anodyne" to the pain caused by our working lives (1963,
43). The "tonic for the troops" I am referring to is different, inspiration
rather than anodyne.

Perhaps we can produce our own entertainment instead of always
having to download, stream, or purchase it from culture industries. There
is ecological promise in homemade music. This exploration is partly
about crafting alternatives, but it is also about communication, entering
into conversation with audiences to create something new. But how does
one communicate meaningful messages in a musical genre where words
barely matter? Boucher's, Frith's, and Ross's cautions about lyrical limitations present us with a dilemma.

On the other hand, topical rock is a separate subgenre. When Neil
Young sings "This Note's for You" (1988), we clearly hear his condemnation of market-driven culture. We know what Toby Keith means when he
sings in favor of the Iraq war (2002). Similarly, at least some proportion
of the Dixie Chicks' audience knows that "Not Ready to Make Nice"
(2006) is a musical retort to President George W. Bush and his supporters. I mention these examples in response to musical researchers who
would ignore lyrics altogether. At least in terms of topical rock, lyrics do
matter, especially in recorded form. Fans listen to words over and over on
musical recordings, picking up bits here and there until at least some
message comes through.

Having made the case that lyrics matter in topical rock and folk, however, I have to admit that Boucher's, Frith's, and Ross's cautions about
lyrics apply particularly well to local music. The local musician's words
are typically heard only once by any given audience, and mostly live,
further reducing the lyric's capacity to communicate environmental or
other topical messages. We'll return to that question again later, but the
problem is worth keeping in mind here while focusing on the songwriting process.

As noted above, writing lyrics is a much less linear process than many
listeners imagine. From talking to other composers, it seems that my
songwriting process was fairly typical. In most cases, the first thing that
comes to mind is a general concept and perhaps a starting line or key
phrase as well. Take a silly song called "Dying Like Punks." It started

coming to me when I was driving along Interstate 94 in Wisconsin. I was listening to a story about mounting war casualties, started thinking about my friends playing war growing up, how that childhood fantasy translated, for some, into going off to real war, about some Irish kids I met in Central America during the eighties who asked if I could take them to "see some of the action," and probably several other stream-of-consciousness ideas I've long since forgotten. During all that I saw a dead rabbit beside the road, which cued the chorus. To be honest, I am not completely sure the last part really happened, but it is part of my songwriting memory nonetheless. Unfortunately, it is hard to take notes while songwriting or driving.

Out of all that, "We're dying like rabbits" came to mind. It first took the shape of an antiwar song, but dystopic images of environmental disaster came into the frame as well. Within minutes the song started taking shape. It changed a bit with each new thought, visual image, rhyme requirement, chord concern, or change in mood. Whether "Dying Like Punks" is any good or not, it does illustrate the nonlinear nature of rock and folk composition.

As an aside, many of my informants mentioned gaining inspiration for songs while driving. Folk singer Carolyn Cruso described pulling over to the side of the road to write down entire songs that popped into her head. Maybe this is another reason for the prevalence of road motifs in American popular music. We write while driving.

From the start, writing songs is rarely a matter of explicit cognition. Even after starting with the odd inspiration detailed above, "Dying Like Punks" never fulfilled my original intent, whatever that was. Interceding between the first germ of an idea and the finished song were several generations of lyrics, notes, erasures, edits, chord shifts, and events that inspired additional meanings. For example, in rehearsal, a band member took exception to one line about a "dumb GI." I intended the line to be from the perspective of a character, probably a fellow GI, talking about the stupidity of going to war. However, my bandmate saw it as condescending toward soldiers. Recognizing that the audience would probably make the same read, I changed the line. A song is like a Rubik's Cube: changing one element changes all of the rest as well. After a song is supposedly finished, it accrues new meanings through rehearsal, performance, and recording. What remains of the initial seed is perhaps nothing more than a general concept or catchy phrase buried deep within a totally new text. The stone helps make the statue.

Songs are somewhat like children: the parent starts out with an idea of what the child might become, and guides him or her accordingly, but the child usually turns out quite differently. Granted, a song that starts out as a war anthem probably will not become a light little ditty about sex on the beach. Nevertheless, meaning tends to shift through the song-writing process, often radically changing the meaning of a song. After it is recorded or performed, audiences interpret the song for themselves. Once audiences get ahold of them, songs about war can become just about anything.

Musical Meanings and Stage Personas

Genre expectations play an important role. As a middle-aged man, I was already the worst kind of rock anachronism, so I consciously tried to steer toward folk. That was a mistake: it just wasn't me (though "some of my best friends" are folk singers). The more folk my songs became, the more they revealed a forced, conscious element. While folk-tinged, the music I write tends to come out as rock, with a strong dose of country western and some residual punk elements. Americana, more or less.

A performer can never be sure how his or her music will be received. Audiences do not take in local bar music the same way they listen to recordings or big-name concerts. Information from audiences reaches a musician in disjointed bits and pieces. For example, at one bar gig I noticed that the soundman was listening with particularly focused attention—which is not always a given. This guy was rapt. When we finished our set, he put Steve Earle on the sound system as a segue to the next band. I nodded in recognition. He smiled back and gave the thumbs up. Clearly, he could hear Earle's influence in my music. As a band of middle-aged guys, we look and sound fairly comfortable in that niche. His reaction was a sign that we were starting to find our genre. People dancing and clapping was another.

When things went well, listeners often reflected back our intent, confirming that they understood that we weren't taking ourselves too seriously. Few local groups get away with gravitas, and serious reflection is not the purpose local rock serves best. And there are age expectations as well. More than once I have watched a group of middle-aged men and women rocking out and thought to myself, "That's kind of sad." Now I think that at least once per show, about myself.

That is one reason I mainly play acoustic guitar. Although the electric guitar is much more forgiving of technical errors, acoustic guitar helps signal "old guys having fun" as opposed to "old guys trying to act cool." Frankly, the rest of the band could probably pull off cool, but I can't. Never could. Also, as noted earlier, acoustic instrumentation more easily signals environmental intent. Having said that, I have started playing electric again. Rock sounds so much better that way.

Who cares what audiences think? Certainly anyone who wants his or her music to be more than an exercise in self-indulgence. Musicians need to have a contradictory, double orientation to the audience. First, they have to be aware of what resonates. However, if all they care about is seeing fans dancing and having fun, they are probably too concerned about getting the audience's approval. Might as well be a cover band.

Generations of rockers have taken stigmatized identities, amplified them onstage, and used them to advantage. Effeminate men like Iggy Pop made glam not only cool, but also "tough." Janis Joplin and Patti Smith broke free from feminine strictures onstage and off. Probably no successful rock musician exhibits the same personality in public and in private. If they did, they would be either hopelessly boring onstage or inaccessibly two-dimensional everywhere else. Performance requires persona.

My first musical collaborator for this project, Varun Kataria, was incredibly impressive in that regard. Varun and I rehearsed a lot, recorded a little, and performed once. Already an experienced hand drummer, Varun had grown up around rock while hanging out in his uncle's head shop. He knew members of local and nationally known bands, some of whom would take him along to their concerts. Rock is in his blood.

After our musical collaboration, Varun formed a band called Brown Moses. He was the front man, a talented vocalist with theatrical charisma. The most interesting local bands turn marginality into art, and Brown Moses did that expertly. One of their performances started with a five-minute picnic on stage: provocative theater, completely free from the telltale signs of wannabe rock stars.

During one show Varun accidentally stabbed himself with a cymbal stand. He kept bleeding throughout the song, holding up his stigmata in order to parody "balls out" rock star antics. Offstage, he screamed in pain and begged for medical attention. As an audience, we pay to see Varun the rock star, not Varun the fragile human being.

Varun and Brown Moses made a virtue of obscurity. There is great artistic freedom in marginality, and Brown Moses made the most of it. I never had the guts to go as far as Varun, but some day I would like to see what it is like to perform as a completely different person. Without moving into camp, I could see our ragged group of aging men playing up our dystopian revelry as evoked (hopefully) in tunes like "Off to California." Perhaps only aging men and women can pull that kind of thing off.

The flip side of the pathetically middle-aged man trying to look cool onstage is the young kid trying to look world-weary. As Elvis Costello sings in "All Grown Up" (2002), "You haven't earned the weariness that sounds so jaded on your tongue." The Hypoxic Punks' performances, when decent, take advantage of age rather than trying to pretend it does not matter. When I sing from the perspective of a jaded, broken-down, and bemused observer, the performance has a feeling of authenticity. However, the "positive" aspects of maturity mostly end there. The 20- and 30-something musicians with whom we share the stage shine with a power and energy we could never match. It is a joy to watch them light up the stage. We feed off their energy like vampires.

In real life, Varun is subdued, pensive, and quietly creative. His onstage persona is very much the opposite. Audiences do not realize the extent to which almost every musician's public persona differs from his or her backstage self. Take Bob Dylan. The transformation from Hibbing, Minnesota's Robert Zimmerman to America's Bob Dylan was more than mere stagecraft. Taking on a character allowed Dylan to let loose something new and interesting. Theatrical stagecraft is liberating, if not obligatory, in rock, pop, and hip-hop. Whereas folk musicians attempt to present their honest face to the crowd, the rock performer is given leave to act up a bit. Both modes of performance have their advantages.

In sum, being oneself onstage is a losing proposition in rock, especially for audiences. The more authentic the connection between performer and audience, the more likely it is that an artist has adopted a new persona, one that resonates with listeners while protecting the less stage-worthy aspects of the man or woman behind the mask. That is difficult for musicians performing on the local level, because much of our audience already knows us.

"Maybe in our world," musical ethnographer H. L. Goodall Jr. writes, "laughter is a kind of tonic we take against a fear of our true mediocrity, our status as just another pretty good bar band" (2000, 102). Constructing a stage character can enable and protect the performer in the same way laughter does. Some of the most enduring local bands take on humorous stage personas, a bulwark against the perception that they are trying to make it in the "serious" world of rock (and are failing). More importantly, humor adds entertainment value.

The First Concerts: A Decent Start?

So far the description of my ethnographic process has barely mentioned environmental matters. That is because step one was to become a musician. Only after gaining a foothold on stage could I seriously think about bringing environmental activism and music together. In my studies of environmental musicians, I have discovered that there are two basic types: activist musicians and musical activists. The former are professional musicians like Woody Guthrie, Joni Mitchell, Bill Bragg, and Michael Franti. Activist musicians are first and foremost musicians. They do not play music halfway or on the side. For the most part, music *is* their activism. Woody Guthrie's highly fictionalized autobiography defends those, like Guthrie, who play music for a cause during hard times, with vignettes about how music can entertain working people. "Those boys are shore gonna need some music," he exclaims near the end, jumping back onto a fictional freight car to visit yet another fictional work camp (1943, 317). Guthrie saw music as an essential tool for entertaining and organizing farm and labor movements. One can read some defensive guilt into Guthrie's fictionalized account, but if so, it was unnecessary. Activist musicians like Guthrie serve us best by playing music. That is what they do best. When gifted musicians like Woody Guthrie, Billy Bragg, and Gillian Welch work 10 hours a day to perfect a song or performance, it is not a matter of indulgence. We need more of that.

Conversely, the musical activist is first and foremost an activist, dedicated to political organizing, education, and strategic communication. Like making good music, these tasks are all-consuming, so musical activists can only make music on the side. To the extent that music is integrated into their activism, it tends to be in the form of special events and participatory music. We need more of that as well.

The Hypoxic Punks do not put enough work into either activism or music to have earned either title. We are neither "musical activists" nor "activist musicians." By trying and aspiring in music, however, I have learned a great deal about it, as a professional ethnographer. The Sierra Club vignette in the Introduction represents one of several attempts over the course of this research to make music for an explicitly environmental purpose. As part of this research I have performed approximately thirty concerts, some solo but mostly with the band. Of those, the following best illustrate the struggle, the pitfalls, and the potential for making local music work environmentally, especially for those of us with day jobs.

As I mentioned, Varun and I performed just once together in public: three songs on djembe and guitar. The performance was well received at an open mic night. I then formed a band with two other musicians and we became the Hypoxic Punks. Our first concert took place around midnight on Saturday, May 5, 2007, at "Balls Cabaret." The MC, Leslie Ball, told the audience of forty or so that the "Hypnotic Punks" were about to perform. She looked back sheepishly after recognizing that she had mispronounced our name. She tried again, this time coming up with the

"Hypnoxic Punks." I corrected her, while trying not to make her look bad or show my considerable nervousness. "The Hypoxic Punks," I said.

Leslie still looked confused. I asked if she wanted to know what "hypoxia" was. She smiled and said, "Sure." Propelled by stage fright and the fact that I teach for a living, I explained that an organism or ecosystem becomes "hypoxic" when its oxygen supply is restricted. "For example," I continued, "hypoxia takes place when farms and cities in the Upper Midwest send too much fertilizer into the Mississippi River, a situation that leads to massive algae blooms in the Gulf of Mexico, choking out other life." Persisting, I told the audience: "When such a large mass of algae dies, the water is almost completely starved of oxygen. That is the cause of the Dead Zone, a large and growing territory within which nothing can live." (I probably did not in fact explain it that clearly.) "That event happens annually and gets larger and worse each year" (for more information see Dybas 2005).

After I was done with the impromptu lecture, Leslie asked, "So we are causing that?" I thought for a moment and responded, "Yes." Without missing a beat, a man at the back proclaimed, "We're bastards!" Everyone laughed. That kind man turned my dry lecture into a wonderfully funny and entertaining act. I should have hired him on the spot. I could have used him several times since. Pete Noteboom (that's his real name), our guitarist, sarcastically added, "Can you tell Mark's a professor?" That brought out more laughter. We then broke into the song "Dead Zone." We could not have scripted a better intro. If I learned one thing that night, it is that I really need a script.

Our first performance went downhill from there. I had set the volume on my amp too high, but it was way across the stage, so I could not hear it very well. My guitar overwhelmed Desdamona's bass and even Pete's snare. Pete, a talented multi-instrumentalist, was drumming on the first tune, rather than playing guitar. I can take most of the blame, although, in my defense, it was my preference to go amp-less. I have learned, however, that without some form of amplification, bass players tend to be drowned out in acoustic performance. That is why acoustic basses and Mexican bajos sextos are so large, and even those instruments tend to get overtaken by snare drums and steel-string acoustic guitars. Desdamona needed her bass amp, but in the war of escalation that resulted, I failed to achieve a proper balance with my amp. Lesson learned. It was the first and last time we performed with amps but without a PA. Even an acoustic band needs a mixer, PA, and soundperson. Words matter, but sound is primary. That first performance made it clear that performing with a band was going to be even more complicated than I had initially assumed.

I learned a more important lesson that night: music is a great attention-getter. Thanks to my overdriven guitar, the Hypoxic Punks' debut sounded like crap. Nevertheless, 30 or 40 people went away with new knowledge about the damage agricultural and stormwater runoff is doing 2,000 miles downriver. Given that our aim was to use music as a tool for environmental communication, it was a great success. Preaching to the choir? Maybe, but that particular choir was unaware of the Dead Zone and our role in causing it. Reaching 40 citizens at a time will probably do little in terms of producing the large-scale changes in behavior, policy, and infrastructure needed to clean the Mississippi River Watershed and the Gulf of Mexico. However, those citizens are fairly likely to act upon the information. The performance represented a dose of "tonic for the troops," a bit of useful information wrapped into a whole lot of fun. Beats canvassing.

The Hypoxic Punks Get Lost in Clubland

I would like to report that our auspicious start at Balls led to bigger and better things. However, as the Hypoxic Punks' sound got better, we became less effective at communicating environmental messages: partly because of the club venues we chose, and partly because, as the music got better, I paid less attention to our original purpose and more on producing a professional sound. Production values do not always translate into getting a message across, and can even work against it. In media studies seminars, I have been told by several international students that Americans are obsessed with technology and production values. It is true. Sometimes we seem more interested in medium than in message.

To understand what went wrong and then right again, it is important to step back to the pedagogical origins of the project. The band's name comes from a series of performance classes I taught with a very talented colleague, Heather Dorsey, a theater director and instructor in public speaking. Heather and I asked each of our students to choose a song, poem, or other performance piece about the Mississippi River. The entire class was required to perform their work on the Washington Avenue Footbridge, which spans the beautiful Mississippi River Gorge. Because of its unique features, the Twin Cities' Mississippi River Gorge is the only urban area administered by the National Park Service. Yet most residents of the Twin Cities know little about it. As a city, we are just now getting reacquainted with the river and gorge. The students' performances were designed with that goal in mind.

FIGURE 2   Angela Lynch sings for the river on the Washington Avenue Footbridge. *(Photo by Patrick O'Leary, University of Minnesota.)*

In addition to learning poems, music, and monologues about the Mississippi River, students learned about the Gulf of Mexico Dead Zone and its causes. That is why I knew enough about the topic to give an impromptu speech at Balls Cabaret. The bridge performances were framed as environmental interventions, with signage and handouts to inform passersby about the river, water pollution, and the Dead Zone. One performance was entitled "Bridge over Troubled Waters," a metaphor for the pollution we were producing in the Upper Midwest and sending to the gulf. That performance was loosely affiliated with the Friends of the Mississippi (FMR.org), for whom we raised a little money through public donations (Figs. 2–4; see ecomusicology.net for more photos of student performances on the bridge).

Several years after the students' "Bridge over Troubled Waters" event, a controversy erupted over a film similarly entitled *Troubled Waters* (2010). The University of Minnesota funded a documentary about water pollution in the Mississippi River, but a PR official at the university canceled the film's premiere because of concerns that it might portray the agricultural industry inaccurately or negatively. After a public altercation about censorship and academic freedom, the relatively innocuous film was released, and the administrator who caused the ruckus quietly resigned.

FIGURE 3   Renee Barron performs "The Negro Speaks of Rivers" by Langston Hughes.
(Photo by Patrick O'Leary, University of Minnesota.)

For students and instructors alike, the years separating "Bridge over Trouble Waters" and the film *Troubled Waters* witnessed a remarkable increase in institutional attention to, and public awareness of, water issues, thanks largely to the university's Water Resources Center (WRC) and the work of hundreds of student activists, scientists, faculty, and community members. In other words, the U of M has been a good place to be involved in water issues. Yet for some reason, throughout that time I continued to focus mainly on making music for off-campus communities. I forgot that community is primarily wherever one happens to live and work. To go looking for community in a music scene somewhere "out there" beyond one's real, face-to-face community is probably an illusory goal, and perhaps runs counter to the most important goals of environmental music and sustainable music making. Love the ones you're with.

Community music is more about listening than performing, and that starts with listening to whatever and whoever is actually surrounding you. David Rothenberg argues that "we cannot make any kind of music without sensing its resonance in an environment" (2001, 4). Musical "resonance" goes beyond sound. Environmentally integrated, community-based music requires a resonant social connection as well as recognition of shared histories, identities, and a common stake in place. It requires very close listening. The students achieved that with the bridge project.

FIGURE 4   Turtle Boy busks on behalf of the Friends of the
Mississippi River (FMR.org). *(Photo by Tim Busse.)*

I would relearn that lesson as this fieldwork developed. But first I would
get a little lost in clubland.

I played several clubs with Desdamona and Pete, and we did some
recording. I improved as a musician, in large part thanks to performing
alongside these accomplished professionals. Desdamona has made a
living for most of her adult life as a professional bassist. She has a great
voice to boot. I will stop the praise there for fear of gushing. Let's just say
that performing with Desdamona was a wonderful way to start.

When we first met him, Pete was a 19-year-old guitar prodigy. He
auditioned and beat out a number of other musicians for the role of
guitarist-drummer. Whereas many 19-year-old guitarists have average
talent and major professional ambitions, Pete is an exceptional guitarist

with no desire to perform professionally. He would rather teach high school political science. He is also a hard-working political staffer who took part in Senator Al Franken's successful campaign, among others. After more than one gig I witnessed audience members and fellow performers trying to persuade Pete to pursue a musical career professionally. He is not interested. I was fortunate to perform with that level of talent.

The biggest problem, from an environmental perspective, was that I took the Hypoxic Punks into the club circuit. I overestimated the political potential of the bar scene. We played a new band night at the Fine Line in Minneapolis, Halloween night at Club Underground, and a few other bar gigs. It did not take long for me to realize that nightclubs are a fairly useless place to make political music. Many readers will disagree and could offer historical examples to refute my claim. From Frida Kahlo's *Friduchos* to Wobblie organizers, bars have been popular meeting places where important political work has been accomplished. That was not apparent during my fieldwork, however. Neither from the stage nor looking up from the audience could I find much evidence of the modern club existing for anything beyond drinking, dancing, socialization, and sex. There is nothing wrong with any of those activities, but there is a virtual proscription against politics within the club scene. The cage of cool precludes it. I base that conclusion on empirical experience as well as interviews and discussions with experienced musicians from throughout the Twin Cities. Audiences come to drink and dance, not to think or be artfully engaged. It is a place for young, single people to become someone else— not a good place for bands to sing about environmental problems.

The club scene has a sort of market authenticity, however. Although privately owned, bars, clubs, and restaurants are among the most authentically "popular" places to hear live local music. The club is a place where people listen to music by choice, and will even pay for it, rather than being conscripted into it by school, church, or civic obligation. But American pop culture eschews politics: it is a sexual turnoff and a detoxicating downer. It hurts the sell. Songs about labor and the environment don't sell alcohol as well as songs about drinking, drugs, and sex. Club owners were always a little suspicious of "political bands" like the Hypoxic Punks, but most let us perform anyway.

Despite their market authenticity, moreover, clubs do not financially sustain the professional music scene. Local musicians sustain the clubs. Few clubs pay enough to keep professional musicians afloat, but volunteering musicians do keep the clubs in business. Local musicians mostly make their living at private parties, weddings, and corporate events. Nevertheless, bands play the clubs in order to feel viable as creative artists and perhaps keep alive the notion that something better awaits in the future. Clubs are not the gateway to success they once were, but they allow local and small-time touring artists to remain creatively relevant.

Unfortunately, bar and club gigs are anathema to environmental art. To understand why, it is useful to examine their primary cultural function and economic underpinnings. From the owner's perspective, clubs are designed to sell alcohol. That is how clubs survive. For customers, the club scene provides ritual intoxication, social lubrication that facilitates a sense of togetherness, escape, and, of course, a meeting place to find new friends and sexual partners.

For bands, the club scene presents a gateway toward "making it," even though hardly anyone does. However, the tricky part is that bands are not supposed to show overt interest in popular success, but rather must master the postmodern art of ironic detachment. Must be hard being them. From the start, however, our little trio clearly did not fit into the club scene. To the extent that we did fit, it was because we abandoned our environmental and political goals.

Occasionally feeling like a fool is the price of taking part in public performance, but never did I feel more foolish than when performing in clubs. Perhaps biker bars or other age-appropriate drinking establishments would make more sense, especially now that the Hypoxic Punks comprises four middle-aged men, but the contradictions between message, medium, and context have dogged the Hypoxic Punks from the beginning. Folk singer Larry Long explained the problem in an interview with Desdamona:

> I used to be a bar musician. I haven't played in clubs for 20 years. I chose to get out of it because . . . what are you selling? You're selling liquor. That's why a bar stays open, because you're selling liquor.

We experienced the same contradiction between medium and message. I greatly respect Long's decision.

Joe Hill recognized the importance of going wherever working people socialize. Unfortunately, the drinking hall has changed in the last hundred years. *Bowling Alone* (Putnam 2000) describes how people live now. Fewer and fewer gather habitually in their local pubs. If they go out on a Friday night, they are as likely to travel ten miles as two blocks. Digital home entertainment has made it less likely that they will go out at all. The growing workday and workweek have undone the weekend for many adults. As a result, bars are filled with little more than young men and women who go out in order to hook up, a liminal rite-of-passage that leads toward more domestic, and often less public, life. The "meat market" metaphor has become even more accurate in the last 20 years.

Furthermore, digital mobility has made it possible, and for many preferable, to build communities online rather than create one in the shared space of a local pub, club, or bowling alley. There is nothing wrong with that, but it makes the club a hard place for local musicians to perform politically or environmentally meaningful music (Pedelty and Racheli 2009).

Musical Community, Ecology, and Ritual

Rehearsing with Desdamona and Pete, I began to realize that local music is as much about interacting with other musicians as about performing for audiences. When making music, it is necessary to be "in time" with others, to have a strong sense of shared space and time rather than allowing one's mind to wander off. Getting too wrapped up in the past is particularly dangerous. Even thinking about the mistake you made in the last measure can take a musician out of that sense of immediate present and shared presence that you need to hit the next beat correctly. That sense is everything, making one intimately aware of others' presence as well. "What all music offers us," argues Frith, "is a way of being present" (1996, 145).

All social activities require some sense of here-and-now, but in the continuum from mind-wandering labor—daydreaming while making copies, for example—to the intricate choreography of ballet, making music is much closer to the latter. It takes all of one's focus and energies to do well. The reflexive aspect of doing ethnographic fieldwork sometimes got in the way of achieving that unreflexive mental state. I would start to think about what a performance meant, culturally, rather than doing it well. As Charles Keil warns, "too much consciousness of 'how to groove' can get in the way" of actually feeling the music and becoming part of the musical moment (2010, 9). I found myself either getting into the music and losing consciousness of my ethnographic goals or else becoming too aware of my participant-observer status and forgetting words or chords, and losing the "groove."

One of the most difficult stages in musicianship is not the "ten thousand hours of practice" required to get good, but rather the next step, which is to forget all of that training in order to perform. Repetitious practice is in large part intended to produce muscle memory and instant recall. The final goal is to limit conscious override, including any sense of past or future. Musical performance is a ritualized method for capturing the ineffable present. No temporal state is more difficult to comprehend.

When all goes well, that special sense of time and place is shared with the audience. Nigel Osborne provides an insightful description of the musical present (2009, 551):

> We hear a beat, it catches our attention, we hear it again and already we know its cycle. By the third beat we have entered a frame where we have no need to remember what has gone before and we anticipate exactly what is going to come—and we may well be impelled to move our body. In one sense we are locked physically and mentally into an illusory "timeless" unchanging present. In another we are scrupulously marking the passage of time, and engaged in, paying attention to, its dynamic processes. If this is the case, then the presence of pulse offers a kind of "homeostasis" or self-stabilizing and ordering to consciousness, a place where it can "play," and "hang out" with others. We, individually and collectively, are synchronized, activated and reconciled with our personal and sympathetic human chronobiology.

Jessica Phillips-Silver and colleagues are among those who refer to musical synchronization as "entrainment," the "spatiotemporal coordination resulting from rhythmic responsiveness to a perceived rhythmic signal process" (Phillips-Silver, Aktipis, and Bryant 2010, 5). Charles Keil and Steven Feld's concept of "groovology" is similar, albeit presented in more lyrical language (Keil and Feld 2005).

Groove, the palpable sense of here and now, can translate into a strong sense of community. It can connect us to each other and help us to create a shared sense of place. However, it can do bad things as well. Musical ritual includes the Yaqui Deer Dance, Mexica sacrifice, half-time-show fly-overs, and military marches. In other words, the fact that there is pleasure in the groove or entrainment does not automatically make it good.

We are fairly well entrained into our society (Groom 1996), and not always toward positive ends. Rowland Atkinson's analysis of the urban soundscape (2007) complements Tagg's (2006) description of urban rock. However, whereas Tagg celebrates music's triumph over the city's chaotic noise, Atkinson argues that urban sound is highly organized and often oppressive (2007, 1907):

The implication of this relatively ordered soundscape is not only that it is in some sense organised, but also that it is socially organising. While we are often not aware of it, sound and music not only exist in differing configurations and volumes, so too does this aural envelope guide, invite, deter and otherwise subtly influence our patterns of sociability, modes of transport and interactions in urban space—influences we are often not aware of.

Atkinson describes deleterious aspects of urban sound patterning. Some of the soundscapes he discusses are unconsciously patterned at the structural level. In other cases, urban sound is designed to disempower (ibid., 1911):

Functional music has thereby been used strategically for the purpose of creating untroublesome and socially useful subjects, as citizens, workers or consumers in territories where control of the soundscape may also be connected to the control of production and consumption functions.

Soundscapes are made for us, encouraging us to buy, work, or play, but rarely to resist.

Precious few songs directly call our attention to soundscape, to help us reflect upon, and therefore change the contexts in which we listen. We are to simply lose ourselves in the consumer utopia that is modern life. Ke$ha and Kid Rock ask us to give in, forget, and adopt the dream.

Nor do many songs call our attention to unpleasant realities, such as military adventures in Vietnam, Nicaragua, El Salvador, Colombia, Iraq, Afghanistan, Pakistan, Bahrain, and so on. The exceptions, such as Toby Keith's rousing war anthem "Courtesy of the Red, White, and Blue" (2002), tell us that the USA will "put a boot in your ass" if you defy it. Such songs are laudable in their brutal honesty. In fact, we need more Toby Keiths willing to explicitly engage political questions through music. Critically engaged songs, left, right, or otherwise, are rare. Most of our music tells us everything is fine—just dance, drink, and forget about it. That is perhaps the most powerful form of entrainment, dominating the soundscape of home entertainment, shopping malls, and clubs.

Given this strident criticism of clubland and mainstream popular music, it is ironic that one of the Hypoxic Punks' most successful events took place in a dingy little club. However, I will save that story for the end.

Bands and Bandmates

Most of what I learned in this project came from fellow musicians. Before I mention a few of the lessons learned from bandmates, however, a word is in order concerning bands that shared the stage. Not "the bands that opened for us" or "bands we opened for"—local shows don't work like that. Our preference was always to go first. When I asked a couple of young bands if they would like to do a show with us, they said, "Sure, we'd be glad to open for you." "No," I explained, "most of our fans are in bed by 10 P.M."

Coastwest Unrest is a band with incredibly strong audience appeal, artful lyrics, and impressive musicianship. They performed with us while traveling to a show in Chicago from their home base in Las Vegas. With a CD released on Reclaim Records, they may be a bit too far ahead of the curve artistically speaking to make a big splash just yet, but live audiences love their shows. Their 2011 appearance at the Warped Tour could be the start of much bigger things for the band. Coastwest's spare, metallic, acoustic sound evokes life in their desert home, very refreshing in a world of could-be-anywhere songs about love, sex, and whatever (myspace. com/coastwestunrest).

Despite being just three guys with minimal instrumentation, Coast-west Unrest's music is highly dynamic. Guitarist and lead vocalist Noah Dickie supplements brother Josh Dickie's mesmerizing, bone-dry percussion with rhythmic stage stomping. That night the stage almost collapsed as unanchored plywood boards started to bounce out of place underneath Noah's pounding boot. It was a captivating part of his performance. At later shows I found myself starting to stomp while singing as well. Not just tapping or swaying, but more vigorously stomping. I was not consciously imitating Noah, but rather had started to incorporate a bit of what he does into my own performances. It is incredible how much you start to pick up just by watching other musicians and even the audience. At an outdoor show I found myself bouncing back and forth like a kid who was dancing in the crowd. Most of the time, however, I am too stuck inside myself to move much at all.

I have learned from every solo musician and band we've played with, as well as musicians encountered in the studio. For example, I have had the great pleasure of getting to know Gary Hines, director and founding member of the renowned gospel ensemble Sounds of Blackness (sounds ofblackness.com). Gary works hard every day to propel Sounds of Black-ness, arranging recording sessions, developing new performances, calling radio stations, dealing with tour logistics, writing arrangements, and so on. Most fans have no idea how much work goes into turning out high-quality music. That is partly by design: the goal of all the hard work is to make it sound easy.

I could go on, but I'll mention just one more performer we learned from. Carolyn Cruso lives on Orcas Island and performs with guitar and hammered dulcimer throughout the United States and Canada. At least once a year she tours, focusing on the rural West and Midwest. Her songs are very much from the heart and mostly drawn from direct experience.

Of all the musicians we performed with, Carolyn is perhaps the best model in terms of environmental performance, even though she does not explicitly think of her work in those terms. Carolyn has had a deep love for nature since her early days. She majored in environmental studies at the University of New Hampshire, volunteered on Seeger's *Clearwater* as a young woman, and has hiked and explored nature throughout her life. During a recent interview (2011), Carolyn contrasted her music with that of more overtly political musicians:

> I don't think I write anything that is environmental; it's not really political in a direct way. It's more indirect. It's how nature feeds us, feeds our soul so that we can just live more fully. So that might be political indirectly, but it's not political like Bruce Cockburn or Jackson Browne or Jim Page. . . . I tried writing music like that because I really, really appreciated it when I was younger. I still do appreciate it, but I just don't listen to it as much anymore. And I just found I wasn't good at it. . . . It didn't feel like that's where my skills and my talents were, so I'll just leave that to them.

Perhaps because she does not draw political lines, Carolyn's music provides a strong musical connection between listeners and the places where they live. Her music forms part of Orcas Island's musical consciousness. A warm smile comes across the faces of local islanders when they mention Carolyn. Through her music the water, trees, and stones become much more than material substrate; they take on a magical quality as part of the listeners' lives. Music like Carolyn's does place-making work particularly well.

One of Orcas Island's leading musical matchmakers, jazz musician Martin Lund, recommended Carolyn when I asked him who might want to play an environmentally themed folk/rock concert with the Hypoxic Punks. Lund is an accomplished Los Angeles studio musician who has worked with Mel Torme, Isaac Hayes, and hundreds of other recording artists. He also composed *Suite for Turtleback Mountain* (2006), music that pays homage to the endangered landscape described in Chapter 1. He has collaborated with Carolyn on many occasions in the studio and on stage. Lund's recommendation is no small praise.

Given her references to thrushes, crows, and owls in her very Cascadian "Rhythm in the Rain" (2009) and the strong evocations of nature in her dulcimer recordings, it is somewhat surprising that Carolyn does not think of her music as environmental. I get the sense that landscape is so much a part of her musical experience that she does not feel the need to call conscious attention to it. Her song "Flyway Zone" (2000) has a traveler moving across the Minnesota prairie, surrounded by flocks of migrating birds, colorful maples, sun, rain, water, and the changing seasons. In contrast to the familiar, ego-driven road motif, the first-person subject in Carolyn's song plays a very small role within nature's unfolding drama, "waiting for the flocks of birds to show me where to go."

Carolyn's comparisons to more "political" musicians brought to mind a potential gender dimension. I am reminded of Frida Kahlo, whose more personal portraiture contrasted with the didactic murals of her three-time husband, Diego Rivera. Kahlo also attempted to do more public, didactic art early on, but felt that it was too forced. Carolyn's expressions of nature, too, are more personal than the work of the musicians she listed. Her music invites the listener in subtly, rather than offering an overt political challenge; it is a dialogue, not a didactic monologue. That allows listeners to relate to Carolyn's music on a more personal level. Although it is by no means an absolute distinction, it seems that women musicians are more likely to take that more subtle, dialogical approach. Among the ethnographic lessons I learned through listening to Carolyn's live and recorded music, the importance of honestly expressing oneself as a performer stands out.

As for my bandmates, I have learned something from each one. Rather than go down the list, it might be more useful to illustrate their differing perspectives. I chose to work with each of them because of their musical talents. At no point did I have an environmental litmus test. They were interested enough in my music to take part, and I am incredibly grateful for that. I have been lucky to learn from them as informants.

It is probably worth mentioning that I did come up with a little grant money to pay Desdamona and Pete. However, their paid status did not seem to warp their sense of collective ownership onstage or in rehearsal. After her stint with the band was over, Desdamona had this to say about music and the environment, based in part on the Hypoxic Punks, but also on her subsequent experience as a teacher:

I have serious doubts about the power of music to communicate any useful environmental message. At any level, I think people are too poorly educated and inundated with too many pressing messages to see the dire situation our planet faces. When they listen to music (live or on media), their emotional needs are usually other needs: to feel understood, to get happy, to hang out, dance/ get laid, etc.

On the other hand, a mentorship experience, and that's what I think I mostly gained from my experience with the Hypoxic Punx, can have a profound impact. Listening is not enough, but doing becomes a part of your physical and mental muscle memory. If you were, for instance, to take a group of musicians who were also interested in making social change or saving the planet (which in my mind is the same thing) and lead them in a program of public works projects + writing songs about it, you will change the team members. (You will also have done something nice for the environment, hopefully.) The impact on the public will be exponentially decreased because hearing and seeing is not believing. Doing is believing. (Email, 2011)

Desdamona finished by citing "an exponential loss of energy down the chain from performer to audience." That is a very interesting idea, and part of the philosophy behind Pete Seeger's participatory music. Musical consumption as an end product is different from helping to create music in more collaborative fashion. Desdamona is an exceptional musical collaborator; she gets everyone around her involved.

Desdamona pours herself into the creative process. She is the type of musician who will forcefully snap you back into time and place if you find yourself out of step. She is demanding, yet patient and helpful. Truly excellent musicians seem to make each other better and bring each other into a shared time and space.

After Desdamona moved on to finish her degree and focus on teaching, time, money, and logistics forced me to become the front person. I have been a very sorry substitute for Desdamona. It is much, much more fun standing behind and a little to the side of a talented lead singer like Des, watching and reacting, a position I hope to occupy once again someday.

Like most bands, the Hypoxic Punks eventually got greedy, wanting more than a mobile acoustic trio. That was not just my fault. I started with a talented djembe player, Varun, and when he left for New Orleans I recruited Des. Pete joined us to switch back and forth between guitar and snare. We all did a bit of hand percussion. Before Desdamona and Pete moved on, Leon Hsu joined us on violin.

I had already played with Leon on the side; in fact, for a short period he and I became the Hypoxic Punks, offering a few live performances as "the band." Like most quick-and-easy ensembles, we started to want some percussion, and after playing an impromptu concert with drummer Robert Poch, we asked him to join us.

Leon and I told Bob he would only have to play hand percussion. Bob is an expert conga player as well as a kit drummer. It is a luxury for drummers to leave behind the kit and focus on hand percussion. Given the rich textures Bob produces with hand instruments, it was unfair to ask him to drag the whole kit to gigs. That did not stop us from breaking our promise and asking Bob to play the full drum set. Having added an excellent electric bass player, Bryan Mosher, we were reaching a size and complexity that required more and more sonic cohesion, equipment, and mixing abilities. At one point there were seven of us, with Jesse's electronic keyboards, Tim Bornholdt adding hand percussion and backing vocals, and Pete coming back for sessions onstage and in the studio. Quite a zoo, but Bob held us together in expert fashion.

It is common for at-the-ready ensembles like ours to grow and become more technologically encumbered. There are advantages to acoustic ensembles, however. It is good for activist musicians to be able to pick up their instruments and move at a moment's notice. It takes at least a half-hour to move, set up, and mic a full drum kit. Once again, rock consumes a great deal of time and money.

Yet the fully equipped rock band sounds so much better than a spare acoustic group. It provides a much greater range of sound textures and rhythmic possibilities. Bob took our request in stride and now lugs his full drum kit to most gigs.

Bob offered his thoughts on performing in the Hypoxic Punks:

> Personally, playing in a band with environmental awareness and themes creates a sense of personal wholeness by connecting a physical form of artistic expression (percussion) with being an involved citizen who cares deeply about the uses and preservation of environmental resources. Further, it connects me with communities of musicians who are also advocates for wise environmental interaction. In such a way it is possible to bring virtually all of oneself artistically, professionally, and spiritually—to a relationship with the environment and its preservation. (Email, 2011)

I decided to work with musicians who were primarily interested in music and not go around looking for ideological symmetry or shared views on the environment. Therefore, I have been lucky to be surrounded by musicians, like Bob, who actively advance the project's environmental goals as well. When I have become stuck, the band gets me going in the right direction. That is true for all three of my current bandmates.

The improvised tag-team act at Balls Cabaret taught me a lesson that is just now starting to take hold, many years later. It is in the moments before and between songs that you get the best chance to communicate explicit messages. If that time is not abused, it can entertain and inform. I enjoy listening to what my bandmates have to say when they take over the mic between songs to banter, introduce band members, or remind audiences that our CDs are on the bar, for the taking (better to give away many than sell a few).

Bryan is particularly good at it:

My wife calls me an undercover brother. I take that to mean that one might not guess my political leanings from my manner or appearance. Playing bass in a band with an environmental mission keeps me under cover, both musically—because the lower frequencies are often unnoticed—and politically—because I can be involved in something I care about in an indirect way.

On stage, I try to capitalize on the fact that I may not appear to align with the mission of the band. Between songs, while Mark calls attention to the environmental themes in the music, I try to play the part of the foil for humorous effect, for example by contradicting Mark's statements or by acting out advertisements for agri-business. (Email, 2011)

Bryan's musical ideas have greatly improved our sound. His instincts for showmanship help us communicate the environmental message in a much more entertaining way as well.

And then there is Leon, the violinist. I have played with Leon longer than with any of the others. I have on several occasions asked him what he thinks of this or that change in the lyrics. His replies have ranged from "The songs have lyrics?" to "I don't really listen to the words." Of course, that has not stopped him from suggesting changes now and then. Asked to supply his final thoughts on the environmental goals of the musical project, Leon said, after thinking long and hard, "nothing really comes to mind." Leon is the sort of bandmate who keeps you securely grounded—plus, he comes up with amazing violin parts.

In the end, what most music does best is provide pleasure. For local music, in particular, that means satisfying the local musicians' desire to express themselves and form musical communities. Everything else, including a loyal following, is icing on the cake.

The Audience

Most of the Hypoxic Punks' audience consists of family, friends, neighbors, and colleagues, as well as their families, friends, neighbors, and colleagues. That is typical for local bands. I was surprised when an owner of one of the most popular clubs in Minneapolis explained that even for bands performing at his establishment, "most ticket sales go to bands' friends and family." Well-known touring bands on their way through town net full houses, but a true "following" is rare for local bands. Most local bands who talk as if they have a large, exogenous audience are promotional, optimistic, or delusional. It is the job of local media, if they like a band, to foster that collective illusion until it finally, in a few isolated cases, becomes reality.

For most local bands, like us, an audience full of family, friends, neighbors, and colleagues suffices. We have had plenty of people stick around who just happened to be at the bar before we got started, a few who come in from the cold after seeing a flyer, others who decide to check out the show after walking by the club, and of course, the other bands' fans. The Acadia Café, in Minneapolis, is particularly good, because it is located on a city corner with wrap-around windows. Some folks passing by will pop in if the band looks like something they'd be interesting in hearing. The Acadia does not allow cover songs, is relatively small, and has no cover charge. Therefore, it is a great place for a band to play without all the hassles brought on by trying to fill a bigger club.

Local musicians sustain each other. They form communities. Their friends and family play an integral role, and without them at the core of the local audience, it would all just be a glorified rehearsal. For me the highlight at all-ages shows is to look down and see my nieces, the best fans in the world. Although I get even more nervous than usual when performing for them, it is much less fun when they are not there.

In other words, when you scratch the surface of much of the local music scene, it really is community-based, participatory music. I don't want to overstate the case or use it as an excuse for my inability to generate larger audiences for the Hypoxic Punks. From the outset, gaining a following was never a goal or even a realistic hope. Nevertheless, there have been a few surprisingly large audiences along the way, often when least expected.

Through fieldwork performance I have come to realize that audiences are not discovered; they are made. I have seen many promising bands fold their tents after a year or two of seeking out a larger audience and never reaching that elusive goal—not for lack of talent, but more often for lack of resources, an inability to adapt to institutional and audience demands, or both. Not only are there the costs of equipment and sustaining oneself, but there is only so much time in the day and only so many people to do all the work. It is time-consuming enough to write, organize, rehearse, record, and perform music with others. Promotions, booking, management, and media relations are also time-consuming, costly, and boring.

In today's mediated age, "word of mouth" is often mythical. Even "buzz" can be artificially generated. Some bands go as far as to pay hip young "street teams" to subtly promote the band in lines outside clubs. They are instructed to talk loudly about the band's latest show or chat up their CD outside an age-appropriate movie. To the untrained eye, a street team appears no different than any other group of young, good-looking men and women (mainly women) talking about their favorite band in a public place. I first became aware of this marketing tactic when reading Naomi Klein's *No Logo* (2002) but did not realize its extent until I met a number of students at the University of Minnesota employed for that purpose. Bands and music promoters market their wares using the same strategies as companies like Red Bull, Vitamin Water, and Coca Cola. They hire energetic young people, model consumers, to go out and conspicuously consume their products in public places. If that happens in Minnesota, one can only imagine how prevalent the practice is in New York City or Los Angeles. On the other hand, no amount of marketing would be enough to generate a large audience for most local bands. For such guerilla marketing tactics to work, there has to be a lot more going for the band than marketing.

Perhaps it was once as simple as forming a band, performing around town, drawing in audiences, and then catching the eye of a national record company, but I have seen little evidence of that being the case today. For the bands that I have watched make a go of it, at least so far, there has been a reciprocal relationship between institutional support and audience. There is usually at least some underwriting available to them early on. These bands have strong talent as well, and incredible work ethics, or they would not garner that support. However, talent is not enough. As Woody Guthrie sang, you also need a bit of "Do-Re-Mi": financial backing.

For all of those reasons, making music professionally takes a lot of hard work, stubbornness, focus, self-confidence, and an unquenchable passion for music. Those are the impressive and rare qualities that keep someone like Robert Zimmerman going despite all of the early doubters. Most of us love music, but few of us want to invest and risk the time, effort, and money it takes to perform professionally. After all, what if we did all that and still failed? Pre-emptive failure is preferable.

Fortunately, most community musicians are not about "making it" in the business. The majority of working bands are local musicians content to make music locally. Even if they have day jobs, however, someone still has to do management, booking, venue logistics, promotions, website updates, and media relations. Someone has to arrange rehearsal times and spaces, move equipment, mix sound, develop song sets, write charts, record rehearsal demos, contact venues, arrange venue logistics, hammer out money details, schedule sound checks, figure out what equipment to bring, and determine how many direct-in (DI) boxes and microphone stands are provided on site. Someone needs to do post-show follow up, including collecting payment. Someone needs to create, print, and post flyers, list concert dates and information on local music websites, develop and contact online fan lists, work closely with other bands, and find new and more creative ways to get the word out about upcoming concerts. Finally, someone needs to contact media, including local newspapers and radio, in order to further promote shows and recordings, and maybe even get a music reviewer to attend the concert. Bands either hire managers, promoters, and booking agents to do those tasks well, or they distribute the work among themselves in order to do it poorly. One way to gauge the professional potential of a band is the number of professionals they hire to help out.

After every concert I tell myself that I'll do more promotions and media work the next time around. Then the next workday hits, and before long the next concert is upon us. This fieldwork experience was realistic in that regard. I learned how difficult it is to perform music as a side gig. After writing songs, rehearsing, and managing the band, there simply was no time left over for logistics and promotions. Frankly, even if I had had the time, I would have done a poor job. This project gave me incredible respect for the professional managers, booking agents, promoters, and media-relations specialists who make popular music work, at every level. They earn their pay and then some. Fortunately, Ari Winkle volunteered her graphic arts and photography skills, as did Cindy Poch (see ecomusicology.net). In short, this fieldwork experience opened my eyes to how much work it takes, and how many people are required, to launch a band and keep it afloat.

Concerts make all of the hassles worth the effort. Local club audiences are appreciative and responsive, at least in Minnesota. One gets the sense, when a performance goes well, that the audience takes collective ownership. They make it happen. In a world where most cultural products are produced somewhere far, far away, it is a truly rare and wonderful experience when something good is produced locally.

Often as I was hustling to get my equipment offstage after a performance or sitting politely watching the next band, audience members would come up to talk. Such conversations typically begin with genre. New audience members try to fit us into a musical taxonomy, such as acoustic rock, Americana, or folk rock. A producer categorized Des, Pete, and me as "like the B52's meet Peter, Paul, and Mary!" He said that he wanted to use the band in other shows and gave us his card, but as usual I did not have time to follow up.

My favorite shout from the audience was: "Are you guys a family?" Even if we were married, Desdamona and I would not produce a six-foot-five child. Nevertheless, I took that question as a compliment. In a way a band does become a family. When the sound and performance come together, there is an infectious sense of connection. The audience senses that and helps to produce it. Our performances have tended to reflect our audiences. It is a truly awful feeling when you fail to meet a good audience's expectations, but truly wonderful when you are able to reflect the same level of energy back to the audience.

Doe Bay and the Lone Guitar Theory

After a few years of searching for answers onstage, the project finally started bearing fruit. We started to make connections with environmental organizations and leverage the power of music to make a small difference locally as part of a larger environmental movement.

My first solo performance took place at an open mic night in an out-of-the-way café in the San Juan Islands of Washington State. It was early summer in 2008. The rustic room was already bursting with life when it was my turn at the microphone. Seated patrons ate pizza while a standing audience hung around the edges of the room in small groups, engaged in lively conversation. Many had just ended a long workweek at a nearby organic farm that recruits energetic college students from the mainland.

I took the stage with my guitar and harmonica, terrified at the prospect of playing alone, with no one to cover up my mistakes. Although two or three bandmates cannot really cover for you, it is nice to know that when you drop out, the song keeps going. Solo sets offer no such safety net.

The set started with few upbeat songs, and much to my surprise, people started dancing and clapping along. After three songs I started to pack up, to vigorous applause. (They seemed to be applauding the set, not the fact that I was packing up.) *No need to push my luck*, I thought. The audience cheered for more. I ended the set with a fourth tune, "River's Getting Dirty." It also went over well. "This solo stuff is going to be easy," I thought to myself. After shaking hands with the MC, I quickly retreated to the back of the room. A fairly successful performance, one that would leave little room for rumination afterward. Typically after a concert I start thinking things like "how could I forget the last verse?" or "my fingers were way too stiff."

The MC picked up his guitar and kept the night moving with a satirical crowd-pleaser: "Bomb-a, Bomb-a, Bomb-a, Bomb-a, Bomb-a an Iranian" set to the tune of Culture Club's hit "Karma Chameleon" (1983). The musical critique of George W. Bush's saber rattling was well received. A young local farmer borrowed my guitar and tossed in a few upbeat cover tunes.

Before my performance, most of the evening had been devoted to brooding, earnest, introspective singer-songwriter material. Good folk music, but out of synch with the context and crowd. The audience was looking for something a bit more lively. In other words, I got lucky, finding the right crowd in the right place at the right time. I should have learned that night that people make music together, even when one performs solo. The local musician is, at the best of times, a catalyst.

Audiences make music. They build community through integrated sound, movement, and sight. There may even be physiological entrainment involved. Neuroscientist Daniel Levitin argues that "there is every reason to believe that some of our brain states will match those of the musicians we are listening to" (2006, 211). The musical connection works on multiple levels, from neural networks to social networks, possibly on up to ecosystems. The musician gets to play a catalytic role in the larger, communal act of making music, but he or she is no more important than the first brave soul who jumps up to dance, the venue staff, or the promoter. While performing at Doe Bay I have noticed how important the wait staff are to setting the mood as well. Watching Doe Bay servers work inspired the song "Jenny Vang."

I tried to recreate the moment later that summer and fell flat on my face. The first solo performance worked because it was what the audience wanted. The songs and performance did not create the moment; the audience did. Once again, the concert was a tonic for the troops, an upbeat and relevant way to celebrate a week of hard work, congeal a community, and refresh its energy. This was the type of community that lives sustainably and works hard to do so. There have to be rewards for that. The music did not make the moment, but it played its part. In a world where most entertainment comes to us from far beyond, all of us gathered there managed to make our own musical moment, together. In an interview with Des, singer Larry Long explained that "you have to go where people are," especially if you want to communicate a message (Pedelty and Racheli 2009, 273). During that first Doe Bay concert, I went to where the audience was, and they reciprocated.

Later that summer I expected the audience to be there again. Unfortunately, it was not that easy. The set started earlier in the evening, and the more family-oriented crowd had gathered to eat pizza in peace rather than listen to music. Ignoring the lesson I had learned before—people at this place prefer upbeat, positive music—I played a slower, more serious set . . . boring, you might say. I had experienced similar scenes many times before, as part of the captive audience. This was the first time I played the part of "that guy" on stage, desperately trying to impose his musical will on an unreceptive audience. Most of the diners just wanted a nice bite to eat with their families, but they clapped politely nonetheless.

That second night at Doe Bay made me realize just how special the local community concert can be, and how psychologically difficult it is to fail as a performer. Stage fright is, to a certain extent, the memory of social failure. Failure is also how an ethnographer learns, going through the painful process of enculturation.

The lessons learned in the summer of 2008 were threefold: (1) audiences are not just passive receptors—they actively make music; (2) if people want local musicians to do anything at all, it is to perform as cultural catalysts; and (3) music makes place, but place also makes music.

Rock and pop audiences do not listen to local performers in the same way they listen to recorded music. The big-name concert audience has already listened to the performer's music in recorded form, over and over again. Their depth of engagement with the recording artist's sounds and words is much more profound as a result. The medium is the message; recorded music speaks to us very differently than music heard live for the first time. Yet that is also the magic of local music. When music is truly new to the audience and the time and place are right, unique and special moments can be created.

I always feel as if a performance has succeeded when people feel free to talk, walk, dance, and so on. When all eyes face forward, as if waiting for the next sound to form or word to drop, it feels more like musical conscription, with the audience chained to the stage. That is how classical and contemporary folk audiences work, but rock and pop are not about people sitting still and listening to abstracted sound. Rock and pop are about fully embodied participation in a cultural scene.

As for making music sustainably, it is useful to contrast the Sierra Club band concert described in the Introduction with the two solo performances at Doe Bay. Neither of the Doe Bay concerts required a cargo van. I can carry a guitar and harmonica on my back, and much of the audience simply walked over from their fields, yurts, and cabins. Perhaps that is why we have come to associate environmentally oriented music with singer-songwriters or small acoustic ensembles. Ani DiFranco, with her acoustic guitar and minimal electrical encumbrance, looks the part. She does not have to seek accolades for turning some huge stadium show into a supposedly carbon-neutral affair. She doesn't need the stadium, the huge electronic band, or the giant stage to start with.

It seems discordant to hear big, Borg-like bands cranking out rock songs about sustainability. As an audience, we sense that dissonance. As environmentalist musicians, we openly confront the question through our own composition, rehearsal, booking, promotion, and performance practices. The energy requirements of rock concerts go well beyond the collective sweat of musicians, managers, and venue staff; they include gas, electricity, and equipment. Audiences may not run rigorous tests or harshly judge us for our contradictions, but part of the aesthetic assessment goes beyond genre conventions or conscious recognition. We can see and hear the symmetry between low-energy ensembles and environmental messages. Likewise, we can sense contradictions, both material and aesthetic, between energy-intensive bands and environmental messages. That is one of the reasons environmental music has been more closely linked to individuals like John Denver and Ani DiFranco than to the big bands of our time.

This lone guitar theory could be taken a bit further. When you hear the words "political musicians," what comes to mind? There are the Weavers, the Clash, Rage Against the Machine, and Sweet Honey in the Rock, but the more common responses, based on the survey cited in Chapter 2, are solo artists like Joe Hill, Paul Robeson, Woody Guthrie, Pete Seeger, Bob Dylan, Joan Baez, Billy Bragg, Ani DiFranco, Tracy Chapman, Sting, and Michael Franti (Pedelty 2008). Even Neil Young, Bruce Springsteen, and Mutabaruka tend to go solo when crafting more political, topical, and word-focused performances, carrying on the Joe Hill tradition described in Chapter 2. Solo folk artists like Utah Phillips help sustain political, labor, and environmental movements through song. It is easier to do that with a single voice and spare instrumentation, more difficult with a larger ensemble. In local contexts, at least, audiences look toward bands for upbeat entertainment, not lyrical messages.

However, neither cultural tradition nor audience expectations completely account for the time-honored association between solo voice and topical music. Logistical and technological factors favor the lone troubadour as well. A solo voice can be heard much more clearly than the harmonized voice: there is a reason lyric sheets are handed out to audiences at choral concerts. The same is true of instrumentation. Rather than blending in with a battery of instruments, the lone voice is more easily heard and understood when accompanied only by the singer-songwriter's guitar. You can hear the words.

Having one's words heard and understood is less of an issue for recorded music and performances by major recording artists. The star performer's audience is likely to have listened to his or her recordings long before attending the concert. Repeated listening to well-mixed recordings allows audiences to hear the musician's words and understand their meaning despite fuller orchestration. Likewise, concert technology used by major-label performers is far superior to that found in local clubs, where sound systems are rarely sophisticated enough to evenly mix sound throughout the space.

Not a problem for solo acts. A soloist's words can be heard through even the most primitive PA system. Band singers often compete with a vast array of sounds, from the drum kit to screaming conversations at the bar. Lyrical clarity is essential for topical music, including environmental messaging. "I think if the performer is singing clearly," explained folk artist Heatherlyn to Desdamona, "it probably informs audiences" (2009).

There are additional logistical and financial benefits in solo performance. Hauling around and setting up an acoustic guitar is much simpler, not to mention less expensive, than transporting an entire band. There is much less overhead. The local musician can subsist more easily as a soloist than as part of a band. The soloist is more nimble, ready to perform for whatever good cause arises. Paul Metsa is a shining example. Paul makes a good living performing locally in the Twin Cities, touring on occasion and almost always lending his talent to a good cause. In a 2009 interview for our joint project, Paul told Desdamona that he believes "in the idea that one-man-one-guitar" can do great things, perhaps even "defeat an army."

Conversely, political bands are hard to manage and maintain. The odds of political concordance go down drastically with each band member added. Rage Against the Machine is the exception that proves the rule. Rage was formed after Tom Morello advertised for a "Socialist lead singer for Public Enemy-style metal band" (Devenish 2001, 21). Despite their tight political formation, Rage broke apart eight years later. Soloists stay together for a lifetime. Recent reunion tours notwithstanding, the fractious relationship among Rage band members shows how difficult it is to sustain a band, especially when you throw in the political element.

Nevertheless, I much prefer performing with the band. For me, the richer textures and rhythms of ensemble performance communicate something far more important than words. As I demonstrated at the second Doe Bay concert, the wrong guy, in the wrong place, doesn't do much at all. In the right context, however, I have heard sound work magic.

Place Makes Music

Going beyond the lone guitar theory, how might we make better music, more sustainably, together? A third Doe Bay concert added a few clues. This one took place on a Friday night with a full band. The owner of Doe Bay invited me to put together a full show, but Bryan and Bob could not make the trip, so the West Coast version of the Hypoxic Punks included two Orcas Island musicians and Leon, who flew in from Minnesota (Fig. 5).

FIGURE 5 The Hypoxic Punks perform at Doe Bay. *(Photo by Lori Mikolon.)*

The complete ensemble consisted of Leon on violin, Randy Jezierski on drums, and Matthew "Wally" Wallrath on tuba. Wally is originally from Wisconsin and Randy is from Chicago, so even the Orcas Island version had roots in the Upper Midwest. I played guitar and harmonica, and sang lead vocal, as I have been doing since Desdamona moved on. Ever since then I have been looking for a logistically feasible way to bring in a new lead singer. I miss having backup vocals. Tim and Pete took their voices with them when they graduated, leaving us with just one singer. Not only does my voice lack some of the complexities necessary for rock, but it's baritone. There is only room for so many Nick Caves in rock, men who can pull off rock baritone.

Perhaps the best illustration of why baritones don't work in rock comes by way of Garrison Keillor, whose classic radio monologue "Pontoon Boat" (2010) finds a pack of baritone Lutheran ministers ineffectually calling for help. As Bryan pointed out earlier, the lower tones don't carry as well as the upper registers. If the goal is for voice and words to be heard, it is better for the baritone to sing over minimal accompaniment. Better yet, he should get out of the way and let a tenor, alto, or soprano take lead. Unfortunately, recruiting and keeping a fifth musician has involved more work than simply making the best of what we have. In some ways that is the true spirit of local music: make the best of what you have.

I asked Carolyn Cruso to perform at the Doe Bay theme concert as well, and thankfully she did. With an opener like that, it is hard to go wrong. That third Doe Bay concert made for a fun night. The level of audience engagement was somewhere between the rowdy enthusiasm I encountered during the first Doe Bay outing and the polite indifference that met my second solo performance there. Several tables were filled with vacationers, and an enthusiastic couple from Connecticut was front and center. After the show they expressed their pleasure at happening upon the event, and were particularly taken by Leon's dynamic violin performance. Although I tease Leon about being the band's *divo*, he is an incredible musician. Throughout the concert I found myself watching the couple from Connecticut as they, in turn, watched Leon go at it. They were smiling and wide-eyed, sitting barely five feet from Leon's wild bow. Some island residents came to check out the show as well. The remaining tables were taken up by friends and families of the band. It was a fine turnout and a wonderfully enthusiastic audience.

Once again, the musicians on stage were not the only ones making music that night. The audience and the place itself exerted strong influences. Environments do not determine what we do, but they do affect us in various ways. Doe Bay the resort is nestled alongside Doe Bay the place, a beautiful inlet lined with limestone cliffs and towering Douglas fir, hemlocks, and red-barked madronas. Deer snack on the grass while seals play along the shoreline. Bald eagles and osprey circle above.

Songs about the natural environment make sense at Doe Bay. As Denise Von Glahn demonstrates in *The Sounds of Place*, "places can inspire art" and "musical responses can, at some level, evoke those places" (2003, 2). During a Doe Bay concert, musicians and audiences alike can gaze out into the woods and over the water. It is an inspiring place to make and listen to music.

As Claude Lévi-Strauss remarked, a listener unaware of Debussy's intent would not know that *La Mer* is even about the sea, let alone any specific ocean (Krause 2001, 216). However, if *La Mer* were performed by the sea, an audience would probably make the connection between sound structure and place without a need for other cues. Ecology goes beyond linear causation; it is about complex relationships. Song does not evoke meaning on its own; it too is about relationships, contexts, and connections.

Michael McDowell equates environmental ecology to Mikhail Bakhtin's social theory, "a science of relationships" where reality is best represented dialogically, rather than in a more univocal, totalizing theory (1996, 372). To imagine spatial landscapes as silent is as false as the notion that all we need do is listen to them. Nature does not talk or sing in teleological fashion, but seven billion people do. We talk and sing in specific spaces, working in conjunction with surrounding environments to make musical sense out of the places we inhabit.

The point is that the physical environment is more than a neutral player in the formation of soundscapes. Different places capture, evoke, and connote different sounds. Doe Bay would make very different music if it were developed into a large five-star resort. For example, the larger and more developed resort of Rosario, just a few miles down the road from Doe Bay, features a magnificent pipe organ as well as other musical accoutrements that would seem discordant at a smaller, more sedate, and environmentally integrated place like Doe Bay. Rosario's dominion over the local land- and soundscape mirrors the goals of shipping magnate Robert Moran, its founder. Moran started building the impressive Rosario Mansion in 1904, and the complex has since been expanded to include a full marina and resort. Thankfully, Moran donated the rest of his 7,000-acre estate to the state, which turned it into Moran State Park.

Once again, it is a matter of degree. Doe Bay is less invasive than Rosario, yet Rosario is far better integrated into the landscape than most resorts. For example, Rosario is far smaller and more sustainable than obtrusive hotel complexes in the Hawaiian Islands and Jamaica.

All places make music, no matter how complex the relationship between place, performer, and listener. A "traditional" Hawaiian luau at a tourist resort contains radically different social meanings than the indigenous rite it references. At Doe Bay musical performance more directly evokes the living world immediately surrounding the performance space. It is less of a nostalgic look back at environments from the past and more of a celebration of the ecological present. Music can be an important tool for environmental sustainability in that it integrates material and cultural environments, keeping ecological systems vital in the cultural imagination. As such, they have a fighting chance to be cared for well. When local ecologies become culturally discounted, they tend to fall prey to forces that view land, water, and life solely in terms of use-value, as "resources." In other words, how we conceive of local environs may be key to determining what happens to them. In both the aesthetic and moral sense, a place like Doe Bay seems to inspire good music, and that music, in turn, plays a role in stemming runaway development by constantly reminding us how special and rare such places are.

Carolyn's set fit Doe Bay perfectly. Ours may not have. Our merry band of acoustic punks seemed somewhat out of place as we blasted out dystopian songs of development and gluttony, but that might be the point. The Hypoxic Punks illustrate the disjuncture between ecological reality and environmental hope. Like rock itself, however, we seem to fit the city better.

Of course, this description of Doe Bay is somewhat idealized. Rural life in America is more closely linked to urban life than anyone likes to admit. People travel long distances to Doe Bay, mainly as a respite from city life. Permanent residents, many of them retired, travel to the mainland for Costco runs and other business. More than a few sit out the dreary island winter in Arizona or Hawaii. Even without such indulgences, the carbon footprint of the average rural person is still far greater than that of most city dwellers.

Wealthy suburbanites are often the first to colonize attractive, out-of-the-way locations like the San Juan Islands. A quick thumb through *Sunset* magazine illustrates the link between Western wealth and wilderness. Take organic hobby farmers. Few people "have access to the financial means, education, occupational flexibility, and time to carry out" urban back-to-the-land projects (2008, 48), observes Heise. The San Juan Islands are filled with people who ignore the "ecological consequences" of such projects (ibid.). Given the intensive energy inputs required for boutique agriculture (i.e., horticulture), relatively limited caloric outputs, soil amendments, transport, and biodiversity reduction (e.g., fencing out local wildlife and plowing over their habitat), such "thought experiments" are "imaginative dead ends" in terms of environmental stewardship and sustainability (ibid.). They accelerate the destruction of rare and disappearing island ecosystems in order to provide the suburban "farmer" with cultural capital. Of course, these small organic farms are better than large housing or resort developments, and some do achieve the Holy Grail of organic gardening: net benefit to the local food web. Plus, in addition to transitory hobby farms, there are permanent, professionally managed, cooperative farms on the island that provide a good deal of the local produce.

New age philosophies and music are popular in the San Juan Islands. The emphasis is on healing, rather than on critical, ecological insight of the sort Heise offers (2008). Conversely, punks tend to rub listeners' faces in such sordid realities. Both dystopian punk and utopian new age music serve a purpose. One represents life as it is; the other imagines alternatives.

But what is "local" music in a context like Doe Bay? Instead of a purely homemade soundscape, Doe Bay is a meeting place for traveling musical cultures. In that respect, Doe Bay is typical, a local place integrated into regional, national, and global systems. Nevertheless, Doe Bay's occupants seek to retain some of the place's local distinctiveness, even if they sometimes disagree as to what that means. Many express fears of becoming like Nantucket Island, touristy and overdeveloped. However, locals disagree with each other regarding how best to avoid that fate.

What does music do to sustain environmental integrity and biodiversity in a place like Doe Bay? Volunteer musicians join with the owner, management, staff, volunteer gardeners, and visitors to make the resort work. Without their volunteer efforts, Doe Bay would not be the same. For example, the annual Doe Bay Music Festival (doebayfest.com/) has helped sustain the resort financially and socially, and musicians provide a sustainable sense of place at Doe Bay year round.

Environmental Music and Film

One goal of ecomusicology is to capture a more complete sense of what it means to be a music-making species (McDermott 2008). Science is therefore essential. Ellen Dissanayake notes that music helps "individuals cope with anxiety" and argues that it might, therefore, have played an important evolutionary role in hominids (2009, 25), helping individuals survive, prosper, and reproduce more successfully (seems to be the case at rock festivals). Music assuages individual anxieties and, by extension, can have the same effect on group dynamics. Or music may be a byproduct of other genetic adaptations rather than an evolutionary development with direct selective advantage (Sacks 2007, xi).

In addition to finding it an interesting topic for scientific investigation, science educators have found music useful. For example, the Earth Systems Education Activities for Great Lakes Schools (ESEAGLS) curriculum entitled "Shipping on the Great Lakes" uses Gordon Lightfoot's song "The Wreck of the Edmund Fitzgerald" (1976) as a gateway to student inquiry about complex earth systems dynamics (Fortner and Corney 2002). "Since the actual causes of the sinking are unknown and probably additive," explain Rosanne Fortner and Jeffrey Corney, "students are left with an understanding that not everything in science has a correct and knowable answer" (2002, 13). "The excitement of science is in the search," and "science moves forward through the exploration of the unknown" (ibid.). Many scientists have praised the power of music to probe the unknown and inspire creative inquiry. Integrating music into science curricula is one way to do that.

An excellent example is the hip-hop project Get Your Green at St. Paul's High School for the Recording Arts (see ecomusicology.net). The Hypoxic Punks were fortunate enough to perform with the Green Crew, talented students from Get Your Green, on Earth Day weekend in 2011 (Fig. 6). The room came alive thanks to their infectious, youthful enthusiasm, nurtured by a program that combines math, science, language arts, music, and recording into a complete environmental studies curriculum.

Much of the preceding material in this book could be described as "dialectical," an examination of the contradictions and conundrums of scale, genre, and action that have stymied the development of ecological pop. However, dialectical contests between competing cultural ideas and social interests eventually result in new, transformative ideas and institutions. Get Your Green and projects like it might represent a way through some of our most serious deadlocks and contradictions. Some young and older musicians alike are finding new, sustainable ways to integrate sound, technology, and performance. We may be witnessing the start of a new, sustainable movement in music, and the key might be integrative allegiances between the arts, sciences, and community action.

When "idealism and materialism" are practiced in isolation, argues ecocritic Timothy Morton, they "can both generate flat worlds" (2007, 150–151). For example, science does a fairly poor job of understanding the role played by "anthropogenic" factors in ecological systems. Billions

FIGURE 6   The Green Crew. *(Photo by Renee Swenson.)*

of people, artifacts, and institutions overwhelm nonanthropogenic elements in ecological systems. Symbolic constructs (i.e., culture) overdetermine ecosystems. Yet environmental scientists trained in the traditional disciplines tend either to ignore culture or place dominant "anthropogenic variables" into what engineers refer to as a "black box." Human inputs and outputs are measured, but the semiotic and even material complexities of human societies are typically ignored. We are left with little understanding of proximate, let alone ultimate, causes of environmental problems. The result is weak science and an incomplete model of contemporary ecosystems.

Gordon Hempton makes a similar point regarding the science of sound: "We've redefined the problem so many times, and it doesn't change. We know almost everything there is to know about noise. We know how to measure it. We know how to quantify it. We don't know how to stop it" (2009, 297). The same can be said of many environmental problems. Because anthropogenic elements are ignored, underestimated, understudied, or assumed, we often have difficulties dealing with contemporary ecosystems holistically and effectively.

The habit of ignoring the human dimension is partly due to ideology. When it comes to global ecosystems, the ideological language and theories of capitalist "development" are a dominant paradigm, causing many to ignore models that might be more accurate from an empirical perspective, such as world systems theory (Billet 1993; Escobar 1995; Wallerstein 2004). In most social systems, cultural ideas that govern social practices are assumed to be self-evident and natural, whereas alternative models are dismissed as ideological even when they are more scientifically accurate. Even scientists seem to fall prey to dominant ideologies about social systems.

There is, therefore, an important role to be played by social scientists and humanists, researchers who study humans as culture-bearing creatures. Without those perspectives, we will have no idea why water continues to get more polluted, the climate is changing, noise is increasing, and so on. Without including culture in ecological studies, we will provide little more than quantitative chronicles of deleterious change or, at best, identify proximate, material causes. In short, one of the biggest challenges we face "is the difficulty of developing constructive relations between the green humanities and the environmental sciences" (Garrard 2004, 178; Lee, Wallerstein, and Aytar 2004). Music might help.

Some musicians are ahead of the curve: John Luther Adams, for example, brings scientific data into the world of musical sound (Kinnear 2010). If that is possible, then surely it is possible for environmental scientists to consider cultural factors, such as why people prefer Kentucky bluegrass to native plants, how policy decisions are made, what role medical advertising plays in pumping endocrine disruptors into our rivers, or how congressional lobbyists influence environmental regulations. Maybe environmental scientists are, quite reasonably, waiting for social scientists to start doing more such research.

With the above motivations in mind, I became a resident fellow at University of Minnesota's Institute on the Environment (IonE). I proposed a community-based water project. The idea was to organize community volunteers and students in a creative clean-water campaign that would be like the students' "Bridge over Troubled Waters" performances, on steroids. Students would use creative means to encourage local residents to make simple changes to their homes (e.g., repositioning drain spouts), yards (e.g., native plantings), and behavior (e.g., raking leaves and other detritus to make sure it does not get swept into storm drains). The campaign would target one neighborhood for an entire year. A similarly sized neighborhood would be used as the control. Stormwater runoff from both neighborhoods would be measured and compared with runoff from past years to determine the results of the cultural intervention.

From earlier discussions with city and regional water officials I had learned that the requisite water testing was being done to permit such a comparison. Upon receiving the fellowship, I went back to the same public officials to launch the project. Tim Brown, water specialist for the Minneapolis Parks and Recreation Board, told me about Metro Blooms' raingarden project. Volunteers from this community education group were conducting a controlled study in the Powderhorn Park neighborhood. They had planned a more direct intervention than we had in mind, with a high level of institutional support and a strong volunteer base. Their plan was to install 150 raingardens in that neighborhood, using an innovative citizens-based approach. They would compare the results of their intervention with readings from a control neighborhood of equal size that also drains into Powderhorn Lake. Whereas most water work has been infrastructural and policy-driven, taking place via government channels, Metro Blooms' idea was to have residents play an active role in cleaning up their watershed, starting with their own front and back yards. After all, most property in the United States is private.

Becky Rice, Metro Blooms' executive director, asked if I would like to participate. The group's enthusiasm was infectious, so I joined forces with them rather than execute my own study from scratch. I suggested that my students and I could work on recruiting residents via music and other creative means. Metro Blooms' leadership felt that recruiting residents would be less of a challenge than documenting the project as it developed and telling others about it afterward. They asked me to make a film about their Neighborhood of Raingardens project.

I had never made a film before, but the IonE fellowship would make it possible. I hoped that the film would do more than document Metro Blooms' successes and failures and would perhaps become another means of engaging the community along the way. That seemed to work rather well. Project leaders, volunteers, and residents willingly gave their time to the film, and early versions were used in project workshops. Season one of the film made it onto Twin Cities Public Television's (TPT) Minnesota Channel, a network with statewide reach. It was presented three times, including twice on Earth Day, 2009. The final film, *A Neighborhood of Raingardens*, was released on September 9 at a premiere sponsored by the Film Society of Minneapolis/St. Paul. The audience was populated by members of groups affiliated with the project, as well as interested others. *A Neighborhood of Raingardens* can now be viewed in its entirety online (via links at ecomusicology.net or raingardenmovie.org). The film project did more than anything else to help me understand the potential links between music, community, and sustainability.

Documentarians typically pay little attention to music. There are three basic ways to score environmental documentaries, each fairly trite. Natural imagery is accompanied by birdlike flute, cascading piano arpeggios, and so on. Conversely, droning dirges connote environmental threat and the ecological Armageddon to come. Triumphant, upbeat music underscores the heroic acts of environmental movements as they begin to turn the tide, leaving the audience with a renewed sense of purpose and hope. It seems that no matter what the topic, that narrative prevails. Beyond that basic narrative, the generic recordings used in most documentaries do little to advance the story, communicate information, or provide a more complete sense of the soundscape. Most documentary soundtrack scores appear to be an afterthought.

A notable exception is *Waterlife* (2009), a beautifully orchestrated film about water problems in the Great Lakes. *Waterlife* features compelling and relevant music by Sam Roberts, Sufjan Stevens, Sigur Ros, Robbie Robertson, and Brian Eno. Bucking other conventions, polluted images are given their own aesthetic appeal in *Waterlife*. Whereas many films make it seem as if we have reached nearly irredeemable dystopia, *Waterlife* shows that there is true beauty in the present, even within and around polluted lakes, rivers, and beaches. Likewise, it shows humans living, working, and playing along the lakes: people are part of, rather than apart from, the natural beauty of the Great Lakes. *Waterlife* is highly recommended viewing and listening. It is a prime example of what music can do when performed or placed into environmentally rich contexts.

Unfortunately, local documentarians cannot afford Sigur Ros or Brian Eno. I decided to use the Hypoxic Punks for the film soundtrack because other options were too time-consuming or expensive. Once again, I am in no position to judge quality, but using our music proved very useful from an ethnographic perspective. Putting music to film forced me to think about the ways in which songs change meaning with medium. For example, music that makes no denotative references to environmental issues becomes environmentally relevant as part of the film. Conversely, more than one song with overtly environmental content had to be removed because it distracted from the visual narrative. In fact, I decided to use purely instrumental versions for that very reason. Quite simply, words got in the way. My major regret is not paying sufficient attention to soundscape. I would have liked to integrate ambient sound into the musical score.

Thus far, several viewers have favorably mentioned the soundtrack, including several Powderhorn Park residents. After a screening of season one, one resident asked if the music was made "by local musicians." The soft-spoken, middle-aged woman was very pleased to hear that our music was made nearby. Musical provenance seemed to matter to that particular Powderhorn resident, gardener, and viewer as much as or more than the specific qualities of our music. She and others seemed to take on a sense of collective ownership. They cleaned up lakes and rivers through gardening, and we made a film and recorded music to document their creative efforts. Together, we made music and transformed the urban environment. Our music became theirs; their gardens became ours. Together, we created a more sustainable soundscape.

A few examples from the film demonstrate how music works in the electronically mediated world of the modern soundscape. Karl Demer, the film's main editor, suggested that I use "Brand on My Heart" to score the introductory montage. It is our only love song and seemed an unlikely choice. Yet that song is another musical element of the film that viewers seem to respond to favorably. This taught me, once again, what became a recurrent lesson throughout the fieldwork: music is rarely a denotative or autonomous art. It provides a structure of feeling that facilitates, and is in turn empowered by, listening environments and intertextual associations. Film, a narrative and message-driven medium, provides one such context.

Another viewer suggested that one of our songs gave her the sense of "being in the BWCA" (Boundary Waters Canoe Area Wilderness). I remember that comment in part because, remarkably, the song was composed on a camping trip in the BWCA. There were probably no specific sonic clues to lead that listener back to the Boundary Waters. It is extremely common for Minnesotans to venture north to the BWCA, so it is not surprising that both composer and listener shared the BWCA as an environmental touchstone. However, that example shows how music can work in relation to place. The musical collaboration—composing, performing, recording, and listening—expressed, reinforced, and synchronized our collective connection to that special place. In such moments I began to glimpse the possibilities for music to build stronger communities and more sustainable ecologies. Metro Blooms volunteers, film participants, and audiences have helped me to better understand the various roles music can play in building sustainable communities, in sustaining communities, and in fostering biodiversity and environmental integrity.

The happenstance application of music in an environmental film appears to have succeeded, whereas several of my more intentional attempts at environmental music making failed. For example, "Brand in My Heart" was not written to deliver an environmental message, but it became an environmental song in practice. There might be a lesson in that: creating a more sustainable society might not require bold moves or creative genius, but instead, simply reorienting ourselves to what already surrounds us. Put a downspout on the driveway, and detritus rushes toward the river, becoming a pollutant. Move it toward the lawn, and most of the runoff will get filtered out into the soil. How we conceive of our environment—as lawn, walk, or raingarden—might determine how we act within it, such as whether we consider it important enough to redirect our downspouts. Music can play a role in resignifying the local environment and making us more ecologically aware.

The soundtrack was not a complete success. One viewer disliked what she referred to as a "weird country song" (accurate) underscoring an overly long montage in the middle. After hearing that feedback, I cut that scene and song. Another viewer complained after I cut the song, stating that she had enjoyed hearing it in the earlier, shorter version of the film on TPT. Turns out that gardeners have strong ideas about both film and music.

Like music, gardening is a fascinating medium and art form (S. Ross 1998). R. Murray Schafer used the garden as a "soniferous" metaphor in his soundscape studies (1994, 246–252) and did the same with water (247–250). Gardens have inspired countless poems and songs (Von Glahn 2003, 248–250). In the case of Metro Blooms, gardening was the means through which people transferred a hobby into environmental activism. Bob Wolk, a master gardener and Metro Blooms board member, refers to gardening as a "gateway drug" for environmental action on a community-wide level. Local, environmentally relevant music might play a similar role. Combining the arts—gardening and music—is particularly rewarding.

The film has just begun to enter national distribution. It is not clear what it will do there. It is out of my control, but I am guessing that the film will be screened in a few environmental studies classes and local film festivals. However, as a means of local engagement, the film and its music have already made a small contribution to Metro Bloom's very large community project. Metro Blooms' Neighborhood of Raingardens project has brought activists, scientists, community volunteers, artists, legislators, homeowners, and city officials together to deal with local water problems.

The language of science has been central to that project, but it does not engage individuals or create active communities on its own. Art plays an important role in environmental education, communication, and expression. The film experience expanded my thinking, taking me from a narrow focus on making music for environmental purposes toward a more nuanced understanding of what music might do as part of ongoing community projects. The Powderhorn Park project illustrated Larry Long's suggestion to "go where people are" with music. Taking part in

Metro Blooms' ambitious experiment was one of the most rewarding experiences of this project, both from an ethnographic perspective and in terms of environmental outcomes.

Environmental Redemption in Clubland?

The Hypoxic Punks have continued to perform, but the last concerts documented here took place in December of 2010. The first was a fundraiser for Metro Blooms; the second was part of the National Center for Earth-Surface Dynamics' (NCED) Sip of Science series at the Aster Café in Minneapolis.

When I heard that NCED was starting a lecture series at a café just a few blocks from my home, I suggested that the Hypoxic Punks perform before the program, as people filtered in. We would bring a pared-down, acoustic setup and get out of the way as soon as the lecture started. We completed a half-hour set with purely acoustic instruments rather than full drum kit. Bryan, our bass, could not make the show, so we were a trio that night: Bob played hand percussion, Leon performed on the violin, and I juggled the guitar, harmonica, and vocals.

It felt a bit naked, given that the Hypoxic Punks had grown into a more complete rock band. However, lessons about matching instrumentation, place, and purpose were finally sinking in. Rather than the overblown electronics we injected into Balls Cabaret or the big rock band aesthetic we brought to the Sierra Club concert, that night we were a small, unassuming acoustic trio. The initial crowd included folks finishing up their meals and drinks before heading home. Then our core audience started arriving: my wife, Karen; our friend, Annette; my brother, Kevin; my sister-in-law, Joan; my mother, Jane; nieces Griffin and Samantha. (Their older sister, Veronica, could not be there, but she created a music video for "Georgie's War," available on ecomusicology.net). Once again, our families, friends, and colleagues made up a sizable chunk of the audience.

Gradually others arrived, the audience for the main event, Mark Seeley's talk concerning weather and climate change. By the time we played our last song, a full crowd was gathered to hear Mark. They reacted fairly well to the music, although it was only intended to be background music before the lecture. Unfortunately, Mark was detained, so we were asked to play one more song. We did so. Never good at going off script, I somehow forgot the middle verse and chord progression to "River's Getting Dirty." No one seemed to mind that much, but it bugged the hell out of me. That is not the mindset of a true musician. For example, one of the

FIGURE 7 The Hypoxic Punks play Rock for Raingardens. *(Photo by Karl Demer.)*

best moments in John Prine's famous live recording of "Dear Abby" (1973) occurs when the veteran folk singer forgets the words and makes a joke out of it. Seasoned performers are expert at improvisation. Instead, I tend to make a mess out of it. Fortunately, most nights the drops are fairly minor, or I would never be able to get back up there again. It is frightening enough when things go right; I could not handle getting back on stage if things ever got too far off the rails.

Deborah Hudleston, "knowledge transfer director" and science writer for NCED, directed the Sip of Science series. Following the event, she asked if we would like to help her plan future events with environmental art, music, poetry, and film. Located just around the corner from my condo, such concerts nicely fulfill the combined goals of this project: to produce music sustainably, to use music to communicate environmental messages, and help build active communities through music. We are hoping to do more such events in 2012 and 2013.

The final concert I would like to discuss here was a benefit for Metro Blooms on December 2, 2010, an event we called Rock for Raingardens (Fig. 7; see ecomusicology.net for more pictures and video from the concert). The year-end event celebrated Metro Blooms' hard work designing, digging, and planting raingardens in 2010.

Thanks to various logistical difficulties, the event was held late on a winter weeknight. I wanted it to take place in a club near campus with relatively good sound. The sound system was great. Unfortunately, the club owner refused our request to patch into their soundboard to record the concert, so all we have are recordings taken from the back of the bar. However, the club was willing to host the event in exchange for keeping their entire bar take and 30 percent of ticket sales, so we can't complain.

In retrospect, it would have been far better to hold the concert on a Saturday afternoon at a less expensive, more family-friendly venue, such as the University of Minnesota's music club, the Whole, where Leon and I once performed, or the Powderhorn Community Center. Yet, surprisingly, those public facilities are more expensive to rent than private clubs, and less money would have been raised for Metro Blooms as a result.

Four students helped promote the benefit concert, as did Metro Blooms' board of directors. Several students got in for free as part of an extra-credit opportunity (they had the alternative option of hearing rapper Common the next night), but the crowd was mostly made up of Metro Blooms' supporters. Paying customers generated $800 for the group, a pretty good take for a Thursday night concert, late in the evening on one of the coldest nights of 2010.

What distinguished Rock for Raingardens from most of our club concerts? It was presented for a clear purpose. It took place within an active and thriving community. In Chapter 1 we learned that even an event backed by massive corporate resources, like Live Earth, can fail to generate sustained commitment, especially when lacking active community connections. For much of its life, this project involved music in search of community.

We have finally found it with Metro Blooms and related organizations. As Rebee Garofalo explains, "The task of building a better world necessarily entails organizing mass movements" (1992, 55). The same logic applies on the local scale. The task of building a better city entails organizing active communities. Music is not the major motivator or focus for action; it is emotional support for a hard-working community. Once again, music is "a tonic for the troops."

Music and politics are both defined by organization. Drawing on the writings of Edgard Varèse, Levitin distinguishes music from natural sound and noise (2006, 14):

> What do the music of Bach, Depeche Mode, and John Cage fundamentally have in common? On a most basic level, what distinguishes Busta Rhymes's "What's It Gonna Be?!" or Beethoven's "Pathétique" Sonata from, say, the collection of sounds you'd hear standing in the middle of Times Square, or those you'd hear deep in a rainforest? As the composer Edgard Varèse famously defined it, "Music is organized sound."

Similarly, communities are organized people. "Organized sound" is good for building, maintaining, and, especially, renewing community. Musical entrainment and ritual help bring people together, fostering a visceral, cathartic, and collective sense of purpose.

There are myriad examples of environmental expression, action, and advocacy through music on the local level. For example, Mark Mattern (1998, 135) describes a powwow for clean water that was performed in 1991, nine miles downstream from where our Metro Blooms club benefit took place. Co-sponsored by the American Indian Movement (AIM) and environmental organizations, the powwow "featured music as diverse as rap, country-and-western, and folk as well as American Indian" (ibid.). In fact, people have been making music to express environmental hopes, fears, and experience for as long as humans have made music.

This study has, I hope, not only illustrated the challenges involved in making local music matter, ecologically speaking, but also provided a few insights into how one might start doing it, if so inclined. The bottom line is this: if you want to make music matter, just start singing, playing, producing, booking, promoting, organizing, listening, or whatever it is that you like to do. No one can do it alone. Find a few others to play along. Perhaps the greatest surprise in all of this was finding so many musicians willing and even eager to get involved.

Beyond Ethnography: Is There Public Space for Environmental Music?

Typically, the first objection leveled against ethnography is that the participant observer's experience is artificial and unrepresentative of the norm and therefore unable to explain how an informant lives or a social group functions. That is true: ethnography is an artificial act, rather than a truly naturalistic methodology. In fact, there is no such thing as a naturalistic social research method. Every act of social research is its own artificial construct. However, every social phenomenon is an artificial construct, and every human experience is distinct. Nothing is truly representative of the norm, because the norm is illusory. The ethnographic encounter is an intersubjective snapshot of a given set of people at a given moment in time. As ethnographers, we leave generalizable social science to those who conduct experiments on college campuses, subjecting 19-year-old students to surveys, focus groups, and eye-tracking devices. We let them claim universal truth and applicability.

In truth, no social research method can produce generalizable cultural laws or universal social truths. No social science methodology, no matter how good at controlling (more often "ignoring") variables, has discovered anything like the material scientist's physical laws of the universe. The nature of what we study—culture—makes it impossible to claim universal laws of human cognition or behavior. The best we can do is identify central tendencies, and describe and explain various social patterns. In fact, the meaning of those cultural patterns shifts from observer to observer. Frustrating, isn't it?

You will have to decide if this ethnographic account does or does not resonate with your own understanding of music and the environment. My initial argument was that any of us could pick up an instrument or let loose our voices in song, and that such an act might be not only possible but profitable from the standpoint of creating more sustainable societies. To the extent that this ethnographic experiment succeeded, it may have been because of idiosyncratic conditions that do not apply widely. The failures in this field experiment may merely be attributable to my own shortcomings as a musician or ethnographer. Yet I still believe that if I can play music, anyone can. While I may have had slightly greater access to instrumentation, my work leaves little free time for making music. As a musical talent I am perfectly average. Yet through the application of elbow grease, and thanks to a hand up from incredibly talented musicians, the music we made seemed to make some small difference to those around us. A community is made up of hundreds of small differences. A movement is made up of thousands of small communities.

As for becoming a musician, it is important to challenge the widespread belief that some people are born musicians while the rest of us are something else entirely (Levitin 2006, 196–200). If I have learned one thing in teaching performance-based classes, it is that everyone has at least some capacity to produce musical sound and movement. Take the case of Samantha Midler. Sam grew up singing, even entertaining herself while delivering newspapers. However, at one point some unkind soul said, "You can't sing." Like so many people who are told that, Sam stopped singing.

In the process of writing a song for class, Sam's classmates picked up on the possibility that she might not only have musical talent but might even have exceptional skill. They encouraged her to try singing, so she recorded her song, "Unseen Wal-Mart Worker." She recorded it in one take, starting on C and ending there two minutes later, after making compelling, calculated, and controlled movements across major and minor chords, including half-steps that many vocalists would find difficult, certainly when singing a capella. In other words, Sam has perfect pitch, which is the ability to remember and reproduce the pitch of a practiced song without instrumental cueing. Listen to Sam's song at ecomusicology.net.

The class was moved by Sam's performance. Despite the crude recording equipment and conditions, I think you will agree that it is not the voice of a young woman who "can't sing." Sam has a wonderful voice, as do many other people who believe they cannot sing. Since graduating Sam has gone on to perform musically and, as I write this, is training in New York to become an actor. Not everyone has perfect pitch, but most people can produce musical sound vocally, and should. Everyone has the capacity to move rhythmically, learn an instrument, or comprehend music. Music evolved in humans for a reason: as a means of communication, for social bonding, or as a byproduct of some other evolutionary development; and it is a gift no one should waste. People like Sam give the rest of us courage to try.

When Sam came to mind as an example, I decided to get back in touch with her. She offered fond recollections of the class and classmates. "I have been songwriting and I think back to my song about Wal-Mart workers," she said. "I still remember it, 'passing shadows on the wall.'" She enjoys listening to, and talking about, political music and musicians like Imogen Heap. There is a bit of Sam in all of us. We can all sing, dance, or play music. We might even direct a little of our musical effort toward shared goals, as working communities have done throughout human history.

In addition to misconceptions about musicianship, the contemporary, widespread bias against mixing pop and politics tends to inhibit meaningful public expression through music. Too often art and politics are viewed as antithetical, because of marketing considerations and a more longstanding fear in the Western tradition that politics might pollute the purity of art. This attitude makes performing topical music a social risk. A person can feel quite foolish singing an antiwar anthem from a bridge or playing an environmental song in the back room of a dingy club. Everyone I know has some interest in making music, but many fear making fools of themselves in the attempt. That is too bad. We have nothing to lose but our collective inhibitions. Democracy requires uninhibited public discourse. Perhaps the depth and health of our democracy can be measured musically.

The best way to get over one's fear of looking or sounding foolish when performing in public is to do so with a lot of other people. There are some impressive participatory music movements in North America, for example. The Radical Cheerleaders take on logging companies and promote animal rights (radcheers.tripod.com). "Honk" street bands provide musical support to peace, human rights, and environmental movements (honkfest.org/bands). And then there are the Raging Grannies (raginggrannies.com). The Canadian Gulf Islands chapter put out the *Raging Grannies Songbook* (1993), a useful resource that includes "Ecological Grannies" (ibid., 35) and a number of other environmentally oriented songs. They rewrite the words to popular songs (much as Joe Hill did with popular hymns a century ago) and sing them at public meetings and protests. In the early 1990s they sang "Ecological Grannies" (to the tune of "Side by Side") to protest against the Weldwood Logging Company's operations in British Columbia. The final verse goes as follows:

> Oh, we're just a gaggle of Grannies
> And we've gotten off of our fannies
> We're telling you chumps
> We're sick of your stumps
> We want to save our trees
> We really mean it
> Save the trees
> We'll say it nicely
> Save the trees . . . (please)
> We mean precisely
> SAVE THE TREES!

The Radical Cheerleaders, Raging Grannies, and activist street bands perform music in the public domain (e.g., traditional folk songs and marches). Their goal is to inspire others to join them, duplicate their efforts elsewhere, and grow the participatory music movement. Like songwriters who "copyleft" their compositions, the goal of these participatory music organizations is to help everyone become an activist-musician, regardless of experience.

As Heise reminds us, "local identity" is both an "essentialist myth" and "a promising site of struggle" (2008, 7). Yes, it is possible to overemphasize and even fetishize "the local." Contemporary environmental challenges reach far beyond local horizons. All ecological systems are, ultimately, global. Nevertheless, the most important struggles over environmental policy and stewardship continue to take place on a local level. Some strategic essentialism is warranted, perhaps even necessary, in local activism. Myth making is part of every meaningful human endeavor, including the stories we tell ourselves about our local communities and environments.

Local environments represent some of the greatest environmental exigencies and provide some of the most tangible results. As Heise points

out, environmental activism has been particularly successful at the local
level (ibid., 8). The Raging Grannies, Radical Cheerleaders, and activist
street bands are less concerned about philosophical dangers like essen-
tializing nature than they are with stopping logging companies from
clear-cutting forests or keeping developers from paving over biodiverse
wetlands.

Many musicians get nervous when politics and art combine. However, the same musicians who turn up their noses at overtly political
artistry have no problem chasing corporate grants and commissions
(classical), accepting lucrative tour sponsorships (rock), selling their
music to advertisers (everyone), and so on. Perhaps this contradictory
aesthetic is a product of modern music's business model, in which he
who pays the piper calls the tune. It is not a matter of Chevron or Wal-
Mart saying, "We don't want popular music to challenge our interests,"
but rather the trickle-down influence of a system predicated on corporate
largess. There is little profit in restoring streams, creating environmental
justice, or marveling at the beauty of an old-growth forest. Therefore, it
might take amateur musicians to bravely go where professionals fear to
tread. In each previous chapter, at each scale of analysis—global, national,
and regional—examples have been provided of professional musicians
whose remarkable courage and exceptional artistry have made a difference. At the local level, we have no one to rely on but ourselves. From
what I have witnessed, everyone is a music maker, activist, and environmental steward in some form or fashion. What we most need are better
ways to coordinate and apply those talents toward the creation and maintenance of cleaner water, clearer air, diverse habitats, and environmental
justice. Maybe that has nothing to do with music. However, I continue to
suspect that the physical health of ecosystems depends in part on the
cultural health of human communities.

Conclusion

After eight years, this research still feels incomplete. Despite a lot of hard work, I feel as if the project is just getting started. Of course, all musicians think that. Almost every musician I have met thinks that he or she is about to write, record, or perform a song that will capture the audience's imagination or finally scratch their artistic itch. As a teenager I met one of the members of the McCoys in a Chicago suburb (not Rick Derringer; he went on to become a bigger rock star). The McCoys recorded the number-one hit "Hang on Sloopy" (1965, 1995). The ex-McCoy was sure that his Holiday Inn band was about to make it big. He never returned to the limelight, but he did make more great music. The tragedy is not that the McCoy in question never made it back to the big time, but that such a talented performer did not seem to realize how much joy his music brought to audiences, regardless of size.

Musical research has a similar dynamic. As investigators, we imagine that the next project will reveal a new key to music's hidden magic. However, the search for sustainable music has just begun. Ecomusicology as a field of study is in its infancy, working through definitions and goals and generating new questions, while finding a few answers along the way. Ethnography is just one way of doing ecomusicological research. Ethnographers seek answers in human experience, the partial, intersubjective, and complex realities of daily life. Such experiences take shape in particular places during specific periods in history, sometimes referred to as the "ethnographic present." My fieldwork and book take place in just one of many possible times and places.

As generations of anthropologists have learned, however, the small places we study ethnographically are integrally connected to more encompassing geographic, temporal, and cultural abstractions. If we want to understand environmental music as performed in specific locales like Stillwater, Minnesota, Orcas Island, Washington, or anywhere else, for that matter, we need to consider the regional, national, and global sound-scapes in which such performances take place. Ecomusicologists consider multiple, interacting levels of life, from local concerts to global sound-scapes, local groundwater to climate change.

This field research indicates that local musicians are heavily influenced by music made on much larger stages. The spirits of Guthrie, Dylan, and DiFranco hang over us all. The truth is that globalized music dominates local soundscapes (Breen 1993; Dawe 1998). There are, of course, local references in globally circulated music; "world-famous" music and musicians have to come from somewhere. However, the global music industry exerts much more influence on what happens in local music scenes than those scenes exert, in return, on the global soundscape. It is not a com-pletely reciprocal system.

"These days if you are traveling to Tuva to study music," Theodore Levin writes, "you're likely to find that Tuva's famous throat-singers are all away on tour" (2006, xii). After finding success, many Tuvan musi-cians decided to take up residence elsewhere. Yet global attention has led to "musical revivalism in Tuva itself, where new ensembles sprang up like wildflowers," thanks to the local style's international success (ibid., 162). This cycle leads to hybrid global-local genres as well. Levin explains that "worldbeat buffs" and "new agers" in Greece, the United States, and else-where have exerted a strong cultural influence on Tuvan musicians and music (ibid., 210). Some Tuvan musicians have become like "rock stars" (ibid.). Their "pop fame" and performances are far removed from the traditional Tuvan cave ceremony (ibid., 211). Yet Tuvan music is one of the local-goes-global success stories. Most local music lacks that level of representation in global markets. However, all local music is influenced by global music industries and markets.

It is similar to the relationship between global nongovernmental organizations (NGOs) and local social movements. Global NGOs create a "market" that directly influences how and where local movements ori-ent their activism (Bob 2005). Similarly, global music markets influence the sound, performance, and consumption of local music. Local musi-cians are seduced into meeting global audiences "at least halfway" (Levin 2006, 217). Global attention can foster local musical traditions, but it greatly modifies them in the process, as it has in the Tuvan case. In short, even cases of local and regional music successfully making it onto the global stage illustrate the overdetermining influence of global markets and industry.

Nevertheless, a romantic notion persists—the belief that local music represents a strong bulwark of resistance to global culture industries (Buell 2005, 65). It is a nice thought, but rarely borne out by evidence. Perhaps that is another reason music researchers ignore ecological contexts. Place resonates less and less in popular music. Distant places, mobile lifestyles, and a general sense of placelessness preside over much of the world's musical imagination. De-territorialization is a hallmark of modern life.

Developing more sustainable ways of life is difficult in a world where culture is increasingly independent of place. Yet ecological knowledge and consciousness are essential, especially for those with economic power and privilege. Much of the world is already living modestly, but not by choice. It is important for us to become more aware of distant others who share our air, water, and ecosystem. In other words, it will be important for cultural imagination to catch up with material reality. Environmental organizations are working hard to foster greater ecological awareness. Their efforts could use a cultural assist. That includes music.

Of course, doing so is more an act of faith than an application of science. Over the past eight years of field research, I read over forty musical biographies and autobiographies, thinking that socially engaged musicians might have some of the answers to these difficult questions. Could performers like Paul Robeson (Duberman 1988), Neil Young (McDonough 2002), Joan Baez (Baez 2009), and Fela (Veal 2000) provide some expert advice on how a local musician might go about making a difference in the world? Although few of them have anything to do with environmental music, their success as politically active performers might provide us with useful models for environmental engagement. Instead, surprisingly, I discovered that they too remain uncertain about what music actually does. Billy Bragg presents the question lyrically in "Waiting for the Great Leap Forwards" (1988, used with permission from Billy Bragg):

> Mixing pop and politics he asks me what the use is
> I offer him embarrassment and my usual excuses.

For a musician, it is never terribly clear what your music does in people's minds, lives, and communities. If Bragg isn't certain, then no performer can be. No musician in the history of rock has done more to articulate music and meaningful action. Bragg is the consummate "movement musician." Yet not even Bragg can be certain just what his musical utterances do in the world. Audiences take ownership the minute music and words leave a singer's mouth. The cultural ecology of music is too complex to understand or explain through systems flow charts or the logic of cause and effect. It is an act of faith.

Nevertheless, music researchers try to better understand what music means and what music does. Among other things, we try to understand how music works by asking people what they think and feel, studying collective expressions and analyzing statistical indicators like music sales data. Unfortunately, most musicologists sidestep the study of music's social effects, perhaps out of fear of functionalism or, worse, having to admit that we know very little about how music actually works in the world. We find ourselves "dancing about architecture" when we try to think and write about music. Does a song about climate change raise awareness, or is it drowned out in an "An Ocean of Noise," to borrow a line from Arcade Fire (2007)? Can music do more than entertain? Does popular music just stoke our desires to fetishize, commoditize, and buy "Mountains o' Things" (Chapman 1988), or can it also help us to sustain healthy communities and ecosystems? When it comes to environmental issues, does music even matter?

The further we move down that list of questions, the hazier things get. There is much greater evidence for popular music's utility as a sales tool than for its capacity to foster sustainable lives and equitable societies. This book is in a sense a desperate search to find and perhaps even create a few positive examples, no matter how small. At no point in the eight years of research did I delude myself into believing that the positive examples could outnumber the negative, neutral, or irrelevant ones.

Nor do I feel epistemological shame at drawing normative judgments about music. Music should be able to play some role in fostering environmental sustainability, biodiversity, and human well-being. That basic value is shared by most ecomusicologists. Every musical genre, act of listening, and research effort is motivated by at least some implicit argument concerning what music is and should be, whether or not we admit it. This book is an argument for adding sustainability to the long list of musical values and expectations. Songs about partying, romance, and fast cars are great, but shouldn't there be more to life and music?

Mark Mattern asked the following question in his research: "To what degree does popular music enable people to make real democratic changes in their lives?" (1998, 6). Ecomusicologists ask a similar question: to what degree does popular music enable people to live sustainably and become better environmental stewards?

Once again, making and studying music are acts of faith. Circulating songs about ecological issues, hosting concerts for renewable fuels, and making guitars sustainably are all acts of faith. It is unclear how much any of this matters, ecologically speaking. Perhaps in the preceding pages I provide some evidence of where, when, and how that faith might be rewarded, or, in other cases, why it might take some time before the tide turns. The unrelenting efforts of concert promoters like Michael Martin, musicians like Jack Johnson, and activists like Metro Blooms provide rays of hope across an otherwise dusky horizon.

"There is no conclusion," writes Michael McDowell, when the goal is to establish a dialogue (1996, 387). Hopefully some clues have been provided as to how we might develop a better dialogue around environmental music, but as McDowell reminds us, there is no solid and singular conclusion. Working below and beyond our methodological radar, music evades simple definitions and explanations. Popular music, which tends toward the carnival side of life, is particularly resistant to utilitarian applications. Yet from money-making Muzak to popular hits, it is impossible to find purpose-free music. Even carnivals serve a purpose.

On the other hand, nothing is more boring than music made solely for the purpose of achieving some simple, tangible effect. Music is about affect rather than effect, a feeling shared between musician and audience, between listener and listener. That is both the challenge and the beauty of music. It is a shared profession of faith, nearly impossible to articulate in words. Music is a hopeful act, a sonic expression of the belief that we can find a shared rhythm and purpose, even when words fail.

Ethnographic research is a humbling exercise, especially when applied to the mysteries of music. We have few firm ideas as to why the capacity for organized sound evolved in humans or why it moves us so. Given that, how could we know how something as mysterious as music relates to something as incomprehensible as an ecosystem? It is dancing about architecture to the extreme. However, in a world where environmental crises are calling everything into question, our music might need some rethinking as well.

As for musicology, I have generally not critiqued the theorists cited here for what they fail to explain. Writing about music is as difficult as making it. All insights are valuable and needed; all musical theories will remain incomplete. Where the literature becomes most problematic is in the tendency toward making narrow judgments. As David Ingram explains, we need to open up ecocritical scholarship to multiple forms of exploration, not close it down before things even get started (2010, 20). We need to listen carefully rather than assume that every utterance or note can be neatly forced into an existing theory, philosophy, or genre. There are more things in heaven and earth, Horatio, than are dreamt of in our musicology.

Ecomusicology needs to look toward music's intertextual connections. Music becomes even more meaningful when joined with other arts, media, and activities. Ecomusicology might call into question the Western art world's tendency to treat music as a museum piece, to isolate sound rather than appreciating and experiencing it in various contexts, including ecological contexts. Ansel Adams said that learning to play the cello was his most important artistic influence, giving spirit and life to his photography (Strauss 1996, 128). As Adams discovered, music holds great potential to enliven other arts and activities. Similarly, music and musical research might enhance our understanding of ecosystems and how we live within them.

References

ABC News. 2007. Critics: Live Earth not so green. September 7. Available at http://abcnews.go.com/GMA/JustOneThing/story?id=3358200&page=1.

Accountancy. 2007. Live Earth called to account. *Accountancy* 140 (1368): 61.

Adams, Douglas. 1984. *So long, and thanks for all the fish.* New York: Ballantine Books.

Adams, John Luther. 2009. *The place where you go to listen: In search of an ecology of music.* Middletown, CT: Wesleyan University Press.

Aldin, Mary Katherine. 1999. Way down yonder in the Indian Nation: Woody Guthrie, an American troubadour. In *Hard travelin': The life and legacy of Woody Guthrie,* ed. Robert Santelli and Emily Davidson, 3–13. Hanover, NH: Wesleyan University Press.

Allen, Aaron. 2010. "Local forests, global instruments: Connecting ecological and cultural sustainability." Paper presented at Society for Ethnomusicology Annual Conference, Los Angeles. November 11–14.

———. 2011. Ecomusicology: Ecocriticism and musicology. *Journal of the American Musicological Society* 64 (2): 391–394.

Althusser, Louis. 2001. *Lenin and philosophy and other essays.* New York: Monthly Review Press.

Alvarez, Robert. 2003. The legacy of Hanford. *The Nation* 277 (5): 31–35.

Anderson, Benedict. 1983. Imagined communities: Reflections on the origin and spread of nationalism. London: Verso.

Anslow, Mark. 2007. From songs to strategy. *The Ecologist* 37 (7): 63.

Appadurai, Arjun. 1996. *Modernity at large: Cultural dimensions of globalization.* Minneapolis: University of Minnesota Press.

Arnold, Chuck. 2007. Live Earth. *People,* December 17: 53–55.

Artisan News Service. 2007. Live Earth performer Chris Cornell stressed about green issues. Available at www.youtube.com/watch?v=xiLpAGhECCc&feature=plcp&context=C3702cdaUDOEgsToPDskKfPVtbAFLkKLEHVln6D8gp. Accessed January 30, 2012.

Atkinson, Rowland. 2007. Ecology of sound: The sonic order of urban space. *Urban Studies* 44 (10): 1905–1917.

Azios, Tony. 2007. Live Earth: A briefing. *Christian Science Monitor,* July 5: 13.

Baez, Joan. 2009. *And a voice to sing with: A memoir.* New York: Simon & Schuster.

Battiste, Harold, Jr. 2010. "Preserving and presenting the music of New Orleans." Panel presentation at the International Association for the Study of Popular Music Annual Conference, New Orleans, April 9.

Benioff, Marc, and Carlye Adler. 2007. *The business of changing the world: Twenty great leaders on strategic corporate philanthropy.* New York: McGraw-Hill.

Bennett, Andy, Barry Shank, and Jason Toynbee. 2006. *The popular music studies reader.* New York: Routledge.

Bennett, Tony, Simon Frith, Lawrence Grossberg, John Shepherd, and Graeme Turner. 1993. *Rock and popular music: Politics, policies, institutions.* New York: Routledge.

Benzon, William. 2001. *Beethoven's anvil: Music in mind and culture.* New York: Basic Books.

Berlin, Irving. 2012. "God Bless America." Available at http://www.scoutsongs.com/lyrics/godblessamerica.html.

Billet, Bret L. 1993. *Modernization theory and economic development: Discontent in the developing world.* Westport, CT: Praeger.

Binford, Leigh. 1996. *The El Mozote massacre: Anthropology and human rights.* Tucson: University of Arizona Press.

Bird, S. Elizabeth. 2010. *The Anthropology of news and journalism: Global perspectives.* Bloomington: Indiana University Press.

Blecha, Peter. 2004. *Taboo tunes: A history of banned bands and censored songs.* San Francisco: Backbeat Books.

Bob, Clifford. 2005. *The marketing of rebellion: Insurgents, media, and international activism.* Cambridge Studies in Contentious Politics. New York: Cambridge University Press.

Boucher, David. 2004. *Dylan and Cohen: Poets of rock and roll.* New York: Continuum.

Bourdieu, Pierre. 1984. *Distinction: A social critique of the judgment of taste.* Cambridge: Harvard University Press.

Boyce-Tillman, June. 2004. Towards an ecology of music education. *Philosophy of Music Education Review* 12 (2): 102–125.

Breen, Marcus. 1993. Making music local. In *Rock and popular music: Politics, policies, institutions,* ed. Tony Bennett, Simon Frith, Lawrence Grossberg, John Shepherd, and Graeme Turner, 66–82. New York: Routledge.

Buell, Lawrence. 2005. *The future of environmental criticism: Environmental crisis and literary imagination.* Malden, MA: Blackwell.

Butler, Richard. 1994. The geography of rock: 1954–1970. In *The sounds of people and places: A geography of American folk and popular music,* ed. George O. Carney, 215–243. Lanham, MD: Rowman & Littlefield.

Carney, George O. 1994. *The sounds of people and places: A geography of American folk and popular music.* Lanham, MD: Rowman & Littlefield.

Carriker, Robert. 2001. Ten dollars a song: Woody Guthrie sells his talent to the Bonneville Power Administration. *Columbia Magazine* 15 (1): 32–36.

Cheng, Fei-Fei, Chin-Shan Wu, and David C. Yen. 2009. The effect of online store atmosphere on consumer's emotional responses: An experimental study of music and colour. *Behaviour and Information Technology* 28 (4): 323–334.

Clarke, Eric F. 2005. *Ways of listening: An ecological approach to the perception of musical meaning.* New York: Oxford University Press.

Cloonan, Martin, and Reebee Garofalo. 2003. *Policing pop.* Sound Matters. Philadelphia: Temple University Press.

Cohen, Aaron. 2006. Pete Seeger, social networking and the decline of mass media. *Billboard* 118 (22): 8.

Cohen, Sara. 2007. "Rock landmark at risk": Popular music, urban regeneration, and the built urban environment. *Journal of Popular Music Studies* 19 (1): 3–25.

Colmeiro, José. 2009. Smells like wild spirit: Galician *rock bravú*, between the "rurban" and the "glocal." *Journal of Spanish Cultural Studies* 10 (2): 225–240.

Coscarelli, Joe. 2010. The 15 most eco-friendly rockers. *Rolling Stone,* December 16. Available at http://www.rollingstone.com/music/photos/the-15-most-eco-friendly-rockers-20101216.

Cray, Ed. 2004. *Ramblin' man: The life and times of Woody Guthrie.* New York: W. W. Norton.

Cross, Ian. 2001. Music, mind and evolution. *Psychology of Music* 29 (1): 95–102.

Crow, Sheryl. 2010. Environmental review. Portland, ME: Reverb. http://reverb.org/project/sherylcrow/SherylCrowSum10Recap_web.pdf. Accessed January 31, 2012.

Cummings, Jim. 2006. Research reports for the ears: Soundscape art in scientific presentations. *Soundscape Writings* (May 12). Available at http://www.acousticecology.org/presentation/intro.html.

Curtis, James, and Richard Rose. 1994. "The Miami Sound": A contemporary Latin form of place-specific music. In *The sounds of people and places: A geography of American folk and popular music,* ed. George O. Carney, 263–274. Lanham, MD: Rowman & Littlefield.

Danner, Mark. 1994. *The massacre at El Mozote: A parable of the cold war.* New York: Vintage Books.

Davies, Chris Lawe. 1993. Aboriginal rock music: Space and place. In *Rock and popular music: Politics, policies, institutions,* ed. Tony Bennett, Simon Frith, Lawrence Grossberg, John Shepherd, and Graeme Turner, 249–265. New York: Routledge.

Dawe, Kevin. 1998. Bandleaders in Crete: Musicians and entrepreneurs in a Greek island economy. *British Journal of Ethnomusicology* 7:23–44.

Deleuze, Gilles, and Félix Guattari. 1977. *Anti-Oedipus: Capitalism and schizophrenia.* New York: Viking Press.

de Rothschild, David. 2007. *The Live Earth global warming survival handbook.* New York: Rodale Books.

De Simone, Claudia Sara. 2008. Hip hopping mad. *Alternatives Journal* 34 (1): 7.

de Soto, Hernando. 2000. *The mystery of capital: Why capitalism triumphs in the West and fails everywhere else.* New York: Basic Books.

Devenish, Colin. 2001. *Rage Against the Machine.* New York: St. Martin's Press.

Diamond, Jared M. 2005. *Guns, germs, and steel: The fates of human societies.* New York: Norton.

Dissanayake, Ellen. 2009. Root, leaf, blossom, or bole: Concerning the origin and adaptive function of music. In *Communicative musicality: Exploring the basis of human companionship,* ed. Stephen Malloch and Colwyn Trevarthen, 17–30. New York: Oxford University Press.

Douglas, Mary. 1966. *Purity and danger: An analysis of concepts of pollution and taboo.* New York: Praeger.

Duberman, Martin B. 1988. *Paul Robeson.* New York: Knopf.

DuBois, Peter. 2006. Modern day Woody Guthrie updates the Columbia River songs. *Friends of Clark County,* January. Previously available at clarkfriends.org/action/documents/dubois.pdf. Site discontinued.

Dybas, Cheryl Lyn. 2005. Dead zones spreading in world oceans. *Bioscience* 55 (7): 552–557.

Electronic Frontier Foundation (EFF). 2011. "JibJab Media v. Ludlow Music." Available at https://www.eff.org/cases/jibjab-media-inc-v-ludlow-music-inc. Accessed December 27, 2011.

Eno, Brian. 2001. Ambient music. In *The book of music and nature: An anthology of sounds, words, thoughts,* ed. David Rothenberg and Marta Ulvaeus, 139–142. Middletown, CT: Wesleyan University Press.

Epstein, Michael, Jeremy Marozeau, and Sandra Cleveland. 2010. Listening habits of iPod users. *Journal of Speech, Language and Hearing Research* 53 (6): 1472–1477.

Escobar, Arturo. 1995. *Encountering development: The making and unmaking of the Third World.* Princeton: Princeton University Press.

Feisst, Sabine. 2010. John Luther Adams: An avant-garde composer in Alaska. Paper presented at Beyond the Centres: Musical Avant-Gardes since 1950, Thessaloniki, Greece, July 1–3. Available at http://btc.web.auth.gr/_assets/_papers/FEISST.pdf.

Feist, Grant W., Molly A. H. Webb, Deke T. Gundersen, Eugene P. Foster, Carl B. Schreck, Alec G. Maule, and Martin S. Fitzpatrick. 2005. Evidence of detrimental effects of environmental contaminants on growth and reproductive physiology of white sturgeon in impounded areas of the Columbia River. *Environmental Health Perspectives* 113 (12): 1675.

Feld, Steven. 1982. *Sound and sentiment: Birds, weeping, poetics, and song in Kaluli expression.* Philadelphia: University of Pennsylvania Press.

———. 2000. A sweet lullaby for world music. *Public Culture* 12 (1): 145.

Fischman, Rajmil. 1999. Global village, local universe: A statement of identity. *Leonardo Music Journal* 9 (1): 53–62.

Forbes, Linda. 2004. Pete Seeger on environmental advocacy, organizing, and education in the Hudson River Valley: An interview with the folk music legend, author and storyteller, political and environmental activist, and grassroots organizer. *Organization and Environment* 17 (4): 513–522.

Fortner, Rosanne W., and Jeffrey R. Corney. 2002. Great Lakes educational needs assessment: Teachers' priorities for topics, materials, and training. *Journal of Great Lakes Research* 28 (1): 3–14.

Freydkin, Donna, Elysa Gardner, and Rachel Grumman. 2007. Around the world with Live Earth. *USA Today,* July 9.

Frith, Simon. 1984. Rock and the politics of memory. *Social Text* 3/4:59–69.

———. 1993. Popular music and the local state. In *Rock and popular music: Politics, policies, institutions,* ed. Tony Bennett, Simon Frith, Larry Grossberg, and John Shepherd, 14–24. New York: Routledge.

———. 1996. *Performing rites: On the value of popular music.* Cambridge: Harvard University Press.

Gardiner, William. 1838. *The music of nature.* Boston: J. H. Wilkins & R. B. Carter.

Garman, Bryan. 1996. The ghost of history: Bruce Springsteen, Woody Guthrie, and the hurt song. *Popular Music and Society* 20 (2): 69–120.

———. 2000. *A race of singers: Whitman's working-class hero from Guthrie to Springsteen.* Chapel Hill: University of North Carolina Press.

Garofalo, Reebee. 1992. *Rockin' the boat: Mass music and mass movements.* Boston: South End Press.

Garofalo, Reebee, Billy Bragg, Tiffany Cheng, Susan Fast, Simon Frith, Holly George Warren, Karen Pegley, and Will Straw. 2005. Who is the world? Reflections on music and politics twenty years after Live Aid. *Journal of Popular Music Studies* 17 (3): 324–344.

Garrard, Greg. 2004. *Ecocriticism.* New Critical Idiom. New York: Routledge.

Giannachi, Gabriella, and Nigel Stewart. 2005. *Performing nature: Explorations in ecology and the arts.* New York: Lang.

Gilbert, Pat. 2005. *Passion is a fashion: The real story of the Clash.* Cambridge, MA: Da Capo Press.

Glotfelty, Cheryll, and Harold Fromm. 1996. *The ecocriticism reader: Landmarks in literary ecology.* Athens: University of Georgia Press.

Gold, John R. 1998. Roll on Columbia: Woody Guthrie, migrants' tales, and regional transformation in the Pacific Northwest. *Journal of Cultural Geography* 18 (1): 83.

Goodall, H. Lloyd, Jr. 2000. *Writing the new ethnography.* Walnut Creek, CA: AltaMira Press.

Gough, Paul J., and Alex Woodson. 2007. Live Earth ratings on cool side. *Hollywood Reporter International Edition* 400 (19): 3–70.

Gracyk, Theodore. 2001. *I wanna be me: Rock music and the politics of identity.* Sound Matters. Philadelphia: Temple University Press.

Graillat, Chris. 2007. After Live Earth: What did the global event mean? *Christian Science Monitor* July 11: 8.

Grant, Alistair. 2009. Have U2 created a monster? *Belfast Telegraph,* July 7.

Green, Johnny, Garry Barker, and Ray Lowry. 1999. *A riot of our own: Night and day with the Clash.* New York: Faber and Faber.

Green, Lucy. 2002. *How popular musicians learn: A way ahead for music education.* Burlington, VT: Ashgate.

Groom, Nick. 1996. The condition of Muzak. *Popular Music and Society* 20 (3): 1–17.

Grossberg, Lawrence. 1992. *We gotta get out of this place: Popular conservatism and postmodern culture.* New York: Routledge.

———. 1993. The framing of rock: Rock and the new conservatism. In *Rock and popular music: Politics, policies, institutions,* ed. Tony Bennett, Simon Frith,

Lawrence Grossberg, John Shepherd, and Graeme Turner, 193–209. New York: Routledge.

Grove Dictionary of American Music, 2nd ed. (Forthcoming). New York: Oxford University Press. [Anticipated publication date: 2013]

Guthrie, Woody. 1941. Letter to Elizabeth and Harold Ambellan, June 10. Correspondence 1, Box 1, Folder 4. Woody Guthrie Archives, New York City.

———. 1943. *Bound for glory.* New York: New American Library. Reprint ed. 1983. New York: Penguin.

———. 1944. Unpublished note for "Folksay Album #1." Manuscript 1, Item 1, Box 1, Folder 19. Woody Guthrie Archives, New York City.

———. 1990. *Pastures of plenty: A self-portrait,* ed. Dave Marsh and Harold Leventhal. New York: HarperCollins.

———. 1991. *Roll On Columbia: The Columbia River collection,* ed. William Murlin, foreword by Pete Seeger. Bethlehem, PA: Sing Out Publications.

Guy, Nancy. 2009. Flowing down Taiwan's Tamsui River: Towards an ecomusicology of the environmental imagination. *Ethnomusicology* 53 (2): 218–248.

Harvard Law Review. 2010. Uncommon goods: On environmental virtues and voluntary carbon offsets. *Harvard Law Review* 123 (8): 2065–2087.

Heise, Ursula K. 2008. *Sense of place and sense of planet: The environmental imagination of the global.* New York: Oxford University Press.

Hempton, Gordon, and John Grossmann. 2009. *One square inch of silence: One man's search for natural silence in a noisy world.* New York: Free Press.

Henry, Jules. 1963. *Culture against man.* New York: Random House.

Hentoff, Nat. 1964. The crackin', shakin', breakin' sounds. *New Yorker.* Available at http://www.newyorker.com/archive.

Hiatt, Brian. 2007. Live Earth. *Rolling Stone,* November 29: 82.

Hogg, Nick, and Tim Jackson. 2009. Digital media and dematerialization. *Journal of Industrial Ecology* 13 (1): 127–146.

Hulme, Mike. 2009. *Why we disagree about climate change: Understanding controversy, inaction and opportunity.* New York: Cambridge University Press.

Ingalls, Wayne B. 1999. Traditional Greek choruses and the education of girls. *History of Education* 28 (4): 371–393.

Ingraham, Laura. 2003. *Shut up and sing: How elites from Hollywood, politics, and the UN are subverting America.* Washington, DC: Regnery.

Ingram, David. 2008. "My Dirty Stream": Pete Seeger, American folk music, and environmental protest. *Popular Music and Society* 31 (1): 21–36.

———. 2010. *The jukebox in the garden: Ecocriticism and American popular music since 1960.* Amsterdam: Rodopi.

Irvine, Katherine N., Patrick Devine-Wright, Sarah R. Payne, Richard A. Fuller, Birgit Painter, and Kevin J. Gaston. 2009. Green space, soundscape and urban sustainability: An interdisciplinary, empirical study. *Local Environment* 14 (2): 155–172.

Jackson, Mark Allan. 2002. Is this song your song anymore?: Revisioning Woody Guthrie's "This Land Is Your Land." *American Music* 20 (3): 249–276.

———. 2005. Dark memory: A look at lynching in America through the life, times, and songs of Woody Guthrie. *Popular Music and Society* 28 (5): 663–675.

Johnson, Allen W., and Timothy K. Earle. 2000. *The evolution of human societies: From foraging group to agrarian state.* Stanford, CA: Stanford University Press.

Johnson, Bruce, and Martin Cloonan. 2009. *Dark side of the tune: Popular music and violence.* Burlington, VT: Ashgate.

Johnson, David. 1968. Untitled manuscript sent to Marjorie Guthrie. Woody Guthrie Archives, New York City.

Jones, Stacy Holman. 1999. Women, musics, bodies, and texts: The gesture of women's music. *Text and Performance Quarterly* 19 (3): 217–235.

Keil, Charles. 2010. Groovology and the magic of other people's music. Available at http://musicgrooves.org/articles/GroovologyAndMagic.pdf.

Keil, Charles, and Steven Feld. 2005. *Music grooves: Essays and dialogues.* Tucson: Fenestra.

Kertzer, David I. 1988. *Ritual, politics, and power.* New Haven: Yale University Press.

Kinnear, Tyler. 2010. "Voicing nature in John Luther Adams's *The Place Where You Go to Listen.*" Paper presented at the Society for American Music Annual Meetings, Cincinnati, OH. March 9–13.

Klein, Joe. 1980. *Woody Guthrie: A life.* New York: Knopf.

Klein, Naomi. 2002. *No logo: No space, no choice, no jobs.* New York: Picador.

Knickerbocker, Brad. 1997. Saving an icon of the Pacific Northwest. *Christian Science Monitor,* January 30: 4.

Korten, David C. 2001. *When corporations rule the world.* Bloomfield, CT: Berrett Koehler Publishers.

Kot, Greg. 2009. U2 gets green to offset huge carbon footprint of its 360 tour. *Chicago Tribune.* Available at http://leisureblogs.chicagotribune.com/turn_it_up/2009/09/u2-gets-green-to-offset-big-carbon-footprint-of-360-tour.html.

Krause, Bernard L. 1998. *Into a wild sanctuary: A life in music and natural sound.* Berkeley: Heyday Books.

———. 2001. Where the sounds live. In *The book of music and nature: An anthology of sounds, words, thoughts,* ed. David Rothenberg and Marta Ulvaeus, 215–223. Middletown, CT: Wesleyan University Press.

KUED. 2012. Joe Hill: Songs of hope. Website. http://www.kued.org/productions/joehill/voices/.

Lanier, Jaron. 2001. Music, nature, and computers. In *The book of music and nature: An anthology of sounds, words, thoughts,* ed. David Rothenberg and Marta Ulvaeus, 91–94. Middletown, CT: Wesleyan University Press.

Lee, Richard E., Immanuel Maurice Wallerstein, and Volkan Aytar. 2004. *Overcoming the two cultures: Science versus the humanities in the modern world-system.* Boulder, CO: Paradigm Publishers.

Leppert, Richard D. 1993. *The sight of sound: Music, representation, and the history of the body.* Berkeley: University of California Press.

Levin, Theodore Craig, with Valentina Süzükei. 2006. *Where rivers and mountains sing: Sound, music, and nomadism in Tuva and beyond.* Bloomington: Indiana University Press.

Levitin, Daniel J. 2006. *This is your brain on music: The science of a human obsession.* New York: Dutton.

Lipsitz, George. 1994. *Dangerous crossroads: Popular music, postmodernism, and the poetics of place.* New York: Verso.

Lobos, Anna. 2009. In harmony with nature: Elements of ecology in pedagogy and art. *New Educational Review* 19 (3–4): 383–389.

Loechner, Jack. 2009. *Radio dominant audio device.* Available at http://www.media post.com/publications/?fa=Articles.showArticle&art_aid=117009.

Malloch, Stephen, and Colwyn Trevarthen. 2009. *Communicative musicality: Exploring the basis of human companionship.* New York: Oxford University Press.

Manes, Christopher. 1996. Nature and silence. In *The ecocriticism reader: Landmarks in literary ecology,* ed. Cheryll Glotfelty and Harold Fromm, 15–29. Athens: University of Georgia Press.

Mann, Charles, and Mark Plummer. 2000. Can science rescue salmon? *Science* 289 (5480): 716–719.

Marcus, George E., and Michael M. J. Fischer. 1986. *Anthropology as cultural critique: An experimental moment in the human sciences.* Chicago: University of Chicago Press.

Marshall, Josh. 2009. Very poor choice. *Talking Points Memo,* January 19. Available at http://talkingpointsmemo.com/archives/2009/01/very_poor_choice.php.

Margolick, David. 2000. *Strange fruit: Billie Holiday, café society, and an early cry for civil rights.* Philadelphia: Running Press.

Marqusee, Mike. 2003. *Chimes of freedom: The politics of Bob Dylan's art.* New York: New Press.

Matless, David. 2005. Sonic geography in a nature region. *Social and Cultural Geography* 6 (5): 745–766.

Mattern, Mark. 1998. *Acting in concert: Music, community, and political action.* New Brunswick, NJ: Rutgers University Press.

McCollam, Douglas. 2010. Slick on slick. *New York Times,* November 7.

McCormick, John, and Jonathan Matusitz. 2010. The impact on U.S. society of noise-induced and music-induced hearing loss caused by personal media players. *International Journal of Listening* 24 (2): 125–140.

McDermott, Josh. 2008. The evolution of music. *Nature* 453 (7193): 287–288.

McDonough, Jimmy. 2002. *Shakey: Neil Young's biography.* New York: Random House.

McDowell, Michael. 1996. Bakhtinian road to ecological insight. In *The ecocriticism reader: Landmarks in literary ecology,* ed. Cheryll Glotfelty and Harold Fromm, 371–391. Athens: University of Georgia Press.

Media Literacy Clearinghouse. 2010. Pop is still king of the world's music genres. Available at http://www.frankwbaker.com/mediause.htm.

Mellers, Wilfrid Howard. 2001. *Singing in the wilderness: Music and ecology in the twentieth century.* Urbana: University of Illinois Press.

Minard, Lawrence. 1992. Cruising with Woody Guthrie. *Forbes* 149 (10): 192–193.

Montaigne, Fen. 2001. A river dammed. *National Geographic,* April: 2–33.

Morris, Desmond, 1984. *The naked ape.* New York: Dell.

Morrow, Lance, and Nathan Thornburgh. 2002. This land is whose land? *Time International,* July 8: 73.

Morton, Timothy. 2007. *Ecology without nature: Rethinking environmental aesthetics.* Cambridge: Harvard University Press.

Moyo, Last. 2010. The global citizen and the international media. *International Communication Gazette* 72 (2): 191–207.

Music and Copyright. 2010. Pop is still king of the world's music genres. Available at http://musicandcopyright.wordpress.com/2010/08/11/pop-is-still-king-of -the-world's-music-genres/.

Naughton, George P., Christopher C. Caudill, Matthew L. Keefer, Theodore C. Bjornn, Lowell C. Stuehrenberg, and Christopher A. Peery. 2005. Late-season mortality during migration of radio-tagged adult sockeye salmon (*Oncorhynchus nerka*) in the Columbia River. *Canadian Journal of Fisheries and Aquatic Sciences* 62 (1): 30–47.

New Musical Express. 2009a. David Byrne disses U2 tour spending. July 28. Available at http://www.nme.com/news/david-byrne/46359.

———. 2009b. U2 defend environmental impact of world tour. August 15. Available at http://www.nme.com/news/david-byrne/46359.

Osborne, Nigel. 2009. Towards a chronobiology of musical rhythm. In *Communicative musicality: Exploring the basis of human companionship,* ed. Stephen Malloch and Colwyn Trevarthen, 545–564. New York: Oxford University Press.

Pedelty, Mark. 1995. *War stories: The culture of foreign correspondents.* New York: Routledge.

———. 2004. *Musical ritual in Mexico City: From the Aztec to NAFTA.* Austin: University of Texas Press.

———. 2008. Woody Guthrie and the Columbia River: Propaganda, art, and irony. *Popular Music and Society* 31 (3): 329–355.

———. 2009. Musical news: Popular music in political movements. In *The anthropology of news and journalism: Global perspectives,* ed. Elizabeth Bird, 215–237. Bloomington: Indiana University Press.

Pedelty, Mark, and Linda Keefe. 2010. Political pop, political fans?: A content analysis of music fan blogs. *Music and Politics* 4 (1): 1–11.

Pedelty, Mark, and Desdamona T. Racheli. 2009. Is the political troubadour dead?: Markets versus politics in local music. *Journal of Popular Music Studies* 21 (3): 266–283.

Peet, Richard, Paul Robbins, and Michael Watts. 2010. *Global political ecology.* New York: Routledge.

Petrilli, Susan. 2009. Semiotics as semioethics in the era of global communication. *Semiotica* 173 (1–4): 343–367.

Petrilli, Susan, and Augusto Ponzio. 2003. *Semioetica.* Rome: Meltemi.

Phillips-Silver, Jessica, C. Athena Aktipis, and Gregory A. Bryant. 2010. The ecology of entrainment: Foundations of coordinated rhythmic movement. *Music Perception* 28, no. 1 (9): 3–14.

Pitt-Brooke, David. 2004. *Chasing Clayoquot: A wilderness almanac.* Vancouver: Raincoast Books.

Postman, Neil. 2006. *Amusing ourselves to death: Public discourse in the age of show business.* New York: Penguin Books.

Pratt, Ray. 1994. *Rhythm and resistance: The political uses of American popular music.* Washington, DC: Smithsonian Institution Press.

Prusher, Ilene R. 2009. The "Elders" arrive in Israel to boost Mideast peace. *Christian Science Monitor,* August 25: 6.

Putnam, Robert D. 2000. *Bowling alone: The collapse and revival of American community.* New York: Simon & Schuster.

Raging Grannies. 1993. *The Raging Grannies songbook.* Gabriola Island, BC: New Society Publishers.

Redfield, Robert. 1930. *Tepoztlán, a Mexican village: A study of folk life.* Chicago: University of Chicago Press.

Reed, T. V. 2005. *The art of protest: Culture and activism from the civil rights movement to the streets of Seattle.* Minneapolis: University of Minnesota Press.

Rehding, Alexander. 2002. Review article: Eco-musicology. *Journal of the Royal Musical Association* 127 (2): 305–320.

Reuss, Richard A. 1968. *A Woody Guthrie bibliography, 1912–1967.* New York: Guthrie Children's Trust Fund.

Reuss, Richard A., and JoAnne C. Reuss. 2000. *American folk music and left-wing politics, 1927–1957.* Lanham, MD: Scarecrow Press.

Richards, Chris. 2010. Tough year for concert sales may push ticket prices down. *Washington Post,* December 31.

Rivard, Nicole. 2007. Ad community rallies around Al Gore's Live Earth campaign. *SHOOT,* July 20: 4–22.

Rogers, Heather. 2010. Offset buyers beware. *The Nation,* June 3: 20–22.

Roper, Emma Rose. 2007. Musical nature: Vocalisations of the Australian Magpie (*Gymnorhina tibicen tyrannica*). *Context* 32:59–72.

Rosenthal, Debra J. 2006. 'Hoods and the woods: Rap music as environmental literature. *Journal of Popular Culture* 39 (4): 661–676.

Ross, Alex. 1997. The pavement tapes. *New Yorker,* June 26: 85.

Ross, Stephanie. 1998. *What gardens mean.* Chicago: University of Chicago Press.

Rothenberg, David. 2001. Introduction: Does nature understand music? In *The book of music and nature: An anthology of sounds, words, thoughts,* ed. David Rothenberg and Marta Ulvaeus, 1–12. Middletown, CT: Wesleyan University Press.

———. 2005. *Why birds sing: A journey through the mystery of bird song.* New York: Basic Books.

———. 2008. *Thousand mile song: Whale music in a sea of sound.* New York: Basic Books.

Rothenberg, David, and Marta Ulvaeus. 2001. *The book of music and nature: An anthology of sounds, words, thoughts.* Middletown, CT: Wesleyan University Press.

Sacks, Oliver W. 2007. *Musicophilia: Tales of music and the brain.* New York: Knopf.

Santelli, Robert, and Emily Davidson. 1999. *Hard travelin': The life and legacy of Woody Guthrie.* Hanover, NH: Wesleyan University Press.

Savage, Jon. 2002 (1992). *England's dreaming: Anarchy, sex pistols, punk rock, and beyond.* New York: St. Martin's Griffin.

Schafer, R. Murray. 1977. *Five village soundscapes.* Vancouver, BC: A. R. C. Publications.

———. 1994. *The soundscape: Our sonic environment and the tuning of the world.* Rochester, VT: Destiny Books. First published 1977 as *Tuning of the world.*

Scott, Alan. 2009. Talking about music is like dancing about architecture. Available at http://home.pacifier.com/~ascott/they/tamildaa.htm.

Sharp, Chesla. 1992. Coal-mining songs as forms of environmental protest. *Journal of the Appalachian Studies Association* 4:50–58.

Sheffner, Ben. 2009. HBO backs off YouTube takedowns of inaugural concert footage. January 23. Available at http://copyrightsandcampaigns.blogspot.com/2009/01/hbo-backs-off-youtube-takedowns-of.html.

Silko, Leslie Marmon. 1996. Landscape, history, and the Pueblo imagination. In *The ecocriticism reader: Landmarks in literary ecology,* ed. Cheryll Glotfelty and Harold Fromm, 264–275. Athens: University of Georgia Press.

Smith, Gibbs M. 1969. *Joe Hill.* Salt Lake City: Peregrine Smith Books.

Spitzer, Nick. 2000. "This Land Is Your Land." Radio program and transcript. National Public Radio, *All Things Considered.* Available at http://www.npr.org/templates/story/story.php?storyId=1076186.

Stahl, Matthew. 2003. To hell with heteronomy: Liberalism, rule-making, and the pursuit of "community" in an urban rock scene. *Journal of Popular Music Studies* 15 (2): 140–165.

Steinbeck, John. 1939. *The Grapes of Wrath.* New York: Viking Press.

Stephens, Mitchell. 1988. *A history of news: From the drum to the satellite.* New York: Viking.

Strauss, Susan. 1996. *The passionate fact: Storytelling in natural history and cultural interpretation.* Golden, CO: North American Press.

Stringer, Ernest T. 2007. *Action research.* Los Angeles: Sage Publications.

Tagg, Philip. 1982. Analysing popular music: Theory, method and practice. *Popular Music* 2: 37–68.

———. 2006. Subjectivity and soundscape, motorbikes and music. In *The popular music studies reader,* ed. Andy Bennett, Barry Shank, and Jason Toynbee, 44–49. New York: Routledge.

Toliver, Brooks. 2004. Eco-ing in the canyon: Ferde Grofe's *Grand Canyon Suite* and the transformation of wilderness. *Journal of the American Musicological Society* 57 (2): 325–367.

Tougaard, Jakob, and Nina Eriksen. 2006. Analysing differences among animal songs quantitatively by means of the Levenshtein distance measure. *Behaviour* 143 (2): 239–252.

Turner, Frederick. 1996. Cultivating the American garden. In *The ecocriticism reader: Landmarks in literary ecology,* ed. Cheryll Glotfelty and Harold Fromm, 40–51. Athens: University of Georgia Press.

Turner, Victor Witter. 1969. *The ritual process: Structure and anti-structure.* Lewis Henry Morgan Lectures. London: Routledge and Keegan Paul.

Vannini, Phillip. 2004. The meanings of a star: Interpreting music fans' reviews. *Symbolic Interaction* 27 (1): 47–69.

Veal, Michael E. 2000. *Fela: The life and times of an African musical icon.* Philadelphia: Temple University Press.

Verplanck, William E., Moses Wakeman Collyer, and George Davis Woolsey. 1908. *The sloops of the Hudson: An historical sketch of the packet and market sloops of the last century.* New York: G. P. Putnam's Sons.

Vogel, I., C. P. van der Ploeg, J. Brug, and H. Raat. 2009. Music venues and hearing loss: Opportunities for and barriers to improving environmental conditions. *International Journal of Audiology* 48 (8): 531–536.

Von Glahn, Denise. 2003. *The sounds of place: Music and the American cultural landscape.* Boston: Northeastern University Press.

Waddell, Ray. 2008. Live Earth: A look back. *Billboard* 120 (13): 34–35.

Wald, Elijah. 2001. *Narcocorrido: A journey into the music of drugs, guns, and guerrillas.* New York: Rayo.

Wallerstein, Immanuel Maurice. 2004. *The modern world-system in the longue durée.* Boulder, CO: Paradigm Publishers.

Waterman, Ellen. 2007. Sound escape: Sonic geography remembered and imagined. *Ecumene* 7 (1): 112–115.

Watkins, Holly. 2011. Musical ecologies of place and placelessness. *Journal of the American Musicological Society* 64 (2): 404–408.

Webb, Jimmy. 1998. *Tunesmith: Inside the art of songwriting.* New York: Hyperion.

Webster, Rebecca. 2010. Protecting country music's home. *E—The Environmental Magazine* 21 (5): 10.

Weinstein, Deena. 2006. Rock protest songs: So many and so few. In *The resisting muse: Popular music and social protest,* ed. Ian Peddie, 3–16. London: Ashgate.

Weissmann, Gerald. 2007. Trashing "America the Beautiful": From she to shining she. *FASEB·Journal* 21 (13): 3399–3403.

Westerkamp, Hildegard. 2002. Linking soundscape composition and acoustic ecology. *Organised Sound* 7 (1): 51–56.

White, Lynn, Jr. 1996. The historical roots of our ecologic crisis. In *The ecocriticism reader: Landmarks in literary ecology,* ed. Cheryll Glotfelty and Harold Fromm, 3–14. Athens: University of Georgia Press.

Wilson, Edward O. 1998. *Consilience: The unity of knowledge.* New York: Knopf.

Wissmar, R. C., and S. D. Craig. 2004. Factors affecting habitat selection by a small spawning charr population, bull trout, *Salvelinus confluentus*: Implications for recovery of an endangered species. *Fisheries Management and Ecology* 11:23–31.

Yardley, William. 2009. Obama follows Bush on salmon recovery. *New York Times,* September 16.

Yi-Nuo Shih, Rong-Hwa Huang, and Han-Sun Chiang. 2009. Correlation between work concentration level and background music: A pilot study. *Work* 33 (3): 329–333.

RECORDINGS AND ONLINE PERFORMANCES

Abreu, Sharon, with Michael Hurwicz. 2002. "Calling the Salmon Home." Tony Ultimate, composer. *Seeking Sanctuary.* Eastsound, WA: Irthlingz.

———. 2002. "Wild, Wild River." *Seeking Sanctuary.* Eastsound, WA: Irthlingz.

———. 2010. "The Food Chain Song." Available at http://www.youtube.com/watch?v=ronChTzB2Ak.

Adams, John Luther. 1994. *Earth and the Great Weather*. New York: New World Records.

———. 1998. *In the White Silence*. New York: New World Records.

Arcade Fire. 2007. *Neon Bible*. New York: Merge.

Artists United against Apartheid. 1985. *Sun City*. Hollywood: Manhattan Records.

Banana Slug String Band. 1989. "Solar Energy Shout." *Dirt Made My Lunch*. Available at http://bananaslugs.bandcamp.com/album/dirt-made-my-lunch.

Band Aid. 1984. *Do They Know It's Christmas?* New York: Columbia.

Beach Boys. 1971. *Surf's Up*. Burbank, CA: Brother Records.

Boomtown Rats. 1979. *A Tonic for the Troops*. New York: Columbia.

———. 1981. *Mondo Bongo*. New York: Columbia.

Bragg, Billy. 1988. *Workers Playtime*. New York: Elektra.

Byrne, David, and Talking Heads. 1988. *Naked*. New York: Sire.

Cake. 2001. *Cake's Comfort Eagle*. New York: Columbia.

Cale, J. J. 1976. *Troubadour*. Los Angeles: Shelter Recording Co.

Capitol Steps. 2006. *Between Iraq and a Hard Place*. Self-published.

Chapman, Tracy. 1988. *Tracy Chapman*. New York: Elektra.

Clash. 1978. *The Clash*. New York: Epic.

———. 1980. *Sandinista!* New York: Epic.

Cruso, Carolyn. 2000. *As Clear a Hue*. Eastsound, WA: Blue Heron.

———. 2009. *Have You Ever?* Eastsound, WA: Blue Heron.

Culture Club. 1983. *Karma Chameleon*. New York: Virgin.

Denver, John. 1971. *Poems, Prayers and Promises*. New York: RCA.

———. 1972. *John Denver: Rocky Mountain High*. New York: RCA.

———. 1974. *Back Home Again*. New York: RCA.

———. 1975. *Windsong*. New York: RCA.

DiFranco, Ani. 2001. *Reveling Reckoning*. Buffalo, NY: Righteous Babe Records.

Dixie Chicks. 2006. *Taking the Long Way*. New York: Columbia.

Doors. 1967. *The Doors*. New York: Elektra.

Dylan, Bob. 1962. *Bob Dylan*. New York: Columbia.

Eagles. 1976. *Hotel California*. Los Angeles: Asylum Records.

Earle, Steve. 2004. *The Revolution Starts Now*. New York: Artemis.

Fogerty, John. 1968. *Proud Mary*. Hollywood: RCA.

Fogerty, John, and Creedence Clearwater Revival. 1989. *Best of Creedence Clearwater Revival*. Miami: Belwin.

Fugazi. 1990. *Repeater*. Washington, DC: Dischord.

Gaye, Marvin. 1971. *What's Going On*. Detroit: Hitsville.

Geldof, Bob, and Midge Ure. 1984. *Do They Know It's Christmas?* London: Phonogram.

Grofé, Ferde. 1932. *Grand Canyon Suite*. New York: Robbins Music Corporation.

———. 1947. *Mississippi River Suite*. Bridgeport, CT: Columbia Masterworks.

———. 1955. *Hudson River Suite*. New York: Columbia.

Guthrie, Woody, and Millard Lampell. 1972. *A Tribute to Woody Guthrie*. New York: Ludlow Music.

Hensley, Hunter. 2010. *Requiem for the Mountains*. Available at http://www.youtube.com/watch?v=g8gJrTe2O18.

Holiday, Billie. 1972. *Strange Fruit.* New York: Atlantic.

Hypoxic Punks. Available at hypoxicpunks.org.

Jackson, Michael, and Janet Jackson. 1995. *HIStory.* New York: Epic.

Keillor, Garrison. 2010. "Pontoon Boat." In *Pretty God Bits.* Minneapolis: High-
 bridge. Available on iTunes.

Keith, Toby. 2002. *Unleashed.* Nashville: DreamWorks.

Kern, Jerome, and Oscar Hammerstein. 1941. *Show Boat.* New York: Columbia.

Lund, Martin. 2006. *Suite for Turtleback Mountain.* Eastsound, WA: MLM Records.

Lynyrd Skynyrd. 1974. "Sweet Home Alabama." *Second Helping.* Universal City,
 CA: MCA Records.

McCoys. 1965. *Hang on Sloopy.* New York: Legacy.

Men They Couldn't Hang. 1988. *Waiting for Bonaparte.* London: Magnet.

Midnight Oil. 1987. *Diesel and Dust.* Los Angeles: CBS.

———. 1990. *Blue Sky Mining.* New York: Columbia.

Minowa, Craig, and Cloud Cult. 2010. *Light Chasers.* Minneapolis: Earthology.

Mitchell, Joni. 1970. *Ladies of the Canyon.* Burbank, CA: Reprise.

Mos Def. 1999. *Black on Both Sides.* Los Angeles: Rawkus.

Newman, Thomas, Michael Crawford, Louis Armstrong, and Peter Gabriel. 2008.
 WALL-E. Burbank, CA: Walt Disney Records.

Nirvana. 1991. *Nevermind.* Los Angeles: DGC.

NYOil. 2007. *Y'All Should All Get Lynched.* New York: Petroleum Empire Music
 Group.

Prine, John. 1973. *Sweet Revenge.* New York: Atlantic.

Robeson, Paul. 1990. "I Dreamed I Saw Joe Hill Last Night." *Live at Carnegie Hall.*
 New York: Vanguard Records.

Seeger, Pete, and Malvina Reynolds. 1966. *God Bless the Grass.* New York: Columbia.

Soundgarden. 1989. *Louder Than Love.* London: A&M.

Spears, Britney. 2004. *Britney Spears, Greatest Hits: My Prerogative.* Miami: Warner
 Bros.

Special AKA. 1984. *Free Nelson Mandela.* New York: Chrysalis.

Young, Neil. 1970. *After the Gold Rush.* Burbank, CA: Reprise.

———. 1992. *Harvest Moon.* Burbank, CA: Reprise.

———. 2005. *Prairie Wind.* Burbank, CA: Reprise.

———. 2006. *Living with War.* Burbank, CA: Reprise Records.

Young, Neil, and The Bluenotes. 1988. *This Note's for You.* Burbank, CA: Reprise.

Young, Neil, Crazy Horse, and The Mountainettes. 2003. *Greendale.* Burbank, CA:
 Reprise.

FILMS

Filmmakers Collaborative, Smithsonian Institution, and Public Broadcasting
 Service. 1998. *The Mississippi, River of Song.* Washington, DC: Smithsonian
 Institution.

Guthrie, Woody, and Leadbelly. 1988. *Folkways, a Vision Shared.* New York:
 Columbia.

Kopple, Barbara, Cecilia Peck, David Cassidy, and Cabin Creek Films. 2006. *Dixie Chicks: Shut Up and Sing.* New York: Weinstein Company.

Lorentz, Pare. 1938. *The River.* New York: Stackpole Sons.

Matthews, Denise, and Mike Madjic. 1999a. Videotaped interview with Elmer Buehler. Woody Guthrie Archives, New York City.

———. 1999b. Videotaped interview with Stephen Kahn. Woody Guthrie Archives, New York City.

McMahon, Kevin. 2009. *Waterlife.* Ottawa: National Film Board of Canada and Primitive Films.

McPhee, Larkin. 2010. *Troubled Waters: A Mississippi River Story.* Minneapolis: Bell Museum.

Metsa, Paul. 2011. "This Land Is Your Land." Available at http://www.youtube.com/watch?v=7AV2wqPQR_Y.

Murlin, Bill. 2005. Filmed interview with Elmer Buehler. Woody Guthrie Archives, New York City.

Pedelty, Mark. 2011. *A Neighborhood of Raingardens.* Minneapolis: Atomic K Studios. Available at raingardenmovie.org.

von Fritsch, Gunther. 1939. *Hydro.* Portland, OR: Bonneville Power Administration.

———. 1948. *The Columbia.* Portland, OR: Bonneville Power Administration.

WEBSITES OF INTEREST

All At Once. Allatonce.org
Cascadia Project. Discovery.org/cascadia
Ecomusicology. Ecomusicology.net
Hypoxic Punks. Hypoxicpunks.org
Riverkeeper. Riverkeeper.org

Permissions

LYRICS

Woody Guthrie lyric (pages 51–52)
"This Land Is Your Land," words and music by Woody Guthrie. WGP/TRO-©
Copyright 1956, 1958, 1970, 1972 (copyrights renewed) Woody Guthrie Publications, Inc. and Ludlow Music, Inc., New York, NY. Administered by Ludlow Music,
Inc. Used by permission.

Ani DiFranco lyric (pages 75–76)
"Your Next Bold Move," words and music by Ani DiFranco. © 2001 Righteous
Babe Music (BMI)/Administered by Bug Music. All rights reserved. Used by permission. Reprinted by permission of Hal Leonard Corporation.

Woody Guthrie lyric (page 92)
"Roll On, Columbia," words by Woody Guthrie. Music based on "Goodnight,
Irene," by Huddie Ledbetter and John Lomax. WGP/TRO-© Copyright 1936, 1957,
1963 (copyrights renewed) Woody Guthrie Publications, Inc. and Ludlow Music,
Inc., New York, NY. Administered by Ludlow Music, Inc. Used by permission.

Woody Guthrie lyric (page 93)
"The Biggest Thing That Man Has Ever Done" (Great Historical Bum), words and
music by Woody Guthrie. WGP/TRO-© Copyright 1961, 1963, 1976 (copyrights
renewed) Woody Guthrie Publications, Inc. and Ludlow Music, Inc., New York,
NY. Administered by Ludlow Music, Inc. Used by permission.

Woody Guthrie lyric (page 94)
"Pastures of Plenty," words and music by Woody Guthrie. WGP/TRO-© Copyright
1960 (renewed), 1963 (renewed) Woody Guthrie Publications, Inc. and Ludlow
Music, Inc., New York, NY. Administered by Ludlow Music, Inc. Used by permission.

Woody Guthrie lyric (page 105)
"Talking Columbia," words and music by Woody Guthrie. WGP/TRO-© Copyright 1961 (renewed), 1963 (renewed) Woody Guthrie Publications, Inc. and Ludlow Music, Inc., New York, NY. Administered by Ludlow Music, Inc. Used by permission.

Carolyn Cruso lyric (page 167)
"Flyway Zone," by Carolyn Cruso. "As Clear a Hue," 2000. All rights reserved.

Billy Bragg lyric (page 201)
"Waiting for the Great Leap Forwards," by Billy Bragg. Lyrics © Billy Bragg, 1988.

TEXT

Portions of Chapter 3
Mark Pedelty, "Woody Guthrie and the Columbia River: Propaganda, Art and Irony," *Popular Music and Society* 31 (3): 329–355, www.tandfonline.com.

PHOTOGRAPHS

Cover image
Photo by David Ramage.

Figure 1 (page 4)
Photo by Kevin Pedelty.

Figure 2 (page 157)
Photo by Patrick O'Leary, University of Minnesota.

Figure 3 (page 158)
Photo by Patrick O'Leary, University of Minnesota.

Figure 4 (page 159)
Photo by Tim Busse.

Figure 5 (page 179)
Photo courtesy of Lori Mikolon.

Figure 6 (page 185)
Photo courtesy of Renee Swenson.

Figure 7 (page 192)
Photo by Karl Demer.

Index

228

Index

Ritual (*continued*):
failure, 28–30; intoxication, 161–162; politics and ideology, 54–58, 161–164, 192; musical concert as, 9–10, 28–30, 54–58, 161–164; persona, 103; place, 184; protest, 62–64 (*see also* Environmental activism; Protest music)
Rivera, Diego, 167
Robeson, Paul, 60, 67, 201
Roper, Emma Rose, 117
Rosenthal, Debra, 66
Ross, Alex, 148
Rothenberg, David, 6, 117, 118, 158. *See also* Bird song; Whale song
Rovics, David, 113

Sacks, Oliver, 117, 118, 184
Savage, Jon, 69. *See also* Punk music
Schafer, R. Murray, 6, 41, 70, 131, 190. *See also* Soundscape studies
Seeger, Charles, 101. *See also* Seeger, Pete
Seeger, Pete: activism, 62, 111–114, 177; environmental music, 46–47; Hudson River, 111–114, 166 (*see also* Hudson River); Joe Hill, 60; Obama inaugural concert, 54–58; participatory music, 39, 168 (*see also* Participatory music); songbook, 138. *See also* Guthrie, Woody
Semioethics, 78
Sex Pistols, 69–70. *See also* Punk music
Sierra Club, 2–3, 62
Sigur Ros, 188
Simulacra, 29, 37
Society for Ethnomusicology (SEM), 45
Songwriting, 139–140, 147–151, 193
Soundgarden, 14–16. *See also* Cornell, Chris
Soundscape studies: animal, 117 (*see also* Bird song; Whale song); applied, 6, 9–10; comparative, 110; consumption, 164 (*see also* Consumers; Consumption); documentary film, 188–189 (*see also* Documentary film music); electronic music, 41; ethnographic research, 131; garden, 190; listening, 41 (*see also* Waterman, Ellen); local vs. global, 200; noise, 20, 81 (*see also* Noise pollution); place, 82, 181 (*see also* Place; Space); silence, 68 (*see also* Hempton, Gordon); sustainability, 40, 84, 189 (*see also* Sustainability); urban, 163–164. *See also* Shafer, R. Murray

Sounds of Blackness, 165–166
Space, 20, 84, 190. *See also* Place
Springsteen, Bruce, 52, 54–58, 60, 62, 177
Stage fright, 176
Stahl, Matthew, 145–146
Steinbeck, John, 101
Sting, 177
Street teams, 172. *See also* Marketing and promotions
Sustainability: aesthetics, 18–20; community, 125–127, 176, 189, 201; consumption, 18, 113 (*see also* Consumer; Consumption); cultures of, 18, 27, 176; development, 182–184; ecomusicology, 11 (*see also* Ecomusicology); environmental activism and movements, 5 (*see also* Environmental activism; Environmental stewardship); ethics, 11, 24, 73–74, 81; food, 23; forestry, 91; local, 7–8; musical, 5, 10–12, 15, 116, 177, 192; musicology, 11, 199; place, 201 (*see also* Place; Space); rhetoric, 18, 58, 73–74; ritual, 30, 35 (*see also* Ritual); soundscape, 189 (*see also* Soundscape studies); tourism, 182
Sweet Honey in the Rock, 177

Tagg, Philip 4–5, 163
"This Land Is Your Land," 49–58, 62, 64, 82, 106, 109
Thoreau, David, 51, 123, 125
Tibetan Freedom Concerts, 23
Ticketmaster, 38. *See also* Live Nation
Timbre, 135–136
Toliver, Brooks, 119
Topical music, 141–142, 149, 196. *See also* Protest music
Transportation, 1, 3, 16, 177, 178. *See also* Sustainability
Troubled Waters, 157–158
Turner, Frederick, 78–79
Tuva, 28–29, 81, 135, 200

U2, 1–2, 5, 16–19, 61

Valens, Ritchie, 34
Vannini, Phillip, 39
Van Ronk, Dave, 94
Varèse, Edgard, 193
Virtuosity, 137, 139
Von Glahn, Denise, 119–120, 127, 128, 181, 190

Mark Pedelty is an Associate Professor of Mass Communication and Anthropology at the University of Minnesota. To learn more, visit his website Ecomusicology.net.